T0271181

Survival
GLOBAL POLITICS AND STRATEGY
Volume 66 Number 6 | December 2024–January 2025

'More than any other major American political figure since the inception of the Great Debate, Trump has consistently, vehemently and publicly questioned the relevance of NATO and America's continued commitment to it.'

Charlie Laderman, With Trump's Return, the Transatlantic 'Great Debate' Resumes, p. 11.

'In truth, Nasrallah had deeply misread Israel's mood after 7 October. He had calculated that Israel would not risk a two-front war, underestimating how the fear that Hizbullah, a more powerful foe than Hamas, might conduct a similar operation and inflict much greater casualties would shape Israel's resolve.'

Emile Hokayem, The Death of Nasrallah and the Fate of Lebanon, p. 34.

'Historically, Pyongyang has been a supplicant who would ask Russia for subsidised oil or debt relief. Putin would occasionally th row a bone to Kim Jong-un's reclusive father by inviting him for lunch at his flat in Moscow as a gesture of goodwill. Now the tables are turned.'

Victor Cha and Katrin Fraser Katz, Crisis and COVID in North Korea, p. 105.

Survival
GLOBAL POLITICS AND STRATEGY
Volume 66 Number 6 | December 2024–January 2025

Contents

Survival
GLOBAL POLITICS AND STRATEGY

The International Institute for Strategic Studies

2121 K Street, NW | Suite 600 | Washington DC 20037 | USA
Tel +1 202 659 1490   Fax +1 202 659 1499   E-mail survival@iiss.org   Web www.iiss.org

Arundel House | 6 Temple Place | London | WC2R 2PG | UK
Tel +44 (0)20 7379 7676   Fax +44 (0)20 7836 3108   E-mail iiss@iiss.org

14th Floor, GFH Tower | Bahrain Financial Harbour | Manama | Kingdom of Bahrain
Tel +973 1718 1155   Fax +973 1710 0155   E-mail iiss-middleeast@iiss.org

9 Raffles Place | #49-01 Republic Plaza | Singapore 048619
Tel +65 6499 0055   Fax +65 6499 0059   E-mail iiss-asia@iiss.org

Pariser Platz 6A | 10117 Berlin | Germany
Tel +49 30 311 99 300   E-mail iiss-europe@iiss.org

Survival Online www.tandfonline.com/survival and www.iiss.org/publications/survival

Aims and Scope *Survival* is one of the world's leading forums for analysis and debate of international and strategic affairs. Shaped by its editors to be both timely and forward thinking, the journal encourages writers to challenge conventional wisdom and bring fresh, often controversial, perspectives to bear on the strategic issues of the moment. With a diverse range of authors, *Survival* aims to be scholarly in depth while vivid, well written and policy-relevant in approach. Through commentary, analytical articles, case studies, forums, review essays, reviews and letters to the editor, the journal promotes lively, critical debate on issues of international politics and strategy.

Editor **Dana Allin**
Managing Editor **Jonathan Stevenson**
Associate Editor **Carolyn West**
Editorial Assistant **Conor Hodges**
Production and Cartography **Alessandra Beluffi, Ravi Gopar, Jade Panganiban, James Parker, Kelly Verity**

Contributing Editors

William Alberque	**Franz-Stefan Gady**	**Nigel Inkster**	**Benjamin Rhode**	**Robert Ward**
Aaron Connelly	**Bastian Giegerich**	**Jeffrey Mazo**	**Ben Schreer**	**Marcus Willett**
James Crabtree	**Nigel Gould-Davies**	**Fenella McGerty**	**Maria Shagina**	**Lanxin Xiang**
Chester A. Crocker	**Melissa K. Griffith**	**Irene Mia**	**Karen Smith**	
Bill Emmott	**Emile Hokayem**	**Meia Nouwens**	**Angela Stent**	

Published for the IISS by
Routledge Journals, an imprint of Taylor & Francis, an Informa business.

ISBN 978-1-032-80665-5 paperback / 978-1-003-49802-5 ebook

About the IISS The IISS, a registered charity with offices in Washington, London, Manama, Singapore and Berlin, is the world's leading authority on political–military conflict. It is the primary independent source of accurate, objective information on international strategic issues. Publications include *The Military Balance*, an annual reference work on each nation's defence capabilities; *Survival*, a bimonthly journal on international affairs; *Strategic Comments*, an online analysis of topical issues in international affairs; and the *Adelphi* series of books on issues of international security.

SUBMISSIONS

To submit an article, authors are advised to follow these guidelines:

- *Survival* articles are around 4,000–10,000 words long including endnotes. A word count should be included with a draft.
- All text, including endnotes, should be double-spaced with wide margins.
- Any tables or artwork should be supplied in separate files, ideally not embedded in the document or linked to text around it.
- All *Survival* articles are expected to include endnote references. These should be complete and include first and last names of authors, titles of articles (even from newspapers), place of publication, publisher, exact publication dates, volume and issue number (if from a journal) and page numbers. Web sources should include complete URLs and DOIs if available.
- A summary of up to 150 words should be included with the article. The summary should state the main argument clearly and concisely, not simply say what the article is about.

- A short author's biography of one or two lines should also be included. This information will appear at the foot of the first page of the article.

Please note that *Survival* has a strict policy of listing multiple authors in alphabetical order.

Submissions should be made by email, in Microsoft Word format, to survival@iiss.org. Alternatively, hard copies may be sent to *Survival*, IISS–US, 2121 K Street NW, Suite 801, Washington, DC 20037, USA.

The editorial review process can take up to three months. *Survival*'s acceptance rate for unsolicited manuscripts is less than 20%. *Survival* does not normally provide referees' comments in the event of rejection. Authors are permitted to submit simultaneously elsewhere so long as this is consistent with the policy of the other publication and the Editors of *Survival* are informed of the dual submission.

Readers are encouraged to comment on articles from the previous issue. Letters should be concise, no longer than 750 words and relate directly to the argument or points made in the original article.

Survival: Global Politics and Strategy (Print ISSN 0039-6338, Online ISSN 1468-2699) is published bimonthly for a total of 6 issues per year by Taylor & Francis Group, 4 Park Square, Milton Park, Abingdon, Oxon, OX14 4RN, UK. Periodicals postage paid (Permit no. 13095) at Brooklyn, NY 11256.

Airfreight and mailing in the USA by agent named World Container Inc., c/o BBT 150-15, 183rd Street, Jamaica, NY 11413, USA.

US Postmaster: Send address changes to Survival, World Container Inc., c/o BBT 150-15, 183rd Street, Jamaica, NY 11413, USA.

Subscription records are maintained at Taylor & Francis Group, 4 Park Square, Milton Park, Abingdon, OX14 4RN, UK.

Subscription information: For more information and subscription rates, please see tandfonline.com/pricing/journal/TSUR. Taylor & Francis journals are available in a range of different packages, designed to suit every library's needs and budget. This journal is available for institutional subscriptions with online-only or print & online options. This journal may also be available as part of our libraries, subject collections or archives. For more information on our sales packages, please visit librarianresources.taylorandfrancis.com.

For support with any institutional subscription, please visit help.tandfonline.com or email our dedicated team at subscriptions@tandf.co.uk.

Subscriptions purchased at the personal rate are strictly for personal, non-commercial use only. The reselling of personal subscriptions is prohibited. Personal subscriptions must be purchased with a personal cheque, credit card or BAC/wire transfer. Proof of personal status may be requested.

Back issues: Please visit https://taylorandfrancis.com/journals/customer-services/ for more information on how to purchase back issues.

Ordering information: To subscribe to the journal, please contact T&F Customer Services, Informa UK Ltd, Sheepen Place, Colchester, Essex, CO3 3LP, UK. Tel: +44 (0) 20 8052 2030; email subscriptions@tandf.co.uk.

Taylor & Francis journals are priced in USD, GBP and EUR (as well as AUD and CAD for a limited number of journals). All subscriptions are charged depending on where the end customer is based. If you are unsure which rate applies to you, please contact Customer Services. All subscriptions are payable in advance and all rates include postage. We are required to charge applicable VAT/GST on all print and online combination subscriptions, in addition to our online-only journals. Subscriptions are entered on an annual basis, i.e., January to December. Payment may be made by sterling cheque, dollar cheque, euro cheque, international money order, National Giro or credit cards (Amex, Visa and Mastercard).

Disclaimer: The International Institute for Strategic Studies (IISS) and our publisher Informa UK Limited, trading as Taylor & Francis Group ('T&F'), make every effort to ensure the accuracy of all the information (the 'Content') contained in our publications. However, IISS and our publisher T&F, our agents and our licensors make no representations or warranties whatsoever as to the accuracy, completeness or suitability for any purpose of the Content. Any opinions and views expressed in this publication are the opinions and views of the authors, and are not the views of or endorsed by IISS or our publisher T&F. The accuracy of the Content should not be relied upon and should be independently verified with primary sources of information, and any reliance on the Content is at your own risk. IISS and our publisher T&F make no representations, warranties or guarantees, whether express or implied, that the Content is accurate, complete or up to date. IISS and our publisher T&F shall not be liable for any losses, actions, claims, proceedings, demands, costs, expenses, damages and other liabilities whatsoever or howsoever caused arising directly or indirectly in connection with, in relation to or arising out of the use of the Content. Full Terms & Conditions of access and use can be found at http://www.tandfonline.com/page/terms-and-conditions.

Informa UK Limited, trading as Taylor & Francis Group, grants authorisation for individuals to photocopy copyright material for private research use, on the sole basis that requests for such use are referred directly to the requestor's local Reproduction Rights Organization (RRO). The copyright fee is exclusive of any charge or fee levied. In order to contact your local RRO, please contact International Federation of Reproduction Rights Organizations (IFRRO), rue du Prince Royal, 87, B-1050 Brussels, Belgium; email ifrro@skynet.be; Copyright Clearance Center Inc., 222 Rosewood Drive, Danvers, MA 01923, USA; email info@copyright.com; or Copyright Licensing Agency, 90 Tottenham Court Road, London, W1P 0LP, UK; email cla@cla.co.uk. This authorisation does not extend to any other kind of copying, by any means, in any form, for any purpose other than private research use.

Submission information: See https://www.tandfonline.com/journals/tsur20

Advertising: See https://taylorandfrancis.com/contact/advertising/

Permissions: See help.tandfonline.com/Librarian/s/article/Permissions

All Taylor & Francis Group journals are printed on paper from renewable sources by accredited partners.

December 2024–January 2025

With Trump's Return, the Transatlantic 'Great Debate' Resumes

Charlie Laderman

'The prime obligation of the defense of.Western Continental Europe rests upon the nations of Europe', thundered the former president of the United States. Until those nations paid up and started spending more on their own defence, the US should not 'land another man or another dollar on their shores'. And if they refused to do so, he suggested, the US could pull back from continental Europe and rely on its air and naval forces to defend its homeland and surrounding oceans.[1] Across the Atlantic, there was uproar and anxiety. 'Where does this leave us poor Europeans?' lamented an editorial in the *Guardian*.[2] From the White House, the Democratic president charged his Republican forerunner with isolationism and lambasted his speech as a gift to Moscow.[3]

Herbert Hoover's speech in December 1950 kicked off what became known as the 'Great Debate' over US foreign and defence policy. For almost a decade, indeed practically ever since Donald Trump descended the golden escalator at Trump Tower, we have been in the midst of a new incarnation of that debate. As in 1950, it centres to a large extent on burden-sharing among allies, and whether the US would be better served focusing its attention on Asia and leaving the defence of Europe to the Europeans. It is a debate that would have continued, in some form and in some tone, regardless of who won the election.

Charlie Laderman is a senior lecturer in international history in the Department of War Studies at King's College London and a Visiting Fellow at the Hoover Institution on War, Revolution and Peace at Stanford University. His most recent book, co-authored with Brendan Simms, is *Hitler's American Gamble: Pearl Harbor and Germany's March to Global War* (Basic Books, 2021). An earlier version of this piece was published by Engelsberg Ideas.

Survival | vol. 66 no. 6 | December 2024–January 2025 | pp. 7–16   https://doi.org/10.1080/00396338.2024.2432189

Complicated precedent

The original Great Debate, arising shortly after the North Atlantic Treaty was passed, sprang from the Truman administration's decision to dispatch a large contingent of US troops to Europe under the command of General Dwight D. Eisenhower, who had steered Allied armies to victory in Europe in the Second World War, as the new head of an integrated NATO force. Alongside Hoover, the principal opponent of the administration's commitment of ground forces was Robert Taft, the senator from Ohio, whose high standing with his colleagues had earned him the nickname 'Mr. Republican'. Though both staunch opponents of the Soviet Union, Taft and Hoover were concerned about expensive overseas commitments and distrustful that Europeans would do enough to help themselves.

With American forces on the back foot in Korea, and the Truman administration already under fire for having 'lost' China, their views struck a chord with considerable sections of a war-weary public. A sizeable number of senators from both sides of the aisle shared their concerns about Congress conceding too much power to an assertive executive. Underlying them was a suspicion that the Europeans were taking advantage of the American security guarantee and a sense that the US would be left holding the bag for the continent's defence.[4]

The Great Debate ended in a clear victory for the Truman administration. Congress approved the deployment of US troops in Europe. Eisenhower returned from Europe and retired from the military, prevailing over Taft for the Republican presidential nomination and then capturing the presidency. As president, Eisenhower helped entrench Harry Truman's national-security doctrine, which contemplated a forward US military presence, a network of international alliances and the concentration of unprecedented power in the executive, including control over the decision to deploy nuclear weapons.[5]

This policy success should not disguise the level of ambivalence that remained among many senior American officials about the sustained presence of US troops in Europe. Reflecting anxiety in the Senate was Resolution 99, which, though it approved sending troops, stressed that Europeans should be responsible for the bulk of NATO's ground forces. It was envisaged that, in time, the US could draw down its land forces and that any additional troops would require Senate approval.[6] Concerns about the uncompensated extension of American military resources were not confined to resolute sceptics like Hoover and Taft. Leading officials in successive administrations also discreetly harboured them.[7] While highly critical of Taft and Hoover in public, Dean Acheson, Truman's fiercely loyal secretary of state, privately took the view that in the long term it was 'probably neither practical nor in [the] best interests of Europe or [the] US that [there] should be a US Commander in Europe or substantial numbers of US forces on [the] continent'.[8]

While Acheson would waver on this point, Eisenhower was more steadfast on the need to draw down the US deployment as soon as practicable. He was a far more committed advocate of American alliances than Taft or Hoover, but he shared their worry that open-ended overseas commitments could financially exhaust the United States. He differed with them over the timing and tactics for drawing down US troops in Europe, but ultimately agreed that a large American contingent could not remain on the continent indefinitely. While commander of NATO forces in 1951, he maintained that 'there is no defense for Western Europe that depends exclusively or even materially upon the existence, in Europe, of strong American units'. The US could not be 'a modern Rome guarding the far frontiers with our legions' and it was imperative that Europeans 'regain their confidence and get on their own military feet'.[9] This continued to inform his outlook as president. Indeed, he told the NATO secretary-general in 1959 that Europeans should be 'ashamed' that they were so reliant on the US for their security and expressed his fear that they were on the verge of 'making a sucker out of Uncle Sam'.[10]

Despite these frustrations, Eisenhower did not significantly draw down the US contingent in Europe. Attempts to establish a European Defence Community that would enable the withdrawal of US troops were thwarted when the French government, which had initially floated the idea, reversed itself in the face of parliamentary opposition, particularly over concerns about German rearmament so soon after the end of the war. In turn, US strategists assessed that only a powerful Germany, with nuclear weapons, would be sufficient to allow the US to withdraw its forces and preserve deterrence against the Soviets. Eisenhower appeared open to the idea, but his successors, beginning with John F. Kennedy, recognised that neither America's allies in Western Europe nor the Soviet Union were prepared to accept a West Germany with nuclear weapons.[11] The only plausible counterbalance to Soviet power in Europe, for friend and foe alike, was therefore the enduring forward US military presence that brought Europe decisively under the American nuclear umbrella.[12]

Pressure for the Europeans to step up their spending and enable at least a reduction in US ground troops still bubbled up intermittently, particularly in the Senate. Especially notable was the campaign led by Senate majority leader Mike Mansfield, a Democrat from Montana, in the late 1960s and early 1970s. Mansfield proposed cutting around half of US troops in Europe, seeing no reason 250 million Europeans could not muster the forces to 'defend themselves against 200 million Russians who are contending at the same time with 800 million Chinese, but [instead] must continue after 20 years to depend upon 200 million Americans for their defense'.[13] This argument appealed to a considerable number of senators, weary with the ongoing war in Vietnam and concerned about the balance-of-payments deficit arising from stationing US forces in Europe. But Richard Nixon's argument that 'as the most powerful member of the Alliance, the United States bears a responsibility for leadership' helped defeat Mansfield's proposals.[14] A majority in the Senate shared the fear, privately expressed by Nixon's national security advisor and later secretary of state Henry Kissinger, that the Europeans would not step up if the Americans pulled back. It was more likely, Kissinger suggested, that 'when big brother even appears to falter, the little brethren will not move forward courageously – as we seem to think – but, on the contrary, they will anxiously take several steps backward'.[15]

This argument held sway for the rest of the Cold War and continues to resonate to this day. In the 1990s, after the collapse of the Soviet Union, US forces were indeed drawn down. But European governments took advantage of the 'peace dividend' to cut their defence spending even more sharply, leaving the continent's defence more heavily dependent on US military power. By 2011, secretary of defense Robert Gates was warning Europeans that, with the US shouldering roughly 75% of NATO's defence spending, their unwillingness to invest sufficiently in their own defence risked dooming the Alliance to a 'dim and dismal future'.[16] Gates was speaking as someone for whom European stability, 'with NATO as the main instrument for protecting that security', had 'been the consuming interest of his professional life'. For him, 'the benefits of a Europe whole, prosperous and free after twice being devastated by wars requiring American intervention was self-evident'. His concern, however, was that 'future US political leaders – those for whom the Cold War was not the formative experience that it was for me – may not consider the return of America's investment in NATO worth the cost'.[17]

Enter Trump

Gates's fear proved prescient. Over the course of his political ascent, Trump has regularly suggested, often vituperatively, that he believes the cost of NATO outweighs the benefits. These views were evident long before. As early as 1987, during an interview with Larry King, Trump declared that 'if you look at the payments we're making to NATO, they're totally disproportionate with everybody else's'. NATO was taking 'tremendous advantage' of the US, according to Trump. Washington's focus should be on 'making lots of profit' to 'defend our homeless, and our poor, and our sick, and our farmers' rather than 'giving it to countries that don't give a damn for us to start off with'.[18] More than any other major American political figure since the inception of the Great Debate, Trump has consistently, vehemently and publicly questioned the relevance of NATO and America's continued commitment to it.

There is no direct analogy between Trump and Truman's opponents. While Hoover and Taft were fiscal conservatives, seeking to rein in expensive overseas commitments in pursuit of a more balanced budget, Trump's scepticism about NATO sits alongside spending plans and tax cuts that are poised to add trillions to America's already unprecedented federal debt, according to the non-partisan Committee for a Responsible Federal Budget.[19] Neither Hoover nor Taft shared Trump's mercantilist approach to trade, nor did they praise any Soviet leader in the way that Trump has extolled Russian President Vladimir Putin.

Despite fears that a second Trump presidency would lead to the US quitting NATO, however, a 'radical reorientation' of the Alliance appears more likely. According to a report in *Politico* based on interviews with parties linked to Trump's national-security team, the strategy that team is developing for NATO bears a close resemblance to the one advocated by Hoover and Taft that emphasised air and naval power, and eschewed substantial ground troops. The US would maintain its nuclear umbrella over Europe but, at the same time, drastically reduce its ground forces, 'significantly and substantially downsizing America's security role'. This would leave the bulk of security provisions almost entirely in European hands short of a full-blown crisis. This is now more necessary than ever, Trump's advisers claim, because China is the principal threat, and the US does not have sufficient military resources to go around.[20]

Some who served in senior national-security roles during Trump's first term, such as A. Wess Mitchell and Jakub Grygiel, agree that resources are stretched, but argue that it would be wrong to deprioritise Europe. In their view, Europe remains America's most significant economic partner, it is geopolitically critical for US power projection across Eurasia, and enduring transatlantic political and cultural ties remain foundational to the American global role. Moreover, they stress, 'whatever its flaws, modern Europe is the greatest accomplishment of US foreign policy'. And the repercussions of failing to contain Russian aggression on the continent would reverberate in other theatres too.[21]

It is unclear whether conservative Atlanticists of this stripe will have any significant role in a new Trump administration, however. In any case, they would be swimming against the tide. An April 2024 Pew poll suggested that 55% of Republicans or those who lean Republican had an unfavourable view of NATO.[22] More reflective of the party's current mood is Elbridge Colby, a senior Pentagon official in Trump's first term who is rumoured to be in line for a senior post in his second administration. Colby has stressed that 'Asia is more important than Europe' and that the US must 'withhold' troops from Europe – even on pain of leaving it exposed to Russian aggression – to focus on deterring China. It is time for NATO, Colby argues, to revert to its 'original idea' and for 'European allies to take primary responsibility for their own defence'.[23] The crucial question now, just as it was during the Cold War, is whether the Europeans are willing or able to step forward to fill the gap. The answer remains unclear.

European mobilisation?

There are some signs that Europe is starting to wake up. Thanks in part to Trump's pressure during his first term and, more significantly, due to Russia's full-scale invasion of Ukraine in 2022, 23 of the 31 non-US NATO members are on track to meet the Alliance's 2%-of-GDP target for defence spending. Poland has gone even further, spending over 4% of GDP and with plans to approach 5% in 2025.[24] But as Polish Prime Minister Donald Tusk recently put it, much more is going to be required of the entire continent regardless of who is the US president. 'Some claim that the future of Europe depends on the American elections', Tusk suggested, but actually 'it depends first and foremost on us ... Whatever the outcome, the era of geopolitical outsourcing is over.'[25] Benjamin Haddad, France's minister for European affairs, voiced similar sentiments on the other side of the continent, maintaining that 'we cannot leave the security of Europe in the hands of voters in Wisconsin every four years'. It was time, Haddad declared, to 'break out of collective denial: Europeans must take their destiny into their own hands, regardless of who is elected president'.[26]

These are strong sentiments, but they need to be turned into substance, and fast. While Poland and the Baltic nations continue to ramp up spending, other members of the Alliance are lagging. Since 2015, France and Germany have only added a battalion's worth of forces and Britain, though from a stronger position, has lost five.[27] More coordinated spending between the European members of the Alliance is required, with a greater focus on developing combat-ready troops, and the continent's defence-industrial base requires revitalisation. The haphazard and sluggish production of arms and shells for Ukraine does not inspire confidence.

The return of large-scale war to the continent has not yet awakened enough European governments to the scale of defence planning and spending required to address Russia's current threat.[28] It remains to be seen whether a president who declared that he would not protect 'delinquent' nations from Russia will in fact do so.[29] What is clear is that Trump believes that the 'prime obligation' for the defence of Europe rests on Europe itself and is likely to predicate continued American protection on Europe's doing more for its own defence.

* * *

The settlement of the original Great Debate ensured a US leadership role in North Atlantic security for more than 60 years. Trump fundamentally challenged that settlement during his first term. It remains to be seen whether it will survive his second term. But it is apparent that the US is again embroiled in a Great Debate, one that will determine the future of transatlantic relations.

Acknowledgements

The author would like to thank the Hoover Institution on War, Revolution and Peace at Stanford University for its support for research on this article, and Alastair Benn for his comments.

Notes

1   Herbert Hoover, 'Our National Policies in the Crisis', 20 December 1950, in Herbert Hoover, *Forty Key Questions About Our Foreign Policy* (New York: Kessinger, 1952), pp. 65–74.

2   Quoted in Richard Norton Smith, *Uncommon Man: The Triumph of Herbert Hoover* (New York: Simon & Schuster, 1984), p. 391.

3   See William S. Williams, 'Hoover Stand Isolationism, Truman Finds, Denouncing It', *New York Times*, 29 December 1950, p. 1, https://www.nytimes.com/1950/12/29/archives/hoover-stand-isolationism-truman-finds-denouncing-it-country-not.html.

4   For an excellent account of the debate in the Senate, see Phil Williams, *The Senate and US Troops in Europe* (London: Palgrave Macmillan, 1985), pp. 43–109.

5   See Charlie Laderman, 'Conservative Internationalism: An Overview', *Orbis*, vol. 62, no. 1, Winter 2018, pp. 13–14.

6   See US Congress, *Congressional Record*, 82nd Congress, 1st Session, vol. 97, 4 April 1951, p. 3,282.

7   See Marc Trachtenberg, 'Is There Life After NATO?', Cato Institute, Policy Analysis no. 982, 22 October 2024, https://www.cato.org/policy-analysis/there-life-after-nato.

8   'Telegram from Dean Acheson to American Ambassador to France David K. E. Bruce', 28 June 1951, available from the US Department of State, Office of the Historian, https://history.state.gov/historicaldocuments/frus1951v03p1/d437.

9   'Dwight D. Eisenhower to Edward J. Bermingham, 28 February 1951', in Louis Galambos et al., *The Papers of Dwight David Eisenhower*, vol. 12 (Baltimore, MD: Johns Hopkins University Press, 1989), pp. 76–7.

10 Quoted in Trachtenberg, 'Is There Life After NATO?', p. 5.

11 See Francis J. Gavin, *Gold, Dollars and Power: The Politics of International Monetary Relations, 1958–1971* (Chapel Hill, NC: University of North Carolina Press, 2004), p. 91; and Marc Trachtenberg, *A Constructed Peace: The Making of the European Settlement, 1945–1963* (Princeton, NJ: Princeton University Press, 1999), pp. 146, 203–4, 209–10.

12 See Gavin, *Gold, Dollars and Power*, especially chapters 2 and 3.

13 Williams, *The Senate and US Troops in Europe*, p. 164.

14 Richard Nixon, 'Statement About United States Military Forces in Europe', 15 May 1971, available from American Presidency Project, https://www.presidency.ucsb.edu/node/239976.

15 Memorandum from Henry Kissinger to President Nixon, n.d. (probably October 1969), quoted in Hubert Zimmermann, 'The Improbable Permanence of a Commitment', *Journal of Cold War Studies*, vol. 11, no. 1, Winter 2009, p. 20.

16 This is the figure that Gates gave in this speech and was in line with NATO's own defence-expenditure data on the total defence spending of all the countries in the alliance. See NATO, 'Defence Expenditure of NATO Countries (2011–2018)', 14 March 2019, https://www.nato.int/nato_static_fl2014/assets/pdf/pdf_2019_03/190314-pr2018-34-eng.pdf. However, such an aggregation does not account for the fact that virtually all European spending is focused on national defence in Europe, while US spending primarily covers other missions and regions.

See Anthony Cordesman, 'NATO and the Claim the U.S. Bears 70% of the Burden: A False and Dysfunctional Approach to Burdensharing', Center for Strategic and International Studies, 25 July 2018, https://www.csis.org/analysis/nato-and-claim-us-bears-70-burden-false-and-dysfunctional-approach-burdensharing.

17 Robert Gates, 'Text of Speech by Robert Gates on the Future of NATO', Atlantic Council, 10 June 2011, https://www.atlanticcouncil.org/blogs/natosource/text-of-speech-by-robert-gates-on-the-future-of-nato/.

18 Quoted in Charlie Laderman and Brendan Simms, *Donald Trump: The Making of a Worldview* (London: I.B. Tauris, 2017), pp. 34–6.

19 Committee for a Responsible Federal Budget, 'The Fiscal Impact of the Harris and Trump Campaign Plans', updated 28 October 2024, https://www.crfb.org/sites/default/files/media/documents/CRFB_The%20Fiscal%20Impact%20of%20the%20Harris%20and%20Trump%20Campaign%20Plans_Final%20Update_10282024.pdf.

20 See Michael Hirsh, 'Trump's Plan for NATO Is Emerging', *Politico*, 2 July 2024, https://www.politico.com/news/magazine/2024/07/02/nato-second-trump-term-00164517.

21 See Jakub Grygiel and A. Wess Mitchell, 'US Strategy Should Be Europe First, Then Asia', *Foreign Policy*, 6 September 2024, https://foreignpolicy.com/2024/09/06/us-strategy-geopolitics-china-russia-europe-asia-threat/.

22 Richard Wike et al., 'Growing Partisan Divisions over NATO and Ukraine',

Pew Research Center, 8 May 2024, https://www.pewresearch.org/global/2024/05/08/growing-partisan-divisions-over-nato-and-ukraine/.

23 Elbridge Colby, 'America Must Face Reality and Prioritise China over Europe', *Financial Times*, 23 May 2024, https://www.ft.com/content/b423aa65-b9cb-4ba5-9c7d-f67dc289a18f.

24 See 'Poland's Government Plans Record Defense Spending in Its 2025 Budget', Associated Press, 28 August 2024, https://apnews.com/article/poland-budget-2025-defense-spending-increase-d1b5d840876df-2cb850a78348887473a.

25 Donald Tusk (@donaldtusk), post to X, 2 November 2024, https://x.com/donaldtusk/status/1852701257267318972.

26 Benjamin Haddad (@benjaminhaddad), post to X, 24 October 2024, https://x.com/benjaminhaddad/status/1849364237161787705.

27 See 'Can Europe Defend Itself Without America?', *The Economist*, 18 February 2024, https://www.economist.com/briefing/2024/02/18/can-europe-defend-itself-without-america.

28 See François Heisbourg, 'Planning for a Post-American Europe', *Survival*, vol. 66, no. 3, June–July 2024, pp. 7–20.

29 See Jill Colvin, 'Trump Says He Once Told a NATO Ally to Pay Its Share or He'd "Encourage" Russia to Do What It Wanted', Associated Press, 11 February 2024, https://apnews.com/article/trump-nato-foreign-aid-russia-2b8054a9fe185eec34c2c541cece655d?.

Trump, Project 2025 and American Grand Strategy

Peter Dombrowski

For much of the 2024 American presidential-campaign season, the Heritage Foundation's Project 2025 – embodied primarily in its self-published, online book titled *Mandate for Leadership: The Conservative Promise*, edited by Paul Dans and Steven Groves[1] – featured prominently in news and social-media accounts of the policy agenda of former president Donald Trump's second term. The book elicited shock and astonishment. In addition to attacking popular Obama and Biden administration programmes such as the Affordable Care Act and student-loan forgiveness, it promised to increase the power of the president while ending what it calls 'radical gender ideology' and eviscerating the civil service in favour of fiercely partisan appointees.[2]

Trump's decisive victory on 5 November raises the urgent question of what the grand strategy of his second term will look like. Early reports suggest that Trump and his key advisers have learned from the false starts of 2017. As *Mandate for Leadership* suggests, Trump is likely to fill key cabinet and second-tier slots with loyalists, purge officials supportive of Biden administration policies and move quickly to take advantage of the election's mandate. With Republicans regaining the Senate, retaining the House and enjoying staunch support in the judiciary from Trump

Peter Dombrowski is the William B. Ruger Chair of National Security Economics at the US Naval War College and the co-author, with Simon Reich, of *The End of Grand Strategy: U.S. Maritime Operations in the 21st Century* (Cornell University Press, 2018). The views expressed here are those of the author and not the US government or any agency thereof.

Survival | vol. 66 no. 6 | December 2024–January 2025 | pp. 17–32   https://doi.org/10.1080/00396338.2024.2432191

appointees, there may be little the Democratic minority can do to moderate Trump's foreign and security policies. Accordingly, it is imperative that American allies, partners and adversaries alike understand what they are likely to be. *Mandate for Leadership* provides the surest guidance. As Maya Angelou said, 'when someone shows you who they are, believe them the first time'.

How radical?

Moderates from both major parties registered profound concern about Project 2025 in general. Larry Hogan, the unsuccessful Republican candidate for the Senate in Maryland who has been critical of Trump, called the project 'radical' and concluded that 'Project 2025 takes many of the principles that have made this nation great and shreds them'.[3] *New York Times* columnist Paul Krugman argued that implementation of Project 2025 'would represent a giant step into the past' in 'replacing much of the federal work force' on the basis of their political loyalty rather than expertise or professional competence.[4] Edward Luce dubbed it 'the *War and Peace* of authoritarian planning'.[5] On the occasion of the Fourth of July, Kevin Roberts, then the Heritage Foundation's president, declared that 'we are in the process of the second American Revolution, which will remain bloodless if the left allows it to be'.[6] Doubters were hardly reassured.

The University of Massachusetts (UMass) at Amherst undertook a broad examination of the electorate's reaction to Project 2025, assessing that

> large majorities of Americans oppose the key pillars of Project 2025, such as the replacement of career government officials with political appointees (68% opposed), restricting a woman's right to contraception (72% opposed) and eliminating the Department of Education (64% opposed). While our politics are usually divided by class, generational, racial, gender and partisan identities, among these groups we find strong opposition to many of the policies associated with Project 2025. Even former Trump voters exhibit opposition to many of these policies, a bad omen for the Republican Party and Trump campaign.[7]

UMass focused on domestic policies, so the degree of public support for most of Project 2025's foreign and security policies remained unclear. The two exceptions involved issues at the intersection of domestic and foreign policy: tariffs and immigration. On these, polling confirmed considerable polarisation. Some 59% of Republicans supported a 10% tariff on all products imported by the US from overseas, versus 21% of Democrats and 37% of independents. And 89% of Republicans against 19% of Democrats and 42% of independents backed building a wall along the border with Mexico.[8]

While the negative attention induced Trump to publicly disavow Project 2025 in July 2024, it has deep and durable ties to Trump's campaign. Many members of the Heritage Foundation's team served in policy positions during the first Trump administration. J.D. Vance, his 2024 running mate, has a close relationship with Roberts, who was compelled to step down after his Fourth of July crack produced outcries.[9] Vance penned the foreword to Roberts's book *Dawn's Early Light*, whose publication was delayed until after the presidential election, noting that 'we are now all realizing that it's time to circle the wagons and load the muskets. In the fights that lay ahead, these ideas are an essential weapon.'[10] Most significantly, the Republican Party platform and the Trump campaign's headline promises plainly resonate with Project 2025.

Obscured by the controversy and political posturing, however, are long sections of *Mandate for Leadership* laying out how a new Republican administration will provide for national defence, pursue foreign policies and reshape the foreign- and security-policy apparatus of the United States. On this score, the authors state that 'development of a grand foreign policy strategy is key to the next Administration's success'.[11] In fact, a close reading reveals the book's acknowledgement and to an extent its acceptance of the power and influence of the entrenched Beltway establishment sardonically known as 'the Blob', which Trump has generally referred to as 'the swamp', an older and more disparaging epithet dating from the 1980s.[12] Perhaps inadvertently, he recognised the Blob's influence in his 2016 campaign, claiming, 'I know the system better than anybody else and I'm the only one up here that's going to be able to fix that system, because that system is wrong'.[13]

Overall, the establishment supports existing American foreign-policy institutions and processes, the liberal-international order, and military and economic activism in international affairs. Its members tend to be drawn from political, policy, bureaucratic, media, think-tank and university elites on the East and West coasts. They often serve on government and non-government commissions and advisory boards, testify before Congress, appear on cable and network news, publish research and policy reports, and place op-eds in prominent outlets. Critics claim the establishment is prone to groupthink and continuity for its own sake, and insufficiently concerned about the domestic consequences of US foreign and security choices. While its direct impact on specific policies is debatable, the establishment still dominates public discourse.

Much of what *Mandate for Leadership* devotes to national defence could have been produced by a range of respected think tanks and policy experts well ensconced in the establishment. But there are three areas in the document – on trade, multilateralism and border security – which suggest that a new challenge to traditional American grand strategy is emerging, fuelled by both the aggressive populism of Trump's political movement and elements of President Joe Biden and Vice President Kamala Harris's foreign- and security-policy agenda that are far less extreme but also qualify as populist.

Convention-adjacent positions

A general reading of the sections of *Mandate for Leadership* devoted specifically to national defence reveal many important consistencies with conventional positions. It exhorts American leaders to 'transform our armed forces for maximum effectiveness in an era of great-power competition'.[14] Late in Barack Obama's second term, of course, American officials began acknowledging that efforts to reset relations with Russia had failed and the rise of an increasingly aggressive China required a concerted response, and *Mandate for Leadership* too recommends prioritising China.[15] While the number of times a particular word appears in a document hardly makes a complete argument, the frequency of the word China in *Mandate for Leadership* so far exceeds that of other geopolitical players as to be significant. According to the Adobe search function, it appears 483 times, in contrast to Russia (108 times), Europe (72), Japan (20), Canada (13), Mexico (34), and Great Britain or the United Kingdom (13). What the Pentagon calls China's 'pacing threat' permeates the international sections of *Mandate for Leadership*, as well as the domestic sections on technological innovation.

In the Project 2025 narrative, China, rather than globalisation or any other macro-factor, is to blame for America's economic troubles. Early on, *Mandate for Leadership* states that 'unfettered trade with China has been a catastrophe'.[16] It then holds China responsible for closed factories, the financialisation of the manufacturing economy, the theft of American intellectual property, addictive video games and, more seriously, 'compromising and coopting our higher education system', as well as 'compromising and coopting corporate America'.[17] While this view may seem over the top, it is in line with the attitudes of many progressive as well as conservative Americans.[18]

Mandate for Leadership is straightforward about the peril Russian President Vladimir Putin's regime poses, noting that 'the United States and its allies also face real threats from Russia, as evidenced by Vladimir Putin's brutal war in Ukraine'.[19] In keeping with prioritising China, however, two paragraphs later the document observes that 'others' should 'take more of a lead in dealing with threats from Russia in Europe, Iran, the Middle East, and North Korea'.[20]

The section discussing a new agenda for the State Department forthrightly acknowledges tensions within the conservative movement over how to deal with Russia's war with Ukraine. It then proposes an approach whereby 'continued U.S. involvement must be fully paid for; limited to military aid (while European allies address Ukraine's economic needs); and have a clearly defined national security strategy that does not risk American lives'.[21] On its face, this stance is not diametrically opposed to the Biden administration's, and *Mandate for Leadership* rejects the conservative position that the United States has no vital national interests at stake in the conflict and prescribes a negotiated settlement between Russia and Ukraine. But it is difficult to reconcile it with Trump's statements during the campaign, which explicitly urged negotiation. On a call with Ukrainian President Volodymyr Zelenskyy and in a subsequent Truth Social post, Trump said that, were he to win a second term, both sides would be 'able to come together and negotiate a deal that ends the violence and paves a path forward to prosperity' despite the Ukrainian president's rejection of initiatives to negotiate with

Russia while its forces occupy Ukrainian territory.[22] Thus, it appears likely that the incoming Trump administration would diverge from *Mandate for Leadership* on Ukraine, though increased defence burden-sharing by NATO Europe could conceivably change its calculations.

Defence burden-sharing, especially within NATO, has been a hobby horse of Trump's. In 2016, he famously suggested that the US commitment to supporting allies under Article 5 of the North Atlantic Treaty was contingent on members 'paying their bills'.[23] During his presidency, he contemplated the United States' withdrawal from NATO. Recently, he raised the ante by suggesting that NATO members should commit to spending 3% of GDP on national defence – 50% more than the standard 2% benchmark. *Mandate for Leadership* reinforces this aggressive stance, stating that 'the new Administration will also want to encourage nations to exceed that pledge'.[24] Of course, US administrations predating Trump's consistently pressured European members of NATO to shoulder a greater share of the defence burden, and Russia's invasion of Ukraine has prompted many to ramp up their defence budgets and defence-industrial output. In this light, conservative hawkishness on burden-sharing may be more a makeweight talking point than an indicator of major substantive differences.

Like most of the policy community, *Mandate for Leadership* takes for granted that China is undertaking a 'dramatic expansion of its nuclear forces that could result in a nuclear force that matches or exceeds America's own nuclear arsenal'.[25] Consequently, any president should concentrate on 'modernizing and expanding the U.S. nuclear arsenal'.[26] Specific recommendations include expanding and modernising the US nuclear force sufficiently to deter Russia and China simultaneously and to preclude serious nuclear coercion at theatre level, as well as ensuring the resilience of nuclear command and control in the face of new threats such as cyber weapons.[27] While the former aim is well within mainstream Blob thinking, that of thwarting nuclear coercion at theatre level is contested. Theatre-level, much less tactical, nuclear weapons have long been out of favour. The Biden administration confirmed this bias when it cancelled the sea-launched nuclear cruise missile (SLCM-N), opponents of which believe there are other nuclear systems capable of providing a regional or theatre-level deterrent that, unlike the SLCM-N, would not lower the threshold for nuclear war fighting. *Mandate for Leadership* also pushes farther than many strategists would in advocating that the United States develop new nuclear weapons and naval nuclear reactors, but in the short and medium terms these efforts would be confined to research and development as opposed to operational employment and would not immediately affect strategy.[28]

Although border security is often viewed as a domestic policy issue, building a wall, restricting flows of legal and illegal immigrants, and possible mass deportation manifestly implicate grand strategy.[29] *Mandate for Leadership* equates border security with safeguarding sovereignty and protecting the domestic economy such that 'illegal immigration should be ended, not mitigated; the border sealed, not reprioritized'.[30] Sealing US borders and deporting both illegal and legal immigrants would affect several of the United States' neighbours – especially Mexico and Canada – and potentially complicate bilateral relations more broadly. When critics characterise Trump's foreign policy as isolationist, his aggressive position on immigration is often invoked. The fact remains that Democrats as well as Republicans understand that a tighter and more coherent immigration policy is a political if not an economic necessity, as evidenced by the tough bipartisan immigration bill that Trump prevailed on the House of Representatives to reject in early 2024 solely to deny the Democratic Party a political win in an election year.

> Mandate for Leadership *advocates new nuclear weapons*

Mandate for Leadership's defence agenda smacks of what Hal Brands, Peter Feaver and William Inboden called the 'stodgy hawkishness' that Ben Rhodes mocked in his characterisation of the Blob.[31] Unlike Trump and Vance's rhetorical grenades, it emphasises largely accepted strategic themes that are embraced by liberal internationalists and measured restrainers alike, and echoed in the official national strategic and defence documents of both the Trump and the Biden administrations. The document reflects an international environment shaped by great-power conflict that requires greater burden-sharing among partners and allies, a promptly strengthened defence-industrial base, and increased military-technical innovation to prepare for a possible high-technology, high-intensity war, especially in the Indo-Pacific.

Discordant notes

Notwithstanding its nods to strategic orthodoxy, *Mandate for Leadership* also charts a populist course that is antithetical to the Blob mindset. The most jarring section is the one on foreign economic policy.[32] Kent Lassman's chapter, 'The Case for Free Trade', lodges conventional support for free trade, advocating 'tariff relief', the separation of other domestic and international objectives from trade policy, and what amounts to deregulation in international transactions. Yet in 'The Case for Fair Trade', Peter Navarro, a staunch Trump loyalist who served as his senior trade advisor and went to prison for ignoring subpoenas to testify and provide documents to Congress about the 6 January 2021 insurrection, blames China and the World Trade Organization (WTO) for undermining American prosperity. According to Navarro, the WTO has facilitated 'unfair and nonreciprocal trade' via higher tariffs institutionalised by most-favoured-nation standards.[33] This is in line with Trump's view of foreign trade as zero-sum and tariffs as coercive instruments for serving American strategic and economic interests.

The policies Project 2025 urges regarding multilateral organisations are also disruptive. It accepts their importance but hedges any support by asserting that 'membership in these organizations must always be understood as a means to attain defined goals rather than an end in itself', calling for more accountability usually without specifying how this will be accomplished.[34] This general prescription may not be terribly different from what hard-right conservatives such as John Bolton – Trump's second national security advisor – espoused well before Trumpism or Project 2025 materialised.[35] But *Mandate for Leadership* takes it in unprecedented directions – for instance, recommending the insertion of anti-abortion language in all grants and cooperative agreements.

Regarding international financial institutions – specifically, the World Bank and the International Monetary Fund – *Mandate for Leadership* is especially blunt and unnuanced. Firstly, it recommends that countries that are American adversaries or do not share American values should not be members of these institutions. Secondly, it argues that the US should 'withdraw from both the World Bank and the IMF and terminate its financial contribution to both institutions' and that 'if the U.S. is to provide economic assistance or humanitarian aid to other nations, it should do so unilaterally'.[36]

The 16-page Republican Party platform, styled the 2024 *GOP PLATFORM MAKE AMERICA GREAT AGAIN!*, highlighted Trump's 'America First' imperative in its emphasis on strengthening the US military through increased defence spending and promoting the American manufacturing and energy sectors, starkly asserting that the United States is to maintain the world's greatest military and restore the world's greatest industrial economy.[37] In turn, the Trump campaign's website enumerated 20 promises, of which five focused directly on how the United States would operate vis-à-vis the rest of the world in a second Trump administration:

- Make america [*sic*] the dominant energy producer in the world, by far!
- Stop outsourcing, and turn the united states [*sic*] into manufacturing superpower
- Prevent world war three, restore peace in europe [*sic*] and in the middle east [*sic*], and build a great iron dome missile defense shield over our entire country – all made in America
- Strengthen and modernize our military, making it, without question, the strongest and most powerful in the world
- Keep the U.S. dollar as the world's reserve currency.[38]

While these edicts generally echoed *Mandate for Leadership*, their incorporation of Trump's unfiltered lexicon, his jangled syntax, and even his idiosyncratic capitalisation made it shriller and more petulant. At the same time, they could be seen as an attempt to harmonise the primacist call for military supremacy and the isolationist and populist tilt towards protectionism that Project 2025 leaves dangling. This attempt has to be judged a failure because, as the drafters of *Mandate for Leadership* may have tacitly understood, reconciling primacism and populism is practically infeasible. Populist themes do have a long tradition in the United States, dating back at least to Andrew Jackson.[39] But, as Walter Russell Mead observes, Jacksonian populism was 'only intermittently concerned with foreign policy'.[40] Since the Second World War, populist politics have rarely intruded on the discussion, much less the implementation, of US grand strategy.

In the 2024 presidential campaign, however, both Trump and Harris stressed populist themes, one from the right and the other from the left. Trump, despite his personal background and lifestyle, has positioned himself as a proponent of the common person and as anti-elitist. He tends to directly address the people – his 'Make America Great Again' base. His appeal relies heavily on his own charisma and personalistic leadership style. The selection of Vance, author of *Hillbilly Elegy*, as his running mate on balance solidified this position despite obvious inconsistencies such as Vance's Ivy League education and stint as a venture capitalist. Like many populists, both are averse to international institutions and suspect that allies do not contribute sufficiently to their own defence and actively work against American national interests.

Harris, on the other hand, emphasised her own modest, middle-class family background to advocate a return to more progressive taxation and stronger social-welfare programmes, including a higher minimum wage, reduced wealth inequality, corporate accountability and healthcare reforms. At the same time, she refrained from disavowing the economic nationalism espoused by Biden, not least the de facto protectionist industrial policies reflected in the CHIPS Act and the Inflation Reduction Act.[41] And Harris too is wedded to the establishment's consensus behind militarised internationalism, having pointedly refrained from delineating a strategic perspective distinct from Biden's with respect to China, the Russia–Ukraine war and the Middle East conflict set off by the Hamas attack of 7 October 2023.

A populist grand strategy?

Since 2016, a cottage industry has developed around figuring out what grand strategy Trumpist foreign and security policies might entail. His four years in office produced broken agreements, threats to allies and enemies alike, and bipartisan rancour over a number of policy choices. Critics have suggested that true grand strategy is impossible under Trump's intensely transactional approach to international affairs, which Richard Haass, former president of the Council on Foreign Relations, has called 'adhocracy'.[42] Others have tried to frame his policies in more traditional grand-strategic paradigms – isolationist, engagement, deep engagement or primacist. As Colin Dueck explains, however, there remains a disjunction between a Trumpist national-security approach and the Trumpist approach to economic policy.[43] A conventional approach to hard security sits uneasily next to a populist approach to international trade. One pillar of the post-Second World War strategic consensus was that American military power underpinned the liberal-international order that originated at Bretton Woods, and vice versa. *Mandate for Leadership* purports to decouple the two and upend this long-standing synergy.

There is another crucial time-tested synergy, this one between the national-security apparatus and the administrative state. Accordingly, *Mandate for Leadership*'s avowed goal of dismantling the administrative state, likewise a response to Trump's dictatorial impulses, fits awkwardly with its aggressive business-as-usual approach to national defence. As the sociologist Charles Tilly famously observed, 'war made the state and states made war'.[44] In the United States, the rise of the administrative state during the two world wars, the New Deal and the Great Society powered the rise of the national-security state during the Cold War. A US government in thrall to populism could find itself in a situation where the military-industrial complex and national-security state remained well funded and powerful while the regulatory and welfare states were hobbled by staff and budget cuts, as well as legislative dismantling.

In this light, it appears unlikely that Project 2025 could provide a viable basis for a new grand-strategic synthesis that combines 'peace through strength' – Ronald Reagan's shorthand for military power that anchors global hegemony – with populist domestic and economic policies.

*   *   *

For a minute, *Mandate for Leadership* may soothe European and Asian allies because it projects a degree of continuity not found in Trump's bombastic sound bites and social-media posts about leaving NATO, making deals with Russia, or pushing Japan to modify the 'peace constitution'. But its espousal of populism cuts against any reassuring orthodoxy. So does the fact that populism has affected Democratic as well as Republican political calculations. Neither Trump's nor Harris's platform resembled the 'progressive worldmaking' or 'progressive pragmatism' recently articulated by scholars such as Van Jackson. His version of grand strategy embraces both ameliorating domestic economic problems like economic equality and advancing progressive goals such as humanitarianism and anti-militarism as elements of the United States' global agenda.[45] Instead, both Harris and Trump rather casually retained the primacist precepts of the Washington national-security establishment while focusing more tightly on the priorities of domestic political constituencies.

Populist grand strategies are unstable and perhaps even impossible.[46] Populist leaders and those pursuing populist economic agendas may become hostage to the emotions of the populace, which leaves little room for the kind of strategic planning and realpolitik that have enabled great powers to navigate complex and persistent challenges. A relatively technocratic planning process insulated from the vicissitudes of domestic politics stands a better chance of weathering them in the pursuit of a coherent grand strategy.[47]

Moreover, maintaining a large and world-class military would be exceedingly difficult in the long term in the absence of a strong administrative state. A nation committed to primacy requires not only powerful defence and intelligence agencies, but also the ability to mobilise resources with popular assent on a vast scale, which populism tends to frustrate. A populist United States would risk becoming hollowed out, starting out with impressive military might that could ebb fast as federal support waned in the face of countervailing domestic priorities to which the government would have to cater to maintain legitimacy and support. Should the federal government dismantle the Department of Education, disinvest in education and devolve substantial responsibility for it to state and local governments, as recommended in *Mandate for Leadership*, for example, this would likely undermine the focus on science, technology, engineering and mathematics that drives the defence innovation generally considered necessary to sustain American military superiority.

Many now apprehend the foreign-policy establishment with frustration, disdain or both. It is too easy to forget that it originated as a set of visionary post-war ideas advanced by giants of international relations and produced the United States' impressive if deeply flawed performance on the world stage over the course of 80 years. That is why the so-called Blob gained, and deserved, the canonical status that made it a target.[48] Given Project 2025's palliative overlap with the US foreign-policy orthodoxy and its wide embrace by the Republican Party, it is likely to have some staying power and to infiltrate the evolution of American grand strategy. If the American political system were not so polarised, some Democrats might even find its perspective appealing. Populism may be its poison pill. With the country's strategic vocation and leadership thus imperilled, it may be time for the establishment to return to form and step up.

Notes

1   According to the Heritage Foundation's website, Project 2025 consists of four interconnected pillars: 1) a policy book, *Mandate for Leadership: The Conservative Promise*; 2) a personnel database of conservatives to staff a newly elected Republican administration; 3) a Presidential Administration Academy to educate and train personnel for conservative activities; and 4) an implementation playbook to execute the policy ideas outlined in *Mandate for Leadership*. Heritage Foundation, 'Project 2025', https://www.heritage.org/conservatism/commentary/project-2025. This article focuses on *Mandate for Leadership*.

2   See Rachel Barber, 'What Is Project 2025? The Presidential Transition Project Explained', *USA Today*, 10 June 2024, https://www.usatoday.com/story/news/politics/elections/2024/06/10/heritage-foundation-project-2025-explained/74042435007/.

3   Larry Hogan, 'Project 2025 Shreds American Values', *Washington Post*, 19 July 2024, https://www.washingtonpost.com/opinions/2024/07/19/larry-hogan-project-2025-trump-abortion/.

4   Paul Krugman, 'Don't Lose Sight of Project 2025. That's the Real Trump', *New York Times*, 15 July 2024, https://www.nytimes.com/2024/07/15/opinion/trump-project-2025.html.

5   Edward Luce, 'The Appeal of an American Caesar', *Financial Times*, 12 June 2024, https://www.ft.com/content/9a34c080-a1d2-4202-9cc7-54e849339e49.

6   See Ali Swenson, 'A Conservative Leading the Pro-Trump Project 2025 Suggests There Will Be a New American Revolution',

Politico, 4 July 2024, https://www.politico.com/news/2024/07/04/leader-of-the-pro-trump-project-2025-suggests-there-will-be-a-new-american-revolution-00166583.

7   University of Massachusetts Amherst, 'Americans Widely Oppose "Project 2025" According to New UMass Amherst Poll', 8 August 2024, https://www.umass.edu/news/article/americans-widely-oppose-project-2025-according-new-umass-amherst-poll.

8   University of Massachusetts Amherst, 'Trump, GOP, Project 2025, Violence 2024 National Poll', 8 August 2024, https://www.umass.edu/political-science/about/reports/2024-3.

9   Quoted in, for example, Emily Brooks, 'Heritage Faces Blowback After "Bloodless" Revolution Comment', *Hill*, 6 July 2024, https://thehill.com/homenews/campaign/4757210-heritage-blowback-bloodless-revolution/.

10 Alex Shephard, 'Read J.D. Vance's Violent Foreword to Project 2025 Leader's New Book', *New Republic*, 30 July 2024, https://newrepublic.com/article/184393/jd-vance-violent-foreword-kevin-roberts-project-2025-leader-book.

11 Paul Dans and Steven Groves (eds), *Mandate for Leadership: The Conservative Promise* (Washington DC: Heritage Foundation, 2023), p. 193.

12 Ben Rhodes, a deputy national security advisor to Barack Obama, ruefully coined the term 'the Blob'. See Ben Rhodes, 'The Democratic Renewal: What It Will Take to Fix U.S. Foreign Policy', *Foreign Affairs*, vol. 99, no. 5, September/October 2020, pp. 46–83.

13 Josh Dawsey, Rosalind S. Helderman and David A. Fahrenthold, 'How Trump Abandoned His Pledge to "Drain the Swamp"', *Washington Post*, 24 October 2020, https://www.washingtonpost.com/politics/trump-drain-the-swamp/2020/10/24/52c7682c-0a5a-11eb-9be6-cf25fb429f1a_story.html.

14 Dans and Groves, *Mandate for Leadership*, p. 92.

15 *Ibid.*, p. 93.

16 *Ibid.*, p. 11.

17 *Ibid.*, p. 12.

18 For both diagnosis and advocacy, see Tarun Chhabra, Scott Moore and Dominic Tierney, 'The Left Should Play the China Card', *Foreign Affairs*, 13 February 2020, https://www.foreignaffairs.com/articles/china/2020-02-13/left-should-play-china-card; and Ali Wyne, 'How to Think About Potentially Decoupling from China', *Washington Quarterly*, vol. 43, no. 1, Spring 2020, pp. 41–64.

19 Dans and Groves (eds), *Mandate for Leadership*, p. 93.

20 *Ibid.*

21 *Ibid.*, p. 182.

22 'Trump Says He Had "Very Good Call" with Ukraine's Zelenskiy, Pledges to End War', Reuters, 19 July 2024, https://www.reuters.com/world/us/trump-says-he-had-very-good-call-with-ukraines-zelenskiy-friday-2024-07-19/.

23 'Transcript: Donald Trump on NATO, Turkey's Coup Attempt and the World', *New York Times*, 21 July 2016, https://www.nytimes.com/2016/07/22/us/politics/donald-trump-foreign-policy-interview.html?_r=0.

24 Dans and Groves (eds), *Mandate for Leadership*, p. 187.

25 *Ibid.*, p. 93.

26 *Ibid.*

27 *Ibid.*, pp. 95, 123–5.

28 *Ibid.*, pp. 366–7, 372, 399.

29 Zachary B. Wolf, 'Trump Explains His Militaristic Plan to Deport 15–20 Million People', CNN, 1 May 2024, https://www.cnn.com/2024/05/01/ politics/trump-immigration-what-matters/index.html.

30 Dans and Groves (eds), *Mandate for Leadership*, pp. 12–13.

31 See Hal Brands, Peter Feaver and William Inboden, 'In Defense of the Blob', *Foreign Affairs*, 29 April 2020, https://www.foreignaffairs.com/united-states/defense-blob; and Rhodes, 'The Democratic Renewal: What It Will Take to Fix U.S. Foreign Policy'.

32 The text itself acknowledges the section's internal inconsistency. See Dans and Groves (eds), *Mandate for Leadership*, p. 658.

33 *Ibid.*, p. 766.

34 *Ibid.*, p. 263.

35 See John Bolton, *Surrender Is Not an Option: Defending America at the United Nations* (New York: Threshold Editions, 2008).

36 *Ibid.*, pp. 702–3.

37 See Faith E. Pinho, '4 Takeaways from the New Republican Party Platform – Or Trump's Playbook', *Los Angeles Times*, 8 July 2024, https://www.latimes.com/politics/ story/2024-07-08/4-takeaways-from-the-republicans-new-platform.

38 Donald J. Trump, 'Agenda 47', https:// www.donaldjtrump.com/platform.

39 See Walter Russell Mead, 'The Jacksonian Tradition and American Foreign Policy', *National Interest*, no. 58, Winter 1999/2000, pp. 5–29.

40 Walter Russell Mead, 'The Jacksonian Revolt: American Populism and the Liberal Order', *Foreign Affairs*, vol. 96, no. 2, March/April 2017, pp. 2–7.

41 See, for example, Nicholas Crawford, 'The Energy Transition, Protectionism and Transatlantic Relations', *Survival*, vol. 65, no. 2, April–May 2023, pp. 75–102.

42 Quoted in, for example, Yoni Appelbaum, 'Trump's Foreign-policy "Adhocracy"', *Atlantic*, 27 June 2017, https://www.theatlantic. com/international/archive/2017/06/ trumps-foreign-policy-adhoc-racy/531732/.

43 See Colin Dueck, *Age of Iron: On Conservative Nationalism* (Oxford: Oxford University Press, 2019), pp. 114–15.

44 Charles Tilly, 'Reflections on the History of European State-making', in Charles Tilly (ed.), *The Formation of National States in Western Europe* (Princeton, NJ: Princeton University Press, 1975), p. 42.

45 See Van Jackson, *Grand Strategies of the Left: The Foreign Policy of Progressive Worldmaking* (Cambridge: Cambridge University Press, 2024).

46 Ronald R. Krebs, 'Pluralism, Populism, and the Impossibility of Grand Strategy', in Thierry Balzacq and Ronald R. Krebs (eds), *The Oxford Handbook of Grand Strategy* (Oxford: Oxford University Press, 2021), p. 683.

47 Peter Dombrowski, 'Alternatives to Grand Strategy', in Balzacq and Krebs (eds), *The Oxford Handbook of Grand Strategy*, pp. 620–3.

48 See Brands, Feaver and Inboden, 'In Defense of the Blob'. See also Jacob Heilbrunn, 'How the War in Ukraine Is Reviving the Blob', *Politico*, 6 May 2022, https://www.politico.com/ news/magazine/2022/05/06/biden-

foreign-policy-blob-00030443; and Robert Wright, 'Toward a Unified Theory of Blob-dom', Responsible Statecraft, 13 October 2021, https://responsiblestatecraft.org/2021/10/13/toward-a-unified-theory-of-blob-dom/.

The Death of Nasrallah and the Fate of Lebanon

Emile Hokayem

The killing by Israel on 27 September 2024 of Hassan Nasrallah, who had served as Lebanese Hizbullah's charismatic leader since 1992, is a turning point not just for the organisation he led, but for Lebanon and indeed the whole of the Levant, as well as for Iran's strategy of influence. For three decades, he did more than anyone else to shape, through guile and violence, both his country's politics and the security dynamics of the broader Levantine region.

The more Nasrallah grew in stature, the more formidable Hizbullah seemed. Equipped with advanced missile capabilities and uninhabited aerial vehicles (UAVs), and battle-hardened through its many regional adventures, the Shia militant group was often described (including by this author) as the Middle East's most powerful non-state actor. Enabled by Iran and dominant in Lebanon, the group dislodged Israel from southern Lebanon in 2000 and fought it to a standstill in 2006. Later, it came to the rescue of the Assad regime in Syria, mentored Iraqi militias and assisted the Houthis' rise in Yemen. Among Tehran's constellation of partners, Nasrallah came second only to Ali Khamenei, Iran's supreme leader, and was an equal of Qassem Soleimani, an Islamic Revolutionary Guard Corps Quds Force commander who was killed by the United States in 2020.

Still, he proved no match for Israel's superior intelligence and air capabilities. In a matter of weeks, starting with the killing of Fuad Shukr,

Emile Hokayem is Director for Regional Security at the IISS. This article is adapted from an IISS Online Analysis piece that was published on 7 October 2024 at https://www.iiss.org/online-analysis/online-analysis/2024/10/the-israel-hamas-war-one-year-on/.

Hizbullah's most senior military commander, in July 2024, Israel decapitated the group's upper- and mid-level echelons. The tally of killed leaders includes members of the tight-knit guerrilla and terrorist group that began rising through the ranks in the 1980s, such as Ibrahim Aqil. (Its two most famous members, Imad Mughniyeh and Mustafa Badreddine, had already been killed by Israel in 2008 and 2016 respectively.) If not yet broken, Hizbullah is definitely weakened. It is struggling militarily against an Israeli enemy that has moved ruthlessly against it, and has been damaged by its apparent weakness and dimming reputation.

An unwanted war

How did this happen? Hizbullah's arrogance, hubris and miscalculations must share in the blame. Hizbullah was not involved in the 7 October 2023 attack on Israel, but it joined the fight out of solidarity with Hamas, hoping for a short war and a political boost for standing with the Palestinians. Hizbullah believed that its calibrated military response, one that was within the rules of escalation that had prevailed in its conflict with Israel since 2006, and its linking of a ceasefire in Gaza to one that would follow in Lebanon, would somehow keep the armed contest under control.

In truth, Nasrallah had deeply misread Israel's mood after 7 October. He had calculated that Israel would not risk a two-front war, underestimating how the fear that Hizbullah, a more powerful foe than Hamas, might conduct a similar operation and inflict much greater casualties would shape Israel's resolve. By establishing a linkage with a ceasefire in Gaza that Nasrallah expected but that never came, he effectively cornered himself. He also found out that Iranian involvement in the war would be restrained because Tehran could not risk a slide toward a direct confrontation with the US. He was effectively alone in facing Israel even as he hailed the advent of a 'unity of fronts' among Iran-backed militias.

Above all, this was not the war Hizbullah wanted, nor was it the one it was designed to fight. Hizbullah was supposed to be a strategic force that would deter Israel and mentor and guide other Iranian-backed militias in the region. Its full force was to be deployed in case Iran's territory, nuclear sites or leadership came under Israeli or US attack, not in the service of a fellow militia

in occupied Gaza. Its war-fighting concept assumed a rapid and violent conflict that would include a massive exchange of missiles, rockets and drones
to overwhelm Israeli air defences, accompanied by intense ground operations. Hizbullah's occasional display of technological prowess in the current
conflict, such as sending a drone over the port of Haifa and other critical
facilities, and destroying several Israeli military assets, gave a taste of what
the movement hoped to achieve. In its 2006 war with Israel, Hizbullah fired
a daily average of 124 rockets; Israeli and independent studies estimated it
could fire as many as 3,000 in the current war.[1] This would have paralysed
life in Israel, stunning its population and forcing a climbdown that would
have inevitably been interpreted as a success by Hizbullah.

Instead, for 11 months and counting, Hizbullah has been caught in an
Israeli-dictated campaign of attrition of ever-higher intensity based on superior intelligence-gathering and airpower, which has imposed high costs on
Hizbullah's command-and-control structure and weapons stockpiles. This
was the war the Israel Defense Forces (IDF) had been prepared to fight since
2006, one for which Hizbullah had no answer. Israel's superior air defences,
combined with Hizbullah's own inability to articulate escalatory steps that
aligned with its reluctance to risk an all-out war, left the group behind
in the air war. With fighting in Gaza becoming less intense, Israel could
devote more attention and military resources to its northern front. Between
October 2023 and August 2024, for every projectile Hizbullah fired at Israel,
Israel fired four. Importantly, Hizbullah fired far fewer rockets and missiles than expected. Whether this was because of its self-imposed restraint,
the destruction of its capabilities or a mixture of both will remain unclear
until the end of the war. In any case, the damage inflicted on Israel has
been limited compared to expectations. As of October 2024, Israel's critical
infrastructure remained largely unharmed, though 80,000 Israeli residents
could not return to their homes in northern Israel. In contrast, over a million
Lebanese were displaced, while critical infrastructure and dozens of southern villages were partially or totally destroyed.

All of this has caused Hizbullah's carefully curated image to take a
beating. The incredible penetration of its security apparatus, which led to
the detonation of members' pagers and walkie-talkies on 17–18 September,

followed in rapid succession by the elimination of nearly its entire command structure, suggests internal betrayals, abysmal security protocols and communications weaknesses.

In his last televised speech on 19 September, a tired-looking and at times humbled Nasrallah seemed to finally understand that his attempt to restore deterrence against Israel was not working. But he still cast his ability to deny Israel its stated objective – the return of Israeli residents to their homes in northern Israel – as a success. He believed that he had properly assessed Israel's risk appetite and seemed confident that escalation could be managed.[2]

Ten days later, a massive air-bombing operation killed him and other senior commanders, including a senior Iranian Quds Force visitor. The intensification of the Israeli air campaign and limited raids across Lebanon's southern regions depopulated large swathes of territory, creating an overwhelming displacement crisis. By late October, Israel still had not mounted a large-scale ground operation. Instead, it remained focused on destroying Hizbullah's military infrastructure in the area south of the Litani River. Israel was also degrading the civilian infrastructure in the area so as to make it impossible for the civilian population to return in the near term. This scorched-earth approach represents a departure from its behaviour during its two-decade occupation of Lebanon and suggests a different security model than straight-up occupation.

Hizbullah's surviving commanders appear to have relinquished their predecessors' caution and are firing more projectiles at Israel. They have also had to defend against a ground campaign with diminished capabilities, hoping that their preparations, knowledge of the field and agile structure will withstand the Israeli onslaught. The number of Hizbullahi and Israeli casualties in southern Lebanon remains unclear, but the IDF has suffered more significant losses and lost more materiel than in Gaza.

Into the unknown

Nasrallah's death and Hizbullah's weakening have pushed Lebanon into the unknown. Nasrallah's immediate successor, Hashem Safi al-Din, was killed only weeks later. Naim Qassem, who was announced in early November, is a hardline cleric who will have to consolidate what is left of the group while dealing with a tremendous rout. Beyond seeking to ensure Hizbullah's survival, he will try to revive the *muqawama* (resistance) spirit, invoke Nasrallah's ghost to mobilise his constituency and look for support in Iraq, Syria and Yemen. Importantly, he will have to negotiate a new partnership with Iran. Nasrallah had significant political and strategic autonomy because he was trusted and valued by Tehran. Seeing its main partner so battered, the Quds Force appears to have asserted greater operational and strategic control over Hizbullah. Many Hizbullah sympathisers blame Iran for its lack of support and strategic clarity; they also suspect that Iran's lax security protocols are to blame for the intelligence breaches. But the organisation will not be able to rebuild its military and financial strength, nor uphold its ideology, without an Iranian commitment.

The war, unwanted by most Lebanese citizens, has been blamed as much on Hizbullah's recklessness as on Israel's brutality. Many Lebanese do not want to shoulder the risks and costs of Hizbullah's gambles. The fact that Nasrallah so badly misread Israel's intentions and capabilities, at the cost of his own life, has given fodder to his many detractors. There is considerable displeasure with – even hatred for – the Shia movement and how it has forced its *muqawama* agenda onto the country through threats, coercion, assassinations and bloody regional adventures, and how it aligned itself with Iran's priorities and policies. According to the 2024 Arab Barometer, while nearly 80% of Lebanese Shi'ites believed that 'Hizbullah is good for the Arab world', only 12% of Sunnis, 11% of Christians and 16% of Druzes agreed.[3]

Even as it lost allies prior to the war, Hizbullah remained the organising force of Lebanese politics. It dictated political life and, when needed, threatened its rivals. The degree to which it can continue to do so in the face of recent military and reputational setbacks will help shape the next phase of the conflict. Hizbullah's new leadership has already tried to intimidate its local rivals: Qassem reaffirmed the linkage between the war and a ceasefire in Gaza, and ruled out any decision on key matters such as Lebanon's presidential election or the deployment of the military to southern Lebanon until a ceasefire is reached. Even so, other political forces are beginning to challenge its hegemony and to explore alternative political and security arrangements. Lebanese politicians understand that the US remains essential to reaching a sustainable ceasefire despite Washington's support for the Israeli campaign, and have publicly called for the implementation of United Nations Security Council Resolution 1701, which would remove Hizbullah forces from southern Lebanon and replace them with Lebanese army and UN forces. Prior to the September escalation, Hizbullah had resisted the full implementation of this resolution, but had agreed to remove some capabilities. These terms are clearly no longer acceptable either to Israel, which is effectively creating new facts on the ground, or to the US, which, after nearly a year of trying to avoid a regional war, has all but embraced the Israeli campaign in the hope that in doing so, it might still moderate Israel's aims. Indeed, Israel has so far refrained from targeting critical infrastructure in non-Hizbullah regions, such as Beirut's airport or electrical and water plants that were hit in 2006.

Beyond the battlefield, Hizbullah's main concern is to secure the well-being and continuous support of its Shia constituency. Nasrallah had presented himself as Lebanon's shield against Israel and Shi'ites' shield against other communities. Anger at his death will be directed at Israel, but also at domestic rivals. Many members of the Shia community appear disoriented by Nasrallah's absence and the speed with which Hizbullah has been battered. The sectarian anxieties that underpinned Hizbullah's appeal have crystallised among its supporters, who stand to lose significantly in political status and access to resources and services. Much of Hizbullah's constituency has been forced to flee their homes and seek shelter elsewhere; early solidarity in non-Hizbullah regions is giving way to political recriminations and social tensions. This presages bottom-up internal instability.

The Lebanese population has also been sobered to discover that assassinations of political leaders, however divisive, do not translate into political openings, and that callous sectarian gloating poisons communal relations. Regardless of their religious affiliation, Lebanese citizens see Israel's campaign through the prism and horrors of Gaza, and assume that, should Israel invade, it will occupy parts of the country as it has in the past. This would cause further fragmentation of an already fractured Lebanese state and army, and revive Hizbullah's resistance ethos.

Indeed, the hope that Lebanon's government and military could sweep in and stabilise the situation has been undermined by the fact that both institutions are in their worst shape ever. The country has failed to elect a president since 2022, and its economy has been in shambles since the 2019 financial and banking collapse. For its part, the Lebanese Armed Forces' (LAF) readiness has been eroded by low morale, bad pay and a sense of drift. It remains unwilling to take any action that would alienate Hizbullah or pose a risk to force cohesion. Israel has targeted LAF personnel, but the LAF, knowing itself to be outgunned, has been unwilling to respond in case this provokes an escalation it cannot match.

Lebanon's fate will be set by Israel's ambitions. Israel could calculate that its interests are best served by an occupation of southern Lebanon and a continuous campaign to degrade Hizbullah. The resulting chaos and even state collapse would prevent Hizbullah from regrouping or restoring its military strength because the group would have to focus on the needs of its constituency. This, of course, runs the risk of reviving Hizbullah's cause. Israel could also, with US, European and Arab encouragement, end its campaign and seek a diplomatic settlement that conditions support for Lebanon on state control over southern Lebanon in parallel with an international effort to provide conditional economic assistance if Beirut undertakes the hard political and economic reforms needed. A diminished Hizbullah would then have to answer for its immense political and strategic failures.

Notes

[1] Yuval Azulay, 'Fire and Blood: The Chilling Reality Facing Israel in a War with Hezbollah', CTECH, 2 September 2024, https://www.calcalistech.com/ctechnews/article/skcodbmia.

[2] See Tamara Qiblawi, 'In Hezbollah Leader's Speech Are Signs of a Group Driven Deeper Underground', CNN, 19 September 2024, https://edition.cnn.com/2024/09/19/middleeast/lebanon-hezbollah-hassan-nasrallah-speech-analysis-intl-latam/index.html.

[3] See MaryClare Roche and Michael Robbins, 'What the Lebanese People Really Think of Hezbollah', *Foreign Affairs*, 12 July 2024, https://www.foreignaffairs.com/lebanon/what-lebanese-people-really-think-hezbollah.

Playing Defence: Europe and Democracy

Elene Panchulidze and Richard Youngs

The place of democratic values in European foreign policies is shifting. Governments and diplomats are increasingly unsettled by the threats facing democracy both within Europe and globally. Yet on some issues, the challenging international context seems to be pushing them towards more traditional notions of geopolitical self-interest that sideline democratic norms. Debates over the right balance between security and democracy have sharpened as incoming leaders in the United Kingdom and European Union formulate new foreign-policy doctrines and begin to revise strategic priorities.

While security imperatives have become more prominent, European support for democracy has not disappeared. It has, however, changed in significant ways. A so-called 'third wave' of autocratisation has combined with power shifts away from the West to propel the EU and European governments towards a more *defensive* form of democracy support. European approaches to international democracy are today more tailored to holding autocratisation at bay than to fostering new democratic transitions. This shift brings improvements to European security policies but also raises concerns about the place of democratic norms in international relations and geostrategy.

Elene Panchulidze is research coordinator at the European Partnership for Democracy, where she directs work on the European Democracy Hub. **Richard Youngs** is senior fellow at Carnegie Europe, co-founder of the European Democracy Hub and professor of international relations at the University of Warwick. His latest book is *Democratic Crossroads: Transformations in 21st-century Politics* (Oxford University Press, 2024).

Survival | vol. 66 no. 6 | December 2024–January 2025 | pp. 41–47   https://doi.org/10.1080/00396338.2024.2432193

Renewed focus on democracy

Support for democracy has nominally been at the heart of European foreign policies for many years. While European governments never fully lived up to their pro-democracy rhetoric in practice, in the 1990s and early 2000s they did direct significant effort and funding into supporting political-reform processes. They harnessed a relatively positive tide of democratisation around the world and worked to push democratic norms into an expanding circle of countries. The EU crafted an intricate policy toolbox with diverse financial, political and technical instruments to advance democratic norms through external action. Then in the 2010s, amid a global trend of democratic regression and autocratisation, European support for democracy lost traction as other priorities grounded in realpolitik gained in importance.

In another swing of the pendulum, today's more dangerous strategic context appears to have pushed democracy back up the foreign-policy agenda. Russia's war on Ukraine and other geopolitical challenges have formally sharpened the European focus on democratic norms. European governments and EU institutions have come to frame democracy support as a matter of high geopolitical importance in the shadow of war.

European governments have conceived of their support to Ukraine since early 2022 as a defence not just of territorial sovereignty, but also of democratic values.[1] Russia's invasion has pushed the EU to focus on defending both Ukrainian democracy and the embattled place of democracy more widely within the international system. This has spilled over into broader EU security dynamics. The EU's focus on democratic norms has become central to the development of a more assertive and unified set of order-related security policies after the invasion.[2] In the last several years, European states have developed a plethora of new security partnerships with Asian democracies in particular, and have framed these as being about defending democracies from autocratic threats.

A defensive democracy agenda

European governments and EU institutions have not reneged on the democracy agenda, but this agenda has clearly taken on a more defensive character. If, in more liberally optimistic times, classical democracy support was about expanding political pluralism into new areas, such efforts are now more cautious, smaller in scale and lower in ambition. The overall balance of democracy support has shifted towards the far more protective aim of limiting the impact of authoritarian regimes' increasingly assertive efforts to undermine democratic norms.

The most obvious change is that the EU has come to focus far more on defending its own democracy from external attack. Ursula von der Leyen stated at the start of her second mandate as EU Commission president earlier this year that 'Europe cannot control dictators and demagogues across the world, but it can choose to protect its own democracy'.[3] Her flagship initiative, the European Democracy Shield, represents an effort to push back against disinformation and other digital attacks on EU democratic processes.[4] The EU Commission has begun to withhold funding from member-state governments that flout the rule of law, and now funds a €1.55 billion programme of democracy projects inside EU member states.[5]

Even where EU efforts are directed outside its own borders, such support is now infused with a protective ethos. European democracy support has increasingly become a means of battling for influence over the future international order and preserving the role of democracies within it.[6] NATO has warned that 'advancing authoritarianism challenge[s] the Alliance's interests and values'.[7] The UK's Integrated Review Refresh 2023 and Germany's 2023 National Security Strategy likewise identify surging authoritarianism as a threat to be mitigated.[8] Europe's democracy agenda is now directed at stemming attacks on the liberal international order – a very different framing from ten years ago.

This conditions where European funding is directed. Much more 'democracy' funding now goes to bolstering democratic governments' cyber resilience in places such as Armenia and Moldova. Indeed, the lion's share of EU aid is being directed towards the Union's new programme of infrastructure funding, the Global Gateway, which has been billed as a democratic alternative to China's Belt and Road Initiative. Thus, Global Gateway projects are mainly about competing with Chinese infrastructure projects and creating commercial opportunities for European companies. Such funding bears little resemblance to classical democracy support, and yet the EU frames it as part of the struggle for democratic values within the global order.

The US-led Summit for Democracy process is similarly aimed at fostering coordination among democratic nations in defence against rising global authoritarianism. The Biden administration framed this process as an effort to build a coalition of democratic states against authoritarian threats to the global order, and European governments (except Hungary) saw the value in building partnerships to help defend democratic values. After three leaders' summits, however, the process may have lost some momentum, in part because non-Western democracies have been hesitant about its geopolitical tone and have pulled it towards less sensitive areas of lesson-sharing about democracy.

Meanwhile, the war in Ukraine has brought EU enlargement back onto the agenda, now as an explicit strategy to protect a democratic European order from authoritarian attack. Although many aspects of the new accession process reflect a traditional form of EU democracy support through candidates' compliance with EU norms, the European narrative around enlargement has shifted. EU policy debates are now about the need for a different kind of enlargement based on geopolitical priorities and security support for Eastern European states. EU pre-accession aid has begun to fuse democratic-reform projects with security capacity-building.[9]

A shift too far?
In some ways, these shifts are necessary and indeed overdue. For years, the democracy-support agenda unfolded in isolation from mainstream EU foreign-policy aims as a worthy project but not one that was central to the Union's security calculations. European democracy strategies have rightly become more attentive to geopolitical trends and the broader strategic context within which democracy support is nested.

Yet there is a risk that European governments may be tilting too far in their defensive approach to democracy. In some of its aspects, the emerging strategy is not much different than standard realpolitik. The priorities laid out by the incoming EU leadership team say almost nothing about making concrete improvements to democracy policy.[10] Even the 'progressive realism' of the UK's new Labour government evinces more realpolitik than any clear strategy for democracy support.[11]

In the name of defending democracy against China and Russia, European governments and the EU collectively have in recent years intensified their support to many autocratic governments, especially in Central Asia, the Middle East, North Africa and Sub-Saharan Africa. The strategy of supporting autocracies in the name of defending democracy will require an awkward balancing act. It risks pushing the age-old issue of double standards to a new level. Europe's failure to defend democratic self-determination with the same clarity in Palestine as in Ukraine has undermined its credibility as a supporter of democratic norms around the world. Moreover, the strategy is in most cases simply not working: European governments have bolstered support to many non-democratic regimes without these becoming any less hostile towards European foreign-policy aims on Ukraine or other issues.

Beyond protecting European democracy from outside threats and containing authoritarian power, a democracy strategy also needs to offer more positive support for democratic activists and reformers in other countries. Too much securitisation of democracy policy risks overriding the kinds of local dynamics necessary to bring about successful political change. In the last two years, the EU has diverted significant amounts of funding away from support for local reform processes in fragile states and countries suffering major political crises in favour of the Global Gateway and security cooperation with autocratic regimes.[12]

Europe's strategic shift is still embryonic, and much work remains to be done in mapping out exactly how security and democracy strategies can be brought together in a mutually reinforcing fashion. A surface-level focus on containing the authoritarian surge will not suffice to address the root drivers of anti-democratic behaviour. As new leaders begin work in Brussels and London, the key challenge will be for the EU and European governments to develop a democracy policy that ties internal and external initiatives into a seamless whole. Their success will determine whether democracy policies become a core pillar of European strategy or simply wither away at this pivotal geopolitical moment.

Notes

1   See European Commission, '2022 State of the Union Address by President von der Leyen', 14 September 2022, https://ec.europa.eu/commission/presscorner/detail/en/speech_22_5493.

2   See Giselle Bosse, 'The EU's Response to the Russian Invasion of Ukraine: Invoking Norms and Values in Times of Fundamental Rupture', *Journal of Common Market Studies*, vol. 62, no. 5, 2023, pp. 1,222–38.

3   European Commission, 'Statement at the European Parliament Plenary by President Ursula von der Leyen, Candidate for a Second Mandate 2024–2029', Brussels, 18 July 2024, https://neighbourhood-enlargement.ec.europa.eu/news/statement-european-parliament-plenary-president-ursula-von-der-leyen-candidate-second-mandate-2024-2024-07-18_en.

4   See *ibid*.

5   European Union, 'Citizens, Equality, Rights and Values Programme (2021–2027)', https://eur-lex.europa.eu/EN/legal-content/summary/citizens-equality-rights-and-values-programme-2021-2027.html.

6   See Council of the European Union, 'Council Conclusions on Democracy', 14 October 2019, https://data.consilium.europa.eu/doc/document/ST-12836-2019-INIT/en/pdf.

7   North Atlantic Treaty Organization, 'NATO 2022 Strategic Concept', 2022, p. 1, https://www.nato.int/strategic-concept/.

8   UK Government, 'Integrated Review Refresh 2023: Responding to a More Contested and Volatile World', March 2023, https://assets.publishing.service.gov.uk/media/641d72f45155a2000c6ad5d5/11857435_NS_IR_Refresh_2023_Supply_AllPages_Revision_7_WEB_PDF.pdf; and Federal Government of Germany, 'Integrated Security for Germany: National Security Strategy', https://www.nationalesicherheitsstrategie.de/en.html.

9   See Elene Panchulidze and Richard Youngs, 'Beyond the Copenhagen Criteria: Rethinking the Political Conditions of EU Accession', Carnegie Europe, 2024, https://carnegieendowment.org/research/2024/06/rethinking-eu-accession-criteria?lang=en&center=europe.

10 See Richard Youngs and Elene Panchulidze, 'The New European Commission's Distorted Democracy Agenda', Carnegie Europe, 8 October 2024, https://carnegieendowment.org/europe/strategic-europe/2024/10/the-new-european-commissions-distorted-democracy-agenda?lang=en.

11 See David Lammy, 'The Case for Progressive Realism: Why Britain Must Chart a New Global Course', *Foreign Affairs*, May/June 2024, https://www.foreignaffairs.com/united-kingdom/case-progressive-realism-david-lammy.

12 See Alexandra Watson and Johannes Friedrich, 'A Growing Gap: EU Peace and Security Funding Beyond Ukraine', Global Public Policy Institute, 30 September 2024, https://gppi.net/2024/09/30/eu-peace-and-security-funding-beyond-ukraine.

Noteworthy

Middle East tumult

'Simultaneous targeting of thousands of individuals, whether civilians or members of armed groups, without knowledge as to who was in possession of the targeted devices, their location and their surroundings at the time of the attack, violates international human rights law and, to the extent applicable, international humanitarian law.'

United Nations High Commissioner for Human Rights Volker Türk comments on the detonation of thousands of pagers belonging to Hizbullah members in Lebanon on 17 September 2024.[1]

'Hizbullah keeps on sending its missiles against our people endlessly. At the end you have the right to defend yourself.'

Israeli President Isaac Herzog gives an interview to Sky News on 22 September.[2]

'Since October 7, we have also been determined to prevent a wider war that engulfs the entire region. Hezbollah, unprovoked, joined the October 7th attack launching rockets into Israel. Almost a year later, too many on each side of the Israeli–Lebanon border remain displaced.

Full-scale war is not in anyone's interest. Even as the situation has escalated, a diplomatic solution is still possible. In fact, it remains the only path to lasting security to allow the residents from both countries to return to their homes on the border safely.'

US President Joe Biden addresses the UN General Assembly on 24 September.[3]

'It was not strong. It is not promising and it would not solve this problem. I [am] still hoping. The United States is the only country that can really make a difference in the Middle East and with regard to Lebanon.'

Lebanese Foreign Minister Abdallah Bou Habib comments on Biden's UN speech.[4]

'The singling out of the one and only Jewish state continues to be a moral stain on the United Nations. It has made this once-respected institution contemptible in the eyes of decent people everywhere. But for the Palestinians, this UN house of darkness is home court. They know that in this swamp of antisemitic bile, there's an automatic majority willing to demonize the Jewish state for anything. In this anti-Israel flat-earth society, any false charge, any outlandish allegation can muster a majority.'

Israeli Prime Minister Benjamin Netanyahu delivers a speech at the UN on 27 September.[5]

'The Islamic world has lost a noble figure, the Resistance Front has lost an eminent standard-bearer, and Lebanon's Hezbollah has lost an unparalleled leader. However, the blessings from Sayyid Hassan Nasrallah's decades of planning and jihad will never be lost.'

Iranian Supreme Leader Sayyid Ali Khamenei reacts to the killing of Hizbullah leader Hassan Nasrallah on 27 September.[6]

'"If someone rises up to kill you, kill him first." Yesterday, the State of Israel eliminated the arch-murderer Hassan Nasrallah.'

Netanyahu releases a statement on 28 September.[7]

'The death of our leader [Yahya] Sinwar and those [killed] before him will only increase the strength and resolve of our group. We continue on the path of Hamas and the spirit of the Al-Aqsa Flood. Our banner will not fall but will remain raised high.'
Khalil al-Hayya, a senior Hamas leader, confirms Hamas leader Yahya Sinwar's death in Gaza on 16 October.[8]

'My dismissal stems from disagreements on three main issues:

The first is my firm stance that everyone of conscription age must serve in the IDF [Israel Defense Forces] and defend the State of Israel. This issue is no longer just a social matter; it is the most critical matter for our existence – the security of the State of Israel and the people living in Zion.

[…]

The second issue is our moral obligation and responsibility to bring our kidnapped sons and daughters back home as quickly as possible, with as many alive as possible, to their families. Based on my role, experience and the military achievements of the past year, with a clear-eyed view of reality, I state that this is achievable but involves painful compromises that Israel can bear, and the IDF can deal with.

[…]

The third issue is the necessity of drawing lessons through a thorough and relevant investigation. When it comes to the national level – political, security and military – there is a name for uncovering the truth and learning from it: a state commission of inquiry. I have said and I repeat, I am responsible for the security establishment over the past two years – for the successes and the failures. Only sunlight and a truthful investigation will allow us to learn and build our strength to face future challenges.'
Yoav Gallant delivers a statement after being dismissed as Israel's defence minister on 5 November.[9]

Elections: tremors and an earthquake

'We have written a piece of history together today. We have opened a door to a new era.'
Herbert Kickl celebrates the election victory of his far-right Freedom Party (FPÖ) in Austria on 29 September 2024, the first time a far-right party has won the most votes in that country since the Nazi Party. As of this journal's press time, the centre-left Social Democrats (SPÖ) and centre-right Austrian People's Party (ÖVP) were in talks to form a government without the Freedom Party.[10]

'Russia is pouring millions in dirty money to hijack our democratic processes. This isn't just meddling – it's full-blown interference aimed at destabilising our future. And it is alarming … We have a unique opportunity: Moldova has a pro-European president, parliament, and government. The EU [European Union] is open to our membership, with all countries backing accession talks last June. Moldova's survival as a democracy is on the line, and the geopolitical stakes are higher than ever.'
Olga Roşca, a foreign-policy adviser to Moldovan President Maia Sandu, alleges interference in the country's presidential election and referendum on EU membership in October 2024.[11]

'The people of Moldova have spoken: our EU future will now be anchored in the constitution. We fought fairly in an unfair fight – and we won. But the fight isn't over. We will keep pushing for peace, prosperity, and the freedom to build our own future.'
Sandu releases a statement after 50.46% of Moldovans who voted in the referendum approved of an EU-membership bid.[12]

'I am here because the government rigged the elections, stealing our voices and our right to choose our future … We want the world to know that we chose Europe, not Russia. I just hope the world can hear us.'

Kato Bochorishvili, a 21-year-old Georgian, explains why she joined protests against the results of Georgia's parliamentary election on 26 October, in which the Georgia Dream party claimed victory.[13]

'This will truly be the golden age of America. That's what we have. This is a magnificent victory for the American people that will allow us to Make America Great Again … This will forever be remembered as the day the American people regained control of their country.'

Donald Trump claims victory in the United States' presidential election on 5 November.[14]

Zelenskyy unbowed

'We know some in the world want to talk to Putin – to meet, to talk and to speak. But what could they possibly hear from him – that he is upset because we are exercising our right to defend our people, or that he wants to keep the war and terror going just so no one thinks he was wrong? That is insane.

[…]

That is why the war cannot be calmed by talks. Action is needed … Putin has broken so many international norms and rules, and he will not stop of his own accord. Russia can only be forced into peace, and that is exactly what is needed, forcing Russia into peace as the sole aggressor in this war, the sole violator of the Charter of the United Nations.'

Ukrainian President Volodymyr Zelenskyy addresses the United Nations Security Council on 24 September 2024.[15]

Sources

1 United Nations, 'Comment by UN High Commissioner for Human Rights Volker Türk on Explosions Across Lebanon and in Syria', 18 September 2024, https://www.ohchr.org/en/statements/2024/09/comment-un-high-commissioner-human-rights-volker-turk-explosions-across-lebanon.

2 Sky News (@SkyNews), post to X, 22 September 2024, https://x.com/SkyNews/status/1837776107908583646.

3 White House, 'Remarks by President Biden Before the 79th Session of the United Nations General Assembly', 24 September 2024, https://www.whitehouse.gov/briefing-room/speeches-remarks/2024/09/24/remarks-by-president-biden-before-the-79th-session-of-the-united-nations-general-assembly-new-york-ny/.

4 'Lebanon Calls Biden's Remarks on Conflict with Israel "Not Promising"', Reuters, 24 September 2024, https://www.reuters.com/world/middle-east/lebanon-calls-bidens-remarks-conflict-with-israel-not-promising-2024-09-24/.

5 'Full Text of Netanyahu's UN Speech: "Enough Is Enough," He Says of Hezbollah, Also Warns Iran', *Times of Israel*, 27 September 2024, https://www.timesofisrael.com/full-text-of-netanyahus-un-speech-enough-is-enough-he-says-of-hezbollah-also-warns-iran/.

6 Ali Khamenei (@khamenei_ir), post to X, 28 September 2024, https://x.com/khamenei_ir/status/1840061688013283336.

7 Israeli Prime Minister's Office, 'Statement by PM Netanyahu', 28 September 2024, https://www.gov.il/en/pages/spoke-statement280924.

8 'Yahya Sinwar: Hamas Confirms Leader Killed "Fighting on Frontlines"', Middle East Eye, 18 October 2024, https://www.middleeasteye.net/news/hamas-confirms-sinwars-death.

9 'Full Text of Gallant Speech: There Will Be No Atonement for Abandoning the Hostages', *Times of Israel*, 5 November 2024, https://www.timesofisrael.com/full-text-of-gallant-speech-there-will-be-no-atonement-for-abandoning-the-hostages/.

10 Deborah Cole, 'Far-right Freedom Party Finishes First in Austrian Election, Latest Results Suggest', *Guardian*, 30 September 2024, https://www.theguardian.com/world/2024/sep/29/far-right-freedom-party-winning-austrian-election-first-results-show.

11 Pjotr Sauer, '"Russia's Dirty Money Will Hijack Our Democratic Process": How Tiny Moldova Fears Kremlin Is Fixing EU Referendum', *Guardian*, 12 October 2024, https://www.theguardian.com/world/2024/oct/12/moldova-fears-kremlin-fixing-eu-referendum-russia.

12 Maia Sandu (@sandumaiamd), post to X, 21 October 2024, https://x.com/sandumaiamd/status/1848350063606587764.

13 Pjotr Sauer, 'Thousands of Georgians Demonstrate Against Contested Election Results', *Guardian*, 28 October 2024, https://www.theguardian.com/world/2024/oct/28/thousands-of-georgians-demonstrate-against-contested-election-results.

14 Archie Mitchell, '"It's Time to Unite": Donald Trump's Victory Speech in Full', *Independent*, 6 November 2024, https://www.independent.co.uk/news/world/americas/us-politics/donald-trump-president-election-speech-b2642299.html.

15 United Nations Security Council, 'Maintenance of Peace and Security in Ukraine', 9,731st meeting, 24 September 2024, p. 4, https://documents.un.org/doc/undoc/pro/n24/273/23/pdf/n2427323.pdf.

How Evil? Deconstructing the New Russia–China–Iran–North Korea Axis

Christopher S. Chivvis and Jack Keating

In a complex geopolitical environment, simplifying threat concepts can be useful, provided they reflect reality. Monolithic communism was one such concept during the early Cold War, but it had to be cast aside in light of the Sino-Soviet split and to open the door to Richard Nixon's 'triangular' diplomacy. After 9/11, global terrorism was another such concept, but in reality, terrorism was an action, not an adversary. Making it a guiding national-security threat was a recipe for gross American overreach. Today, Washington is again verging on a new threat concept that seems bound to create more problems than it solves. The idea is that America and its allies face a new 'axis of evil' consisting of China, Russia, Iran and North Korea. Voices across the political spectrum want to make this grouping the focus of Western statecraft.[1] The fact is that cooperation among these adversaries is modest overall, and treating them as a coherent bloc ignores important uncertainties about their future bonds. In the process, it risks creating a self-fulfilling prophecy that would ultimately harm US and allied interests.

Each of these states obviously poses a threat in its own right. All four have been problematic for decades. But their cooperation so far has been ad hoc and is easily exaggerated. Their economic ties are limited. They have moved forward on security cooperation, but much of it springs from a single

Christopher S. Chivvis is Senior Fellow and Director of the American Statecraft Program at the Carnegie Endowment for International Peace (CEIP). **Jack Keating** is the James C. Gaither Junior Fellow in the American Statecraft Program at the CEIP. This article is based on research originally conducted for a CEIP working paper titled 'Cooperation Between China, Iran, North Korea, and Russia: Current and Potential Future Threats to America', published in October 2024.

Survival | vol. 66 no. 6 | December 2024–January 2025 | pp. 51–66   https://doi.org/10.1080/00396338.2024.2432198

event – Russia's war on Ukraine. Their growing bond may be an unantici-pated geopolitical cost of the war, but by the same token their cooperation will probably diminish when the war ends.

This doesn't mean their collaboration is not harmful. Their backing for Russia's war on Ukraine, their potential for proliferating nuclear and advanced missile technology, and their collective effort to thwart Western sanctions are all bad news. The real risk, however, is that their cooperation will deepen, setting the stage for real teamwork that could someday trans-form a regional crisis into a global one of proportions extremely difficult for the United States to manage. Washington should therefore monitor their ties. But turning what is a weak partnership at best into a framing concept of American statecraft would be a big mistake. Instead, Washington should seek to prevent these states from growing closer by loosening the ties that bind them. This requires ending the war in Ukraine, which has driven them together. It also means finding levers to weaken China's relationships with the other three – especially Russia. Meanwhile, the United States needs to do a better job of prioritising its global commitments so that it is less exposed to their coordinated attacks.

Backing Russia in Ukraine

Thus far, China, Iran and North Korea's support for Russia's war in Ukraine constitutes the most enduring and problematic form of security coopera-tion in the group. Iran leapt to Russia's support first, selling it thousands of *Mohajer* and *Shahed* drones and ballistic missiles.[2] The drones came at a criti-cal time for Russia, enabling Moscow to cripple Ukraine's infrastructure, saturate its missile defences and preserve missile stockpiles for a possible direct conflict with NATO.[3] The Iranians even sent advisers to Ukraine to educate the Russians on the use of the drones and helped them set up their own drone-production facility in Tatarstan. Russia is now producing drones there, reducing its reliance on Iran.[4]

More recently, North Korea has become another substantial backer of Russia's war effort. Since September 2023, North Korea has sent Russia more than five million artillery shells.[5] This is significant, as estimates suggest that Russia only has the capacity to make about 2–3m shells a year on its own.[6]

Russia has used some North Korean Kn-23/24 ballistic missiles in Ukraine, although their failure rate is reportedly quite high.[7] North Korea has also sent around 10,000 troops to Russia to fight in Ukraine.[8] These are serious contributions, but their actual impact remains to be seen given differences in training and language, and the fact that Russia is already estimated to be losing as many as 1,200 soldiers per day.[9]

China does not offer overt military assistance to Russia, but it also does not want to see Russia lose the war. Washington has accused Beijing of providing important goods to Russia, including machine tools, semiconductors, drone engines and dual-use technology that Russia has employed in cruise missiles.[10] Beijing denies the accusation, but the nature and degree of Chinese support for Russia has become an increasingly contentious issue between the US and China, and added to the long list of other disputes between the two countries.

China, Iran and North Korea have different reasons for supporting Russia's war effort. Russia is believed to have promised to advance Iran's and North Korea's military capabilities. It has reportedly pledged to sell Tehran Su-35 fighter jets and advanced air-defence systems.[11] Some technology, such as Yak-130 aircraft used to train pilots on the Su-35, has made its way into Iran, although the scale remains unclear.[12] Russia has probably also promised conventional military technology to North Korea, which may include advanced aircraft and ballistic-missile technology.[13] Russia might also seek to bolster North Korea's weapons-manufacturing capabilities, both to service its own military needs and to enable North Korea to illicitly spread weapons to America's adversaries.[14]

China's motivations are different. At the strategic level, it fears for the stability of the Russian regime, whose collapse would have dire consequences for China. It also seeks reliable and cheap energy, while at the same time aiming to avoid dependence on Russia. Beijing's support for Moscow affords it influence there, diminishes Russia and thereby solidifies China's role as the chief alternative to American power in the world.

In no case, however, is support for Russia's conflict unconditional. Iran is now in a vulnerable position at home and will not be able to offer Russia more in the future. This probably explains Russia's increased interest in its relationship with North Korea. The fact that China has thus far withheld lethal weaponry, despite a history of extensive arms cooperation with Russia, suggests that it is not wholly committed to Russia's war effort, perhaps because it still fears Western and even global reprisals.[15] Russia reportedly failed to consult with China before it invaded Ukraine, and the invasion is damaging China's relations with Europe.[16]

Security cooperation beyond Ukraine

Outside the war in Ukraine, security cooperation among the group primarily serves political purposes. China and Russia have a long history of conducting high-profile joint military exercises. Since Iran joined the Shanghai Cooperation Organisation, it too has participated in these exercises. Russia and China have conducted naval patrols near Alaska and flew bombers close to Japan during US President Joe Biden's visit there in 2022.[17] But the US intelligence community has judged that most of these exercises serve primarily as political signals and have little operational value to China.[18]

The 25-Year Comprehensive Strategic Partnership signed by China and Iran in 2021 lays out plans for joint weapons-systems development, and it is rumoured that China may have assisted Iran's ballistic-missile programme by providing satellite technology.[19] Iran also allows China to use two of Iran's ports, which could in theory significantly bolster its naval position in the Indian Ocean.[20] Thus far, however, little evidence exists that China has provided any valuable weapons technology to the Iranians. Iran's regional proxies have used Chinese drones, but so has Saudi Arabia, one of Iran's main adversaries.[21]

China is also unwilling to offer North Korea major military assistance, at least in peacetime. China's relationship with North Korea centres on averting a disastrous collapse of the country. An even more belligerent North Korea would be dangerous from Beijing's perspective if it led the United States to bolster its military presence in East Asia or resulted in a war in which North Korea invoked its military treaty with China. Worse yet, North Korea could also lose such a war. This would create a massive refugee crisis on China's border and could see a US ally, South Korea, controlling the whole peninsula.

North Korea and Russia's recent security agreement establishes a strong commitment to collective defence on paper, but its operational implications remain opaque. Russia may in fact have kept the treaty language intentionally vague in order to ensure flexibility should North Korea invoke the treaty.[22] Also vague is whether Russia would divert meaningful resources away from its Ukraine war effort to support North Korea. In addition, China probably fears losing control over North Korea and worries that Russia's backing might encourage it to be even more bellicose.

In short, in terms of depth, commitment and strength, the security linkages between these states pale in comparison to those of the United States' key alliances, which are deeply institutionalised, regularly practise military inter-operability, and enjoy far-reaching political and economic ties.

Narrow economic horizons

The United States shares deep and long-standing trade and investment ties with its allies in Asia and Europe, routinely cooperating with them on questions of global economic governance. In contrast, economic relations among the four 'axis' countries are weak. Beyond energy and weapons, they have little to offer one another economically.

Russia and China have the most productive economic relationship of the group. Trade between the two reached $240 billion in 2023, a large increase from the $190bn from the previous year.[23] This is 22% of Russia's trade, but only 4% of China's.[24] Perhaps most importantly, even as China's trade with Russia has grown, China's trade with Europe and the United States still dwarfs it. Moreover, China has good reason to be sceptical about Russia as a long-term economic partner, given its high levels of corruption and a declining population.[25] Russians, for their part, have long accused the Chinese of both industrial and military espionage.[26]

The energy relationship is more important. China's imports of Russian oil have steadily grown, and Beijing now accounts for 40–45% of all Russian energy exports.[27] But even here, the Chinese have hesitated to accept a deep dependency, as evidenced by their decision to delay the construction of a second natural-gas pipeline linking the two countries.[28]

Meanwhile, China pledged $400bn in investment to Iran under their 25-year strategic partnership, in return for which China receives a heavily discounted supply of Iranian oil.[29] Iran, however, has seen only $185m in

Chinese investment since the agreement was made in 2021, much to the frustration of the Iranian government and private sector.[30] Iran even temporarily withheld oil from China at the end of 2023 when it refused to pay a higher price.[31] Ultimately, China's desire for diversified oil supplies and broad influence across the Middle East will make it hard for it to deepen economic relations with Iran. China's trade with Iran reached only $16bn in 2022.[32] Its trade with the United Arab Emirates and Saudi Arabia, two of Iran's adversaries in the region, stood at $99bn and $87bn, respectively.[33] In fact, in 2023 Iran still only accounted for around 10% of China's total oil imports – a non-trivial number but certainly not great enough for China to risk hurting its relations with the Gulf Arab states, who carry greater strategic weight.[34]

Economic ties between China and North Korea are lopsided. Total trade was about $2.3bn in 2023 – miniscule for China but over 90% of North Korea's trade.[35] Beijing also allows North Korean labourers to stay illegally in China and remit substantial income to Pyongyang, and it facilitates the ship-to-ship transfer of millions of barrels of oil to North Korea.[36] North Korea's economic relationship with Russia is also meagre so far. Russian state-owned news services assess their trade to have grown to about $34m in 2023, meaning that Russia still only accounts for about 1% of North Korean trade.[37]

Russia and Iran have outlined high aspirations for deepening their economic relationship, but the reality is that Russia's economic links with Iran's adversaries in the Middle East are more important to it. Furthermore, both Iran and Russia are energy exporters, which means that they have little to offer each other in trade. While Russia was Iran's fifth-largest trading partner in 2022 and its largest investor, Iran accounted for only 1% of Russia's trade that year.[38] In 2023, bilateral trade actually fell to levels similar to Iran's trade with the European Union, despite sanctions.[39] Russia and Iran have attempted to establish a 'North–South Corridor' – a train, road and sea lane that would facilitate trade between the two countries and with the Caucasus. However, this effort has fallen prey to funding disagreements and remains mired in bureaucratic disputes.[40] Russia's trade with Iran does subvert Western sanctions, which is obviously not helpful from a Western standpoint. But the strategic impact should not be exaggerated in the context of such small totals, and questions remain about the effectiveness of the sanctions regime in changing Iran's behaviour in the first place.

The threat today

China, Russia, Iran and North Korea are divided by geography, limited horizons for economic exchange, close relations with one another's adversaries, different perspectives on nuclear proliferation, major differences in power, mutual suspicion, their own military limitations, the resistance of their bureaucracies, and divergent relations with the West and the rest of the world. They undeniably pose threats to the United States on an individual basis, but it is important not to conflate this set of disparate threats with an overall potential for cooperation, or to imagine that recent steps toward cooperation represent straight and narrow paths to deepening relations in the future.

In the near term, three primary worries about their cooperation are salient. The first and most important is the support Russia is receiving from the other three, which allows it to prosecute a war on NATO's eastern flank. Secondly, their cooperation is loosening US sanctions and, if it continues, could further weaken sanctions as a tool of statecraft for the United States and its allies. Thirdly, their subversive rhetoric on questions of global order complicates the United States' ability to pursue certain global objectives. But joint declarations in which they express criticism of America or grandiose but ultimately vague schemes such as China's Global Security Initiative only marginally increase the pressure the United States is already under to reform global governance. Many states, including Brazil, India and South Africa, are also expressing frustrations with the international order.[41]

The latter two threats are therefore quite limited. The bulk of the damage visited by the so-called axis's cooperation, at least so far, comes down largely to their support for Russia's war on Ukraine. This is of course important, but it is essentially transactional and should not be overhyped as a factor in the geopolitical moment, especially prospectively.

Possible future threats

More serious threats could emerge if cooperation were to deepen in the future. There are two main ways this could happen. Firstly, Russia and China might decide to advance the military capabilities of Iran and North Korea – something they have refrained from doing thus far. They have strong incentives to keep holding back, including their own concerns with escalation and regional stability, and interests in limiting nuclear proliferation to other states. Neither China nor Russia likely wants a nuclear cascade in the Middle East or East Asia. But Russia might reconsider its traditional position if, say, it came to view sophisticated arms transfers to Iran and North Korea as a means of imposing additional costs on the United States in the Middle East and East Asia – doing unto the US in these regions as it perceives the US is doing unto it in Ukraine. North Korea already has nuclear weapons, and this may lead Russian and Chinese leaders to conclude that past efforts to prevent proliferation are now outdated, or at least futile. Similarly, the closer Iran gets to building a nuclear weapon, the greater the chance that Russia and China might view their long-standing counter-proliferation position as overtaken by events and thus embrace a nuclear Iran. This could turn Iranian nuclear weapons into a dangerous source of instability between the world's major powers.

Secondly, and most concerning, these states might opportunistically coordinate their strategies in a crisis. For instance, if China were to attempt a blockade or invasion of Taiwan, Iran might seize the opportunity to attack US forces in the Middle East. Russia might issue threats of its own in Europe, timed to maximise the stress on the United States and thus extract concessions. This coordination would resemble the interplay between Nazi Germany and Japan in the Second World War, although it would be more improvisational.

To be sure, these countries would face major challenges in committing to credible joint action, given their divergent interests and the autocratic nature of their regimes.[42] The timing and circumstances of such action would have to align perfectly for all parties involved. Even if it occurred, this sort of coordination would not approach what the United States and its allies, which are extensively trained for joint military action against common threats, could accomplish. But if an orchestrated crisis did arise, it would stretch US resources, force America to make difficult strategic trade-offs and transform a regional contingency into a global one. America and its allies should therefore be wary.

Loosening the ties that bind

Contrary to popular belief, the four states in question do not share a common ideology or regime. China and North Korea are both Marxist regimes, but China has long understood the importance of a healthy dose of market forces. Russia is a personalist dictatorship, and Iran is a theocratic oligarchy. None share an ideological commitment even close in strength to that which bound the Soviet Union and the member states of the Warsaw Pact and envisioned the overthrow of the capitalist world. What unites them, beyond opportunistic cooperation over the war in Ukraine, is a shared belief that the US-led international order threatens their security. Accordingly, the extent of their alignment will depend in large part on how great a threat they perceive from the United States and the West, and whether they see options for reducing that threat that do not involve drawing closer together.[43]

In this context, China is the key. Not only is China the most powerful player in the group, but it is also the most influential. Beijing will determine the depth and aggressiveness of the group's future cooperation. Without its backing, the other three players lose strategic relevance and will remain isolated from much of the world. Accordingly, the best way to forestall future collaboration among these adversaries and short-circuit what has already taken place is to reduce the incentives China has to align itself with the other three states. While it will be difficult if not impossible to completely break the linkages connecting China with them, weakening China's relations with them is still feasible, even though a reactionary mood in Washington, and increasingly Europe, has turned sharply in the other direction – a trend likely to continue under US president-elect Donald Trump.

Unlike Russia, Iran and North Korea, China has exhibited behaviour that, however problematic, suggests some interest in maintaining positive relations with the West – especially Europe. Europe is particularly well placed to serve as a lever to pry China away from Russia. Not only do European states have the greatest incentive to defang Russia, but they also have a strong reason to seek to maintain a beneficial economic relationship with China. This is becoming more difficult in light of Beijing's unwise decision to attempt to flood the West with cheap electric vehicles – which adds to a long list of antagonistic Chinese trade practices – but it is not impossible. China would prefer to avoid losing access to the European market and European capital. The more Europe sustains positive economic and political relations with China, the lower China's incentives are for supporting Russia in its war on Ukraine and other issues, and the greater the incentives for dialling back relations with Russia and the other two states. Europe should seek to steer its relationship with China in this direction by making clear its interest in maintaining positive economic relations and emphasising that China has an economic interest in preventing Russia from further destabilising European security.

It goes almost without saying that ending the war in Ukraine would dampen cooperation among these adversaries. More often than not, alignments like this weaken when wars end and other interests come to light.[44] China has no interest in seeing Russia destabilise Europe further and could in fact play a helpful role in making an armistice more lasting. The longer the Russia–Ukraine war goes on, however, the more likely the structures that are developing will grow institutional roots, and the more likely negative future scenarios – such as opportunistic cooperation during a crisis – will become.

* * *

At the strategic level, the United States urgently needs to take a hard look at its many accumulated commitments around the world, where it is verging on overreach. Reducing commitments in the Middle East – once a goal of the Biden administration – would help limit America's exposure to Iran's malfeasance. At a minimum, the United States should avoid heavy new commitments in the region, such as a formal defence treaty with Saudi Arabia. Anyone who doubts the positive effects of such retrenchment might consider how difficult it would be to deal with the threats discussed above if America were still in Afghanistan, with its forces strained and vulnerable to not only Russian but also Chinese and Iranian mischief. Continuing to shift burdens to European allies in Europe while eschewing fresh commitments there would also reduce America's vulnerability to Russian coercion.

The United States has seized upon simplifying strategic concepts in the face of foreign threats throughout its history; it fought fascism in Europe and the Pacific during the 1940s, contained communism during the Cold War, and made terrorism the enemy after 9/11. Today, advocates for Ukraine may hope that combining Russia and China into a single threat will garner extra support for Ukraine by associating it with Washington's current anti-China mood. Simplifying concepts can be useful to motivate society and bureaucracies, and to galvanise public will. But it's crucial that the concepts are the right ones. Adopting the wrong threat concept, or adopting one prematurely, could end up encouraging exactly the outcome that America and its allies should be seeking to avoid.

Notes

1   See Daniel Byman and Seth G. Jones, 'Legion of Doom? China, Russia, Iran and North Korea', *Survival*, vol. 66, no. 4, August–September 2024, pp. 29–50; Richard Fontaine and Andrea Kendall Taylor, 'The Axis of Upheaval', *Foreign Affairs*, vol. 103, no. 3, May/June 2024, pp. 50–63; Steny Hoyer, 'The Seats in This House Are Empty Today, While Democracy and Freedom Are Under Siege in Ukraine', 14 December 2023, https://hoyer.house.gov/media/press-releases/hoyer-seats-house-are-empty-today-while-democracy-and-freedom-are-under-siege; 'Transcript: Senate Minority Leader Mitch McConnell on "Face the Nation"', CBS News, 22 October 2023, https://www.cbsnews.com/news/mitch-mcconnell-senate-minority-leader-face-the-nation-transcript-10-22-2023/; Yaroslav Trofimov, 'The War in Ukraine Has Created a New "Axis of Evil"', *Wall Street Journal*, 21 December 2023, https://www.wsj.com/world/the-war-in-ukraine-has-created-a-new-axis-of-evil-cd50a398; and Philip Zelikow, 'Confronting Another Axis: History, Humility, and Wishful Thinking', *Texas National Security Review*, May 2024, https://tnsr.org/2024/05/confronting-another-axis-history-humility-and-wishful-thinking/.

2   See Dina Esfandiary, 'Axis of Convenience', *Foreign Affairs*, 17 February 2023, https://www.foreignaffairs.com/russian-federation/axis-convenience.

3   See Julian E. Barnes, 'Iran Sends Drone Trainers to Crimea to Aid Russian Military', *New York Times*, 18 October 2022, https://www.nytimes.com/2022/10/18/us/politics/iran-

drones-russia-ukraine.html; Danny Citrinowicz, 'Iran Is on Its Way to Replacing Russia as a Leading Arms Exporter. The US Needs a Strategy to Counter This Trend', Atlantic Council, 2 February 2024, https:// www.atlanticcouncil.org/blogs/ iransource/iran-drone-uavs-russia; Esfandiary, 'Axis of Convenience'; Parisa Hafezi et al., 'Exclusive: Iran Sends Russia Hundreds of Ballistic Missiles', Reuters, 21 February 2024, https://www.reuters.com/world/ iran-sends-russia-hundreds-ballistic-missiles-sources-say-2024-02-21/; Aamer Madhani, 'US, G-7 Allies Warn Iran to Back Off Deal to Provide Russia Ballistic Missiles or Face New Sanctions', Associated Press, 15 March 2024, https://apnews.com/article/ russian-iran-ballistic-missiles-ukraine-f12dc454b04f7cbe671d2c401e31390c; and United States Institute of Peace, 'Timeline: Iran–Russia Collaboration on Drones', Iran Primer, 10 August 2023, https://iranprimer.usip.org/ blog/2023/mar/01/timeline-iran-russia-collaboration-drones.

4   See Benoit Faucon, Nicholas Bariyo and Matthew Luxmoore, 'The Russian Drone Plant that Could Shape the War in Ukraine', *Wall Street Journal*, 28 May 2024, https://www.wsj.com/world/ the-russian-drone-plant-that-could-shape-the-war-in-ukraine-7abd5616.

5   'North Korea Sent Russia Millions of Munitions in Exchange for Food: Seoul', Al-Jazeera, 28 February 2024, https://www.aljazeera.com/ news/2024/2/28/n-korea-sent-russia-millions-of-munitions-in-exchange-for-food-says-seoul; and Soo-Hyang Choi, 'North Korea Sent Russia

Millions of Artillery Shells, South Korea Says', Bloomberg, 14 June 2024, https://time.com/6988568/ north-korea-russia-artillery-shell-south-korea-defense-minister/.

6   See Max Boot, 'Weapons of War: The Race Between Russia and Ukraine', Council on Foreign Relations, 24 April 2024, https://www.cfr.org/ expert-brief/weapons-war-race-between-russia-and-ukraine; and Jack Detsch, 'Ukraine Is Still Outgunned by Russia', *Foreign Policy*, 23 April 2024, https://foreignpolicy.com/2024/04/23/ ukraine-war-artillery-shortage-production-military-aid-bill/.

7   See Tom Balmforth and David Gauthier-Villars, 'Exclusive: Ukraine Examines N. Korean Missile Debris Amid Fears of Moscow–Pyongyang Axis', Reuters, 7 May 2024, https://www.reuters.com/ world/ukraine-examines-nkorean-missile-debris-amid-fears-moscow-pyongyang-axis-2024-05-07/; 'Russia Used at Least 20 North Korean Ballistic Missiles in Attacks on Ukraine, Kyiv Says', *Politico*, 22 February 2024, https://www.politico.eu/article/ ukraines-sbu-found-evidence-russia-used-at-least-20-north-korean-missiles-to-attack-ukraine/; Olesia Safronova, 'Ukraine Says Russia Has Launched 24 North Korean Missiles So Far', Bloomberg News, 16 February 2024, https://www.bloomberg. com/news/articles/2024-02-16/ war-in-ukraine-kyiv-says-russia-has-fired-at-least-24-north-korean-missiles?sref=QmOxnLFz.

8   See Edward Wong, 'U.S. Turns to China to Stop North Korean Troops

from Fighting for Russia', *New York Times*, 31 October 2024 (updated 5 November 2024), https://www.nytimes.com/2024/10/31/us/politics/russia-north-korea-troops-china.html.

9   Julian E. Barnes, Eric Schmitt and Michael Schwirtz, '50,000 Russian and North Korean Troops Mass Ahead of Attack, U.S. Says', *New York Times*, 10 November 2024, https://www.nytimes.com/2024/11/10/us/politics/russia-north-korea-troops-ukraine.html.

10   See Kylie Atwood, 'China Is Giving Russia Significant Support to Expand Weapons Manufacturing as Ukraine War Continues, US Officials Say', CNN, 12 April 2024, https://www.cnn.com/2024/04/12/politics/china-russia-support-weapons-manufacturing/index.html.

11   See Robbie Gramer and Amy Mackinnon, 'Iran and Russia Are Closer than Ever Before', *Foreign Policy*, 28 March 2024, https://foreignpolicy.com/2023/01/05/iran-russia-drones-ukraine-war-military-cooperation/.

12   See Joby Warrick, 'Iran Seeks "Billions" Worth of Russian Aircraft and Weapons in Exchange for Drones, US Says', *Washington Post*, 9 June 2023, https://www.washingtonpost.com/national-security/2023/06/09/iran-russia-military-drones/.

13   See Jon Herskovitz, 'North Korea and Russia Accelerate Exchange of Weapons and Resources', *Time*, 27 February 2024, https://time.com/6835478/north-korea-speed-up-weapons-shipment-russia/; and Hyonhee Shin, 'North Korea Received Russian Aid for Satellite Launch – South Korea Lawmakers', Reuters, 23 November 2023, https://www.reuters.com/world/asia-pacific/north-korea-received-russian-aid-satellite-launch-south-korea-lawmakers-2023-11-23/.

14   See Jonathan Corrado and Markus Garlauskas, 'The Arsenal of Autocracy', *Foreign Affairs*, 15 February 2024, https://www.foreignaffairs.com/north-korea/arsenal-autocracy; and Andrew Yeo, 'Expect to See More North Korean Weapons Reach Nonstate Armed Actors in 2024', Brookings Institution, 21 February 2024, https://www.brookings.edu/articles/expect-to-see-more-north-korean-weapons-reach-nonstate-armed-actors-in-2024/.

15   See Alexander Gabuev, 'Putin and Xi's Unholy Alliance', *Foreign Affairs*, 9 April 2024, https://www.foreignaffairs.com/china/putin-and-xis-unholy-alliance.

16   See James Palmer, 'Did Russia Catch China Off Guard in Ukraine?', *Foreign Policy*, 28 March 2024, https://foreignpolicy.com/2022/03/02/china-russia-ukraine-invasion-surprise/.

17   See Alastair Gale, 'China and Russia Sent Bombers Near Japan as Biden Visited Tokyo', *Wall Street Journal*, 24 May 2022, https://www.wsj.com/articles/china-and-russia-sent-bombers-near-japan-as-biden-visited-tokyo-11653402634; and Michael R. Gordon and Nancy A. Youssef, 'Russia and China Sent Large Naval Patrol Near Alaska', *Wall Street Journal*, 6 August 2023, https://www.wsj.com/articles/russia-and-china-sent-large-naval-patrol-near-alaska-127de28b.

18   See Office of the Director of National Intelligence, 'Annual Threat Assessment of the US Intelligence

Community', February 2024, https://www.dni.gov/files/ODNI/documents/assessments/ATA-2024-Unclassified-Report.pdf.

19 See Will Green and Taylore Roth, 'China–Iran Relations: A Limited but Enduring Strategic Partnership', US–China Economic and Security Review Commission, June 2021, https://www.uscc.gov/sites/default/files/2021-06/China-Iran_Relations.pdf; Lucille Greer and Esfandyar Batmanghelidj, 'Last Among Equals: The China–Iran Partnership in a Regional Context', Wilson Center, September 2020, https://www.wilsoncenter.org/sites/default/files/media/uploads/documents/MEP_200831_OCC%2038%20v3%20%281%29.pdf; and Heath Sloane, 'Droning On: China Floods the Middle East with UAVs', *Diplomat*, 2 September 2022, https://thediplomat.com/2022/09/droning-on-china-floods-the-middle-east-with-uavs/.

20 See Scott Harold and Alireza Nader, 'China and Iran: Economic, Political, and Military Relations', RAND Center for Middle East Public Policy, 2 May 2012, https://www.rand.org/pubs/occasional_papers/OP351.html.

21 See Sloane, 'Droning On'; and Jared Szuba, 'Drones Used by Iran-backed Militias Are Coming from China, US Says', *Al-Monitor*, 5 August 2022, https://www.al-monitor.com/originals/2022/08/drones-used-iran-backed-militias-are-coming-china-us-says.

22 See Michelle Ye Hee Lee and Robyn Dixon, 'North Korea's Kim Declares "Full Support" for Russian War in Ukraine', *Washington Post*, 19 June 2024, https://www.washingtonpost.com/world/2024/06/18/russia-vladimir-putin-north-korea-kim-jong-un/.

23 'China–Russia 2023 Trade Value Hits Record High of $240 Bln – Chinese Customs', Reuters, 12 January 2024, https://www.reuters.com/markets/china-russia-2023-trade-value-hits-record-high-240-bln-chinese-customs-2024-01-12/; Laura He, 'China's Largest Oil Supplier in 2023 Was Russia', CNN, 22 January 2024, https://www.cnn.com/2024/01/22/business/china-top-oil-supplier-2023-russia-intl-hnk/index.html; and Simone McCarthy, 'China's Xi Jinping Hails Russia Cooperation as Record Trade Beats $200 Billion Target', CNN, 21 December 2023, https://www.cnn.com/2023/12/21/china/china-russia-relations-record-trade-intl-hnk/index.html.

24 Dmitry Gorenburg et al., 'Russian–Chinese Military Cooperation', Center for Naval Analysis, March 2023, https://www.cna.org/reports/2023/05/Russian-Chinese-Military-Cooperation.pdf.

25 See Jonathan E. Hillman, 'China and Russia: Economic Unequals', Center for Strategic and International Studies, 15 July 2020, https://www.csis.org/analysis/china-and-russia-economic-unequals.

26 See Brian Hart, 'How Deep Are China–Russia Military Ties?', ChinaPower Project, Center for Strategic and International Studies, 4 August 2022, https://chinapower.csis.org/china-russia-military-cooperation-arms-sales-exercises/; and Phillip Ivanov, 'Together and Apart: The Conundrum of the China–Russia Partnership', Asia Society, 11 October 2023, https://asiasociety.org/

policy-institute/together-and-apart-conundrum-china-russia-partnership.

27 Vladimir Soldatkin and Olesya Astakhova, 'Russia Exports Almost All Its Oil to China and India – Novak', Reuters, 27 December 2023, https://www.reuters.com/business/energy/half-russias-2023-oil-petroleum-exports-went-china-russias-novak-2023-12-27/.

28 See Lily McElwee et al., 'Xi Goes to Moscow: A Marriage of Inconvenience?', Center for Strategic and International Studies, 28 March 2023, https://www.csis.org/analysis/xi-goes-moscow-marriage-inconvenience.

29 Farnaz Fassihi and Steven Lee Meyers, 'Defying US, China and Iran Near Trade and Military Partnership', *New York Times*, 11 July 2020, https://www.nytimes.com/2020/07/11/world/asia/china-iran-trade-military-deal.html; United States Institute of Peace, 'Iran and China: A Trade Lifeline', Iran Primer, 5 July 2023, https://iranprimer.usip.org/blog/2023/jun/28/iran-china-trade-lifeline; and Muyu Xu, 'Explainer: Iran's Expanding Oil Trade with Top Buyer China', Reuters, 10 November 2023, https://www.reuters.com/markets/commodities/irans-expanding-oil-trade-with-top-buyer-china-2023-11-10/.

30 Jonathan Fulton, 'China Doesn't Have as Much Leverage in the Middle East as One Thinks – at Least When It Comes to Iran', Atlantic Council, 1 February 2024, https://www.atlanticcouncil.org/blogs/menasource/china-mena-leverage-iran-houthis-yemen/.

31 See Chen Aizhu and Muyu Xu, 'Exclusive: Iran's Oil Trade with China Stalls as Tehran Demands Higher Prices', Reuters, 8 January 2024, https://www.reuters.com/business/energy/irans-oil-trade-with-china-stalls-tehran-demands-higher-prices-2024-01-05/.

32 United States Institute of Peace, 'Iran and China'.

33 *Ibid*.

34 See Erica Downs and Edward Fishman, 'Q&A: Potential Impacts of New US Sanctions on Iran's Oil Sales to China', Center for Global Energy Policy at the Columbia School of International Public Affairs, 28 May 2024, https://www.energypolicy.columbia.edu/qa-potential-impacts-of-new-us-sanctions-on-irans-oil-exports-to-china.

35 'China's Exports to North Korea Return to Growth in November', Reuters, 20 December 2023, https://www.reuters.com/world/china/chinas-exports-north-korea-return-growth-november-2023-12-20/; and Anton Sokolin, 'North Korean Trade with China Doubles in 2023 to Highest Since Pandemic Began', North Korea News, 18 January 2024, https://www.nknews.org/2024/01/north-korean-trade-with-china-doubles-in-2023-to-highest-since-pandemic-began/.

36 See Ben Frohman, Emma Rafaelof and Alexis Dale-Huang, 'The China–North Korea Strategic Rift: Background and Implications for the United States', US–China Economic and Security Review Commission, 24 January 2022, pp. 12–13, https://www.uscc.gov/sites/default/files/2022-01/China-North_Korea_Strategic_Rift.pdf.

37 'Trade Turnover Between Russia, North Korea Up 9 Times in 2023 – Russian Presidential Aide', TASS,

17 June 2024, https://tass.com/economy/1804561.

38 Emil Avdaliani, 'Iran and Russia Enter a New Level of Military Cooperation', Stimson Center, 6 March 2024, https://www.stimson.org/2024/iran-and-russia-enter-a-new-level-of-military-cooperation/; United States Institute of Peace, 'Iran and Russia: Gyrating Trade Flows', Iran Primer, 18 May 2023, https://iranprimer.usip.org/blog/2023/may/18/iran-and-russia-gyrating-trade-grows; and World Trade Organization, 'Iran Trade Profile', 2023, https://www.wto.org/english/res_e/statis_e/daily_update_e/trade_profiles/IR_e.pdf.

39 See 'Iran–EU Trade Rises 8% in Q1 2024', *Tehran Times*, 27 May 2024, https://www.tehrantimes.com/news/499105/Iran-EU-trade-rises-8-in-Q1-2024.

40 See Avdaliani, 'Iran and Russia Enter a New Level of Military Cooperation'; Emile Hokayem et al., 'IISS Roundtable – Russia and Iran: Isolated from the West and Drawing Closer', International Institute of Strategic Studies, 12 October 2022, https://www.iiss.org/en/online-analysis/online-analysis/2022/10/russia-and-iran-isolated-from-the-west-and-drawing-closer/; and Alex Vatanka, 'Russia and Iran Have High Hopes for Each Other', *Foreign Policy*, 28 March 2024, https://foreignpolicy.com/2023/05/02/russia-iran-grain-trade-china-investment-bri/.

41 See Christopher S. Chivvis and Beatrix Geaghan-Breiner, 'Emerging Powers and the Future of American Statecraft', Carnegie Endowment for International Peace, 9 April 2024, https://carnegieendowment.org/research/2024/04/emerging-powers-and-the-future-of-american-statecraft?lang=en.

42 See Michaela Mattes and Mariana Rodríguez, 'Autocracies and International Cooperation', *International Studies Quarterly*, vol. 58, no. 3, September 2014, pp. 527–38.

43 See Mark L. Haas, 'Ideology and Alliances: British and French External Balancing Decisions in the 1930s', *Security Studies*, vol. 12, no. 4, Summer 2003, pp. 34–79; John M. Owen, 'When Do Ideologies Produce Alliances? The Holy Roman Empire, 1517–1555', *International Studies Quarterly*, vol. 49, no. 1, March 2005, pp. 73–100; Stephen M. Walt, 'Alliance Formation and the Balance of World Power', *International Security*, vol. 9, no. 4, Spring 1985, pp. 3–43; and Stephen M. Walt, *The Origins of Alliances* (Ithaca, NY: Cornell University Press, 1987).

44 See Lee J.M. Seymour, 'Why Factions Switch Sides in Civil Wars: Rivalry, Patronage, and Realignment in Sudan', *International Security*, vol. 39, no. 2, Fall 2014, pp. 92–131; and Barbara F. Walter, 'The Extremist's Advantage in Civil Wars', *International Security*, vol. 42, no. 2, Fall 2017, pp. 7–39.

Can the US and China Forge a Cold Peace?

Andrew Byers and J. Tedford Tyler

The United States and China are great powers and peer competitors. They have vast resources, grand ambitions and major disagreements, which is a recipe for unavoidable competition. Bilateral relations have steadily worsened over the last five years and, if this decline is not arrested, a new cold war – with all the risks that entails – seems likely. While both the US and China have important interests in East Asia, their economic interdependence coupled with the region's geography would make great-power conflict there ruinous.[1] A conventional war between the US and China would run the risk of triggering an existentially dangerous nuclear war. Moving away from a cold-war mindset calls for a new way of thinking about the US–China relationship. The United States and China should mutually embrace peaceful coexistence – the stakes are too high for anything else – which requires them to accept that they are locked into a state of competitive interdependence. A cold peace, rather than a cold war, should be the goal.

Moderating strategic ambitions

Matt Pottinger, who worked on China issues in the Trump administration, and former Republican congressman Mike Gallagher contend that the United Stated should stop trying to manage or limit US–China competition

---

Andrew Byers is a non-resident fellow at Texas A&M University's Albritton Center for Grand Strategy. **J. Tedford Tyler** is a foreign-policy program officer at Stand Together Trust.

Survival | vol. 66 no. 6 | December 2024–January 2025 | pp. 67–86   https://doi.org/10.1080/00396338.2024.2432202

and instead embrace confrontation by applying maximal pressure to pre-
cipitate the Chinese Communist Party's (CCP) collapse.[2] They argue that
a similar strategy implemented by the Reagan administration during the
waning days of the Cold War worked against the Soviet Union. But such
an approach would risk dangerous escalation and possibly unintended
nuclear war. Moreover, the China of the 2020s is not the Soviet Union of
the 1980s. From the Brezhnev era through Mikhail Gorbachev's tenure, the
Soviet Union was in steep decline by every measure. Although the Chinese
economy has encountered some speed bumps in recent years, China remains
a growing economic and military power.

While the term 'cold peace' has been used informally for decades to
describe some less tense version of the cold war – *Time* magazine defined the
term in 1952 as a 'sustained truce without a settlement'[3] – it has remained an
elusive concept in international relations. Drawing on the work of Charles
Kupchan, Benjamin Miller and others who have sought to inject conceptual
rigour into the concept, we conceive of a cold peace as a state of international relations in which, while there are major unresolved geopolitical
tensions, the focus is on the use of diplomatic and other non-military means
for resolving conflict and there are conscious attempts to further moderate
the potential for conflict through crisis prevention and negotiation.[4]

This mindset requires that both powers relinquish something they
desire. Neither can single-handedly impose its will on the other, and neither
can achieve everything it wants at a price it is willing to pay. Ryan Hass
and others have introduced the idea of 'competitive interdependence', conceding that major differences will probably always separate Beijing and
Washington while acknowledging that the US and Chinese economies are
inextricably bound.[5] The United States and China will probably never grow
to love each other – their foundational principles and preferences are simply
too divergent – but they cannot live without each other in the globalised
economic environment of the twenty-first century.

China, for its part, must abandon its fantasy that the United States will
exit the ranks of the great powers.[6] While China has made great economic
and military gains over the past several decades, suggesting relative US
decline, the United States is not declining in absolute terms and will remain,

with China, one of the two predominant great powers for the foreseeable future. China should therefore give up any ambitions of being the only Asia-Pacific power able to compel or coerce countries to cooperate. It should accept that its neighbours desire a stable balance of power and want options for working closely with the US when it serves their interests. American power will endure.[7]

In turn, the United States must abandon the delusion of engineering political change within China. Meaningful internal political change, if it ever happens, would have to come from the Chinese people themselves. In this context, US policymakers were foolish to believe that Beijing would become a liberal democracy, placing too much weight on the notion that a wealthy China would awaken to Western political values and norms.[8] While China has grown richer, the CCP still rules it. China's economic advances have yielded a powerful industrial base, which great powers have historically used to build military strength.[9]

The United States will remain a great power in East Asia, where its extra-regional ability to deploy its forces and dominate the region in the maritime domain is unique and durable. At the same time, it is critical that Washington avoid overreacting and triggering a conflict and, more broadly, solidifying a cold-war mindset.

Analytic assumptions

It is hard to be nostalgic for the Cold War owing to the standing existential danger and near calamities that it brought. We favour managed competition and peaceful coexistence between the two powers as the end goal.[10] This approach would moderate the risk of military conflict, an existential danger for both countries and the world.

Underlying our analysis are several assumptions. Firstly, and perhaps most importantly, we assume that China will not invade Taiwan in the near term or otherwise forcibly unify Taiwan with China. If that were to happen, then the United States and China would inexorably be in a new cold war, and the threat of military escalation would rise. Many of China's neighbours might exhibit more interest in joining a balancing coalition to contain China. The economic interdependence between China and the US would overnight become much less meaningful, and, even if all-out war were avoided, real decoupling, rather than rhetorical distancing, would likely begin in earnest, with diplomatic rapprochement becoming infeasible for an indefinite period.

Secondly, we assume that China will not become a meaningful threat to Japan. If Chinese military capabilities (particularly air and sealift) and revisionist intent grew to the point that Japan faced serious peril from China, our analysis would change. While Taiwan, outside of its advanced semiconductor industry, does not have a significant role in the global economy, Japan is a key player. Its potential absorption by China could presage Chinese domination of East Asia and the global economy, and far stronger military countermeasures to deter Chinese aggression would be required.

Lastly, we assume that the US and China will continue to be major economic partners. While the United States' economic vital signs appear stronger than China's, China may soon achieve rough economic parity with the US.[11] The Chinese economy may be undergoing recovery, given the increase in urban consumption rates, decreasing savings rates and shrinking inventories for consumer goods.[12] Some American policymakers and analysts view China's large-scale industrial policy and state planning with trepidation and advocate decoupling and onshoring as responses.[13] But such measures would result in significant supply-chain disruptions and high prices for US consumer goods.[14] This is not to say that sectorial 'de-risking' and economic friction will vanish, but our analysis presupposes stable trade relations. If either or both parties sever them, the possibility of positive change would dry up, and we would be compelled to concede the likelihood of a new cold war between the United States and China.

Cold peace, not cold war

Kupchan defines a cold peace as 'stability based on competition and mutual deterrence'.[15] He suggests that cold peace, though historically a rare outcome of power transitions, might become more frequent because of the prevalence of nuclear deterrence among great powers, whose second-strike nuclear capabilities would check the prospect that military conflict could escalate to the nuclear level.

Benjamin Miller has differentiated among three levels of regional peace – cold, normal and warm – and presented strategies by which each could be achieved.[16] When a region is in a state of normal peace, the main conflicts that might have afflicted that region would be resolved. There would be transnational ties among regional states. While revisionist groups might exist, their influence would be muted and ineffectual. The possibility of deteriorating relations and the return of war in the region would remain, but it would be low barring some significant shift – say, the unexpected rise of a revisionist regime or intervention by an outside power. The Western Hemisphere today approximates normal peace.

In a state of warm peace, not only are there no regional conflicts, but they have also been rendered irrelevant. Highly developed transnational ties would be expected. The possibility of war within the region would be very low, and there would be no substantial revisionist threats. The only region we might presently describe as existing within a state of warm peace would be Western Europe. There, past issues that could have been *casus belli* have been resolved or rendered irrelevant, and it is virtually unthinkable that there could be a return to war within the region. The European Union reflects the implementation of significant and highly developed inter-governmental and other transnational ties.

Neither normal peace nor warm peace is currently plausible for East Asia, given the outstanding regional conflicts, unresolved ambitions on the part of China, the current dispute over the status of Taiwan, the territorial disputes present in the South China Sea, long-standing tension between North and South Korea, and other major sources of conflict. This does not mean that inter-state relations in the region must inevitably decline and slip into war, nor does it dictate that the status quo will persist indefinitely and preclude better relations.

Unlike a cold war, which involves hostility just short of actual war, a cold peace would see both sides avoid using subversion against the other and strive for cooperation – effectively, detente – in selected areas.[17] Great powers present or acting within the region would not necessarily behave coercively; their hegemony could be exerted in benign ways conducive to peace. Underlying conflict issues would persist during a cold peace, but all sides would be committed to moderating and reducing tensions. For example, China and Taiwan could be open to limited cooperation even though their dispute would remain unsettled. Their cold peace could centre on increased economic exchange and an exploration of how Taiwan might feature in international organisations through observer status or some other mutually acceptable formal role. Taiwan, in turn, would take steps to assuage Chinese fears about it pursuing formal independence. While the danger of military conflict would still exist and loom in the background, a cold peace could transition to a normal peace if the relationship improved.

Even in a cold peace, both sides would engage in hedging and balancing behaviour. The general condition of the relationship need not worsen and could improve over time. Regular, institutionalised summits and ongoing official interactions at all levels of government could produce concrete concessions and reduce tension.[18] There would be no efforts to militarily contain the adversary or change the status quo in a cold peace.

Michael Doyle offers several examples of cold peace, including US relationships with fascist Italy and imperial Japan in the interwar years, the US–Great Britain relationship before and after the War of 1812, the Franco-German relationship between 1871 and 1914, and Russo-British relations between the Crimean War and 1918.[19] These historical cases are, of course, as much cautionary tales as exemplars, and sometimes, as Richard Sakwa has noted, amounted merely to 'an unstable geopolitical truce, typically found in inter-war periods, where the "defeat" of the one side is not accepted as legitimate, while the "victory" of the other side cannot be consolidated'.[20] In most of these cases, war shattered the cold peace. In only a few, such as the US–Great Britain relationship in the nineteenth century, did cold peace give way to warmer relations. Accordingly, cold peace can be a prelude to war or a temporary deferment of conflict, or it can lay the groundwork for more peaceable relations. It depends on whether shifting priorities can resolve or diminish tensions.

Forging a cold peace between the United States and China will hinge on finding ways to normalise their relationship. While the concept of cold peace remains under-theorised, lacking clear consensus on how and under what conditions states might collapse into war or advance to enduring peace, we offer one possible pathway for advancing the latter in US–China relations.

Cooperation, not confrontation

To achieve a cold peace, each state must renounce the use of subversion against the other, and both must focus on generating what Lyle Goldstein has called 'cooperation spirals' for mutual benefit.[21] The renunciation of subversion would entail that neither side attempt to destabilise or meaningfully degrade the other's essential political institutions. This does not mean that promoting national interests and other goals deemed critical – such as human rights or the protection of intellectual-property rights – must fall by the wayside. On the contrary, gaining a workable consensus on such matters is more likely under a cold peace than a cold war. Goldstein characterises cooperation spirals as incremental actions and outcomes that reduce tensions.[22] His concept adapts the spiral model of conflict, which theorises that misperceptions about the prospects of future punishment lead two sides to grow ever more hostile.[23] Cooperation spirals follow a similar causal logic but instead coalesce towards greater concord, starting with small concessions or compromises that lead to reciprocal concessions and deeper degrees of cooperation. Both sides must take positive actions for a spiral to continue and trust must be maintained and enhanced over time.

For cooperation spirals to take hold, three conditions must be met. Firstly, cheating and deception must be effectively addressed.[24] Each side needs to be able to, per Ronald Reagan's dictum, 'trust, but verify'. Secondly, the parties must perceive that continued cooperation is likely and will further develop. What each side believes about the future is important and needs to move towards a positive, shared vision over time. Thirdly, both sides have to embrace their relationship as a quid pro quo. While concessions and compromises may not always be even, each side should be getting something it wants. While these conditions need not exist at the outset, they must materialise relatively quickly after a cooperation spiral begins for it to continue. Kupchan conceptualises strategic restraint, which he terms 'self-binding', as an important component of a cold peace. This allows 'trust and reciprocity to build, in turn enabling an incremental cognitive shift toward the mutual attribution of benign character'. For him, this process is about communicating 'benign intentions and a state's willingness to forgo opportunities for individual gain'.[25]

Goldstein's theory specifically contemplated US–China relations, and he made numerous policy recommendations that not only proposed direct changes in the bilateral relationship but also incorporated various moves Washington and Beijing could make through their respective policies vis-à-vis Japan, the Association of Southeast Asian Nations (ASEAN) countries, the Korean Peninsula and Taiwan.[26] Of course, past US efforts to engage more with China often have not borne fruit.[27] But a cooperation-spiral approach could conceivably build the United States' inclination to bring China to the negotiating table for more substantial beneficial arrangements. A deep understanding of the other side – what it wants, what it can live without, what its red lines are, what it might be willing to concede – is key to successful pursuit of cooperation spirals. They are ultimately about strategic empathy.[28]

The US could forgo additional sanctions against China

To take one example of how a cooperation spiral might begin, the United States could invite China to reopen its Houston consulate. As part of a secret negotiation preceding such an invitation, China would agree to allow the reopening of the US consulate in Chengdu within six months. Both parties would obtain something of roughly equal value and, assuming these steps proceeded satisfactorily, the groundwork would be laid for additional measures and generally lower tensions.

In the economic realm, the United States could offer to forgo additional economic sanctions against China. While this might involve domestic political costs to the US administration, it would send an important signal to Chinese manufacturers and investors, vital segments of the Chinese economy. It would also provide relief for US companies worried about retaliatory Chinese economic policies. In return, Beijing might increase the transparency in the business relationship between the CCP and Chinese commercial enterprises. Openness would be challenging for China, given the advantage of hoarding information, but it could also benefit Beijing by removing suspicion about adverse CCP involvement and encourage further economic reforms that would reassure investors.

In the security sphere, a cooperation spiral could involve commitments to decrease the US military presence in the Asia-Pacific provided that China meaningfully reduced tensions in the South China Sea, the site of recent confrontations between China and the Philippines, a US security partner. The June 2024 incident in the Second Thomas Shoal reflected the current state of tension.[29] There are no good crisis-management procedures in place and the situation, if allowed to fester, could escalate. Beginning a cooperation spiral over the area of the shoal would require significant political manoeuvring by the United States and likely need to be handled discreetly. The goal, of course, would be to see both China and the Philippines observe the status quo and continue peacefully negotiating towards a political solution.

The United States might begin a cooperation spiral with China by proposing to remove US military forces or weapons systems from the Philippines in exchange for the China Coast Guard executing fewer patrols when operating in the shoal's vicinity. In July 2024, the United States announced that it was withdrawing a *Typhon* mid-range missile system from the Philippines, while making it clear the system could be brought back at any time. Analysts speculate that Washington intended this gesture as an olive branch to China.[30] If China proves unwilling to come to the negotiating table or to act in good faith, the United States could increase its material support of the Philippines by selling or giving it decommissioned US Coast Guard vessels. If China signals cooperation, the US might dial down its provision of military capabilities to the Philippines and lean on Manila to talk more with Beijing. Although one side might use sticks as well as carrots to bring the other side to the negotiating table, acute calibration would be required.

Rosemary Foot, among others, has pointed out obstacles to the success of the cooperation-spiral approach. They include Chinese and US conceptions of national exceptionalism, radically different domestic political structures and incentives, differing narratives on the possibility of a twenty-first-century power transition and related ideas about national destiny, and long-standing mutual strategic mistrust.[31] It is important to anticipate how these obstacles will come into play, and to craft political and rhetorical landscapes that avoid zero-sum conceptions of East Asia, instead emphasising mutual cooperation.

Deterrence by denial

While cooperation spirals could produce breakthroughs and lead to peaceful coexistence, major war remains too salient a prospect to proceed without a backup plan. As insurance against the cooperation-spiral process not working or taking too long to reduce tensions, the United States should practise deterrence by denial in East Asia. This would involve building up the anti-access/area-denial (A2/AD) capabilities of partners like Taiwan and allies like Japan by selling them air-defence and anti-ship assets among other anti-access systems. But in the pursuit of a cold peace, diplomatic and military elements should be reciprocally adjustable. Leaving aside procurement challenges, the United States should be willing to pause arms sales in the service of a cooperation spiral.[32] If China took steps to reassure Taiwan and other US security partners by, say, unilaterally reducing the number of its amphibious landing craft or redeploying short- and intermediate-range missiles, US arms sales could be reduced commensurately.

In this situation, US military forces in the Asia-Pacific would have a lighter footprint and be dispersed across the region, with local allies shouldering increased responsibility for defending themselves. The US Navy and Air Force would assume more prominent roles, the US Army and Marine Corps less prominent ones.[33] Primary US military missions in Asia would be air-defence and anti-ship operations to supplement the capabilities of partners such as Taiwan and Japan. The US Navy's force structure would have to be reoriented towards fewer large surface ships and more small surface vessels, with its submarine fleet maintained in-theatre. The US Air Force would continue to acquire new combat aircraft and expand its tanker, transport and intelligence, surveillance and reconnaissance capabilities. As large-scale land campaigns would be less likely, army and Marine Corps forces permanently or rotationally deployed in the region would be reduced overall, and those supporting US Indo-Pacific Command made lighter, more mobile and more readily deployable to a high-threat environment on an expeditionary basis.[34]

This deterrence-by-denial approach assumes greater risk than forward-deploying significant US forces. It places greater reliance on local allies to defend themselves and requires tailored US technical assistance and arms sales. This risk should be acceptable if the United States makes the effort to enable regional partners to build their A2/AD capabilities, not least by helping the US defence industry meet the currently overwhelming demand for such capabilities.[35] Given the long lead times involved, it will take several years to ramp up production of key A2/AD systems, but the US will have to replenish its own stockpiles anyway in light of recent weapons transfers to Ukraine and Israel. Until US manufacturing capacity is increased, the United States could relax peacetime-procurement restrictions, use multi-year contracts to purchase munitions, and seek replacements from reliable third parties.[36]

Mitigating the risk of pursuing a cold peace is the apparent lack of compelling evidence that China has short-term intentions to invade or otherwise attack Taiwan, despite the unsupported assertions of some US military officials.[37] A number of factors support this assessment. An amphibious invasion is one of the most complicated types of military campaigns, and the Chinese military, notwithstanding occasional amphibious exercises, is not especially well equipped or practised in undertaking such an operation, especially in the face of a concerted defence. The risks of conducting one would be exceedingly high, especially insofar as it could draw the US military into a conventional war, which makes China especially wary. Taiwan's geography – in particular, its shallow water and mountainous terrain – favours the defender, casting further doubt on prospects for a successful invasion.[38]

The nature of US–China competition

For a cold peace to develop and endure, it is important that the US–China competition be confined as much as possible to the economic and diplomatic spheres. By focusing on statecraft, the United States can offer a new, non-militarised vision for the Asia-Pacific. Above all, Washington must make clear that it is not attempting to contain Beijing, but rather is offering preferred partnerships, which it should not approach with a zero-sum mindset. It should also minimise punishing countries who want to cooperate with China or forcing countries to choose between the two regional powers. Such policies would only encourage the division of the region into rival blocs. This is not in Washington's best interest given that there is no ready-made 'contain China' coalition to be had in East Asia. While many Asian countries object to China's territorial aggrandisement and coercive behaviour, they are not broadly balancing against China. Although Chinese military spending is continuing to increase, most East Asian countries are not increasing their military spending as a share of GDP and are continuing to tighten economic ties with China.[39]

The United States should seek to advance new bilateral trade deals in Asia (and around the world), reduce trade barriers and open up new markets for US goods and services. The goal would be to establish a more robust and diverse array of trading partners.[40] This does not mean just encouraging US firms to exit China, but also incentivising new partnerships and competitive domestic innovation. This will require retooling the US economy and facing the uncomfortable truth that most legacy, Industrial Age manufacturing jobs are not returning. New industries and jobs will emerge, and the US must be prepared to transform its economy by leveraging opportunities afforded by technological change – for instance, growth in human–artificial intelligence (AI) hybrid-workforce arrangements.

The United States should also de-emphasise sanctions as an economic tool. Frequently, they are ineffective and gratuitously antagonise their targets. Furthermore, while China's attempts to economically pressure some US allies and partners have produced short-term gains, Australia, Lithuania, the Philippines and Taiwan have all withstood Chinese coercion and moved closer to the United States. Thus, retaliatory punishment via sanctions, even if effective, does not appear necessary when US and partner interests overlap significantly. Instead, Washington can implement a kind of economic deterrence-by-denial, opening markets and providing investment opportunities to the objects of Chinese aggression.[41] Such an approach could drive home to China that its image is harmed if its coercion continues but improved if it behaves more benignly.

Launching the effort

The United States can readily undertake a series of steps, using all the instruments of national power – political, military, economic and diplomatic – to begin realising this vision. The foundation for a more productive US–China relationship has arguably been built. On her visit to China in August 2023, US Commerce Secretary Gina Raimondo announced that Washington and Beijing would begin a new round of economic dialogues and exchange information on matters such as export controls.[42] Foreign Minister Wang Yi's October 2023 visit to Washington and the meeting between Joe Biden and Xi Jinping at the November 2023 Asia-Pacific Economic Cooperation Summit outside San Francisco prepared the ground for further coopera- tion, even if economic issues were not featured in the public read-out of the Biden–Xi meeting.[43] In any case, the start of a new administration is an ideal time to reset a major relationship. At least in theory, a new president can engage in a cooperation spiral with less fear about looking 'soft' on China.

Despite the tough, anti-China rhetoric across the American political spectrum, the incoming Trump administration, free of immediate political pressure, could pursue a more open-minded approach focused on recon- ciliation rather than confrontation. To do so effectively, the United States would have to initiate a cooperation spiral and wait for China's response. China would find itself under pressure to reciprocate, lest it be seen as uncooperative. If China responded in ways that advanced both countries' interests, the US could take further cooperative action. If China's reply were negative or apathetic, the US would take no further action.

In the political realm, no question is more central to the US–China rela- tionship than that of Taiwan. The United States should make a concerted effort not to openly question the status of Taiwan and encourage its part- ners – especially Taiwan itself – to follow suit. This means, for now, no more official US diplomatic visits to the island. The administration should also try to ensure that Congress follows suit. In addition, the White House and State Department should cease using the 'democracy versus autocracy' framing of the US–China relationship. This is an unnecessarily provocative para- digm that irritates China without yielding any substantive benefit to the United States.[44]

New US policy preferences should be established, centring on a peace- ful resolution of the political conflict between China and Taiwan. It is a US national interest to encourage the two sides to resume talks on that issue, despite Beijing's lack of interest in engaging with Taiwan's Democratic

Progressive Party and Taiwanese President William Lai. If both the mainland Chinese and the people of Taiwan ever want to peacefully unify, then the US should support that outcome. The only potential resolution the US should oppose is forced unification by the mainland.

The United States' responsibility for militarily supporting Ukraine against Russia has compromised its ability to arm Taiwan. There is now a seven-year-long backlog for US-made Joint Standoff Weapon (JSOW) orders for Taiwan. The sale was announced in 2017 and contracted in 2024. Delivery is not expected until March 2028. The total backlog for all US-purchased arms stands at $20.5 billion and continues to accumulate.[45] While the United States shores up its defence-industrial base, Taiwan needs to transform its own defence establishment, strategy and force structure. Taiwan does not require high-end combat aircraft, surface vessels and other prestige systems and platforms to deter and repel a Chinese military invasion. What it needs most critically are A2/AD systems, like maritime mines and anti-aircraft batteries.[46] Helping Taiwan design a force structure with a minimal long-term supporting role for the United States should be a US strategic priority. Washington should not renounce its policy of strategic ambiguity, however.[47] It would be prudent to leave Beijing with lingering questions about whether the US would militarily assist Taiwan in the event of a Chinese invasion, even if many American analysts and officials believe that actually doing so would be unwise and Taiwanese leaders should understand that such assistance probably would not be forthcoming.

The United States should also try to avoid further harm to its economic relationship with China. This means not adding sanctions or raising tariffs. The Biden administration's recent executive order on US outbound investments seems to be tightly scoped, with the aim of placing notifications and restrictions on capital investments in Chinese AI, quantum-computing and semiconductor industries.[48] These constraints align with the administration's attempt to protect 'foundational technologies with a small yard and high fence'.[49] But it is important for the administration to think carefully about the costs of enlarging the yard and elevating the fence. If economic conflicts cannot be resolved bilaterally, the US should first try to settle them through the World Trade Organization's dispute-resolution mechanisms rather than imposing unilateral measures likely to provoke unproductive retaliation from China.

Lastly, on the diplomatic front, the US should explain its revised economic and diplomatic approach to all key players in the region, including China, India, Japan and Taiwan. This would position Washington to better cultivate goodwill via clarity and transparency. As to China specifically, the United States should continue to keep the door open for people-to-people exchanges. For instance, the administration should urge Congress to pass a multiyear extension of the US–China Science and Technology Agreement, which expired in February 2024. Since 1979, this agreement has facilitated scientific collaboration between the two countries. Both countries have tangibly benefited from it. For example, Chinese scientists have learned how to reduce air pollution and US scientists about how folic-acid additives are crucial for preventing birth defects in newborns.[50] Relatedly, it is in the United States' interest to allow educational exchanges with Chinese universities. While risks of the theft of intellectual property for dual commercial and military use via espionage are real, universities such as the Massachusetts Institute of Technology are devising ways to reduce these risks and still allow productive knowledge exchanges.[51]

*   *   *

Critics of engagement have cast US policy as a total failure, but the alternative could have been worse: a more hostile, impoverished, nuclear-armed, Maoist country that never fully entered the global economy and still got rich.[52] China possessed enormous untapped economic capacity and human capital. While Mao Zedong created numerous barriers to unleashing its full economic potential, Deng Xiaoping placed China on the path to productivity relatively quickly. China's population already possessed high levels of education, and even under collectivisation the entrepreneurial spirit stayed alive. China was well positioned to rise on its own, even without expedited access to US markets.[53]

Calibrated US engagement makes sense now, as it did 50 years ago. The fact that China has become a major stakeholder in the economic order places limits on the large-scale geopolitical revisions it might try to engineer. It is in neither the United States' nor China's interest to act as though a new cold war is in the offing. Although that mindset may be slowly crystallising, there are alternative paths forward that need not lead to cold war, or worse, hot war. Finding ways to productively compete with China economically and diplomatically while hedging against military risks could forge a cold peace.

Notes

1 See Robert S. Ross, 'The Geography of the Peace: East Asia in the Twenty-first Century', *International Security*, vol. 23, no. 4, Spring 1999, pp. 81–118.

2 See Matt Pottinger and Mike Gallagher, 'No Substitute for Victory: America's Competition with China Must Be Won, Not Managed', *Foreign Affairs*, vol. 103, no. 3, May/June 2024, pp. 25–39.

3 'COMMUNISTS: Cold War & Cold Peace', *Time*, 29 October 1952, https://content.time.com/time/subscriber/article/0,33009,817112,00.html.

4 See Charles A. Kupchan et al., *Power in Transition: The Peaceful Change of International Order* (Tokyo: United Nations University Press, 2001); and Benjamin Miller, 'Explaining Variations in Regional Peace: Three Strategies for Peacemaking', *Cooperation and Conflict*, vol. 35, no. 2, June 2000, pp. 155–92.

5 See Ryan Hass, *Stronger: Adapting America's China Strategy in an Age of Competitive Interdependence* (New Haven, CT: Yale University Press, 2021), pp. 6–7.

6 See Robert A. Manning, 'Washington's Supposed Consensus on China Is an Illusion', *Foreign Policy*, 27 June 2023, https://foreignpolicy.com/2023/06/27/

united-states-china-consensus-competition-diplomacy-hawks/.

7 See G. John Ikenberry, 'Why American Power Endures: The US-led Order Isn't in Decline', *Foreign Affairs*, vol. 101, no. 6, November/December 2022, pp. 56–73.

8 See Kurt Campbell and Ely Ratner, 'The China Reckoning: How Beijing Defied American Expectations', *Foreign Affairs*, vol. 97, no. 2, March/April 2018, pp. 60–70; Aaron L. Friedberg, *Getting China Wrong* (New York: Polity Press, 2022); and Anne Stevenson-Yang, *Wild Ride: A Short History of the Opening and Closing of the Chinese Economy* (London: Bui Jones Books, 2024).

9 See Paul Kennedy, *The Rise and Fall of Great Powers: Economic Change and Military Conflict from 1500 to 2000* (New York: Random House, 1987).

10 See Bonnie S. Glaser, Jessica Chen Weiss and Thomas J. Christensen, 'Taiwan and the True Sources of Deterrence: Why America Must Reassure, Not Just Threaten China', *Foreign Affairs*, vol. 103, no. 1, January/February 2024, pp. 88–100.

11 See Zoe Zongyuan Liu, 'China's Pensions System Is Buckling Under an Aging Population', *Foreign Policy*,

29 June 2023, https://foreignpolicy.com/2023/06/29/china-pensions-aging-demographics-economy/; Zoe Zongyuan Liu and Benn Steil, 'Xi's Plan for China's Economy Is Doomed to Fail', *Foreign Affairs*, 29 June 2023, https://www.foreignaffairs.com/china/xis-plan-chinas-economy-doomed-fail; and Carl Minzer, 'Xi Jinping Can't Handle an Aging China', *Foreign Affairs*, 2 May 2023, https://www.foreignaffairs.com/china/xi-jinping-cant-handle-aging-china.

12 See Nicholas R. Lardy, 'How Serious Is China's Economic Slowdown?', Peterson Institute for International Economics, 17 August 2023, https://www.piie.com/blogs/realtime-economics/how-serious-chinas-economic-slowdown.

13 See Select Committee on the Strategic Competition Between the United States and the Chinese Communist Party, 'Reset, Prevent, Build: A Strategy to Win America's Economic Competition with the Chinese Communist Party', United States Congress, 12 December 2023, https://selectcommitteeontheccp.house.gov/sites/evo-subsites/selectcommitteeontheccp.house.gov/files/evo-media-document/reset-prevent-build-scc-report.pdf.

14 See Joshua R. Itzkowitz Shifrinson, 'Neo-primacy and the Pitfalls of US Strategy Toward China', *Washington Quarterly*, vol. 43, no. 4, Winter 2021, pp. 79–104; and Jessica Chen Weiss, 'The China Trap: US Foreign Policy and the Perilous Logic of Zero-sum Competition', *Foreign Affairs*, vol. 101, no. 5, September/October 2022, pp. 40–58.

15 Kupchan et al., *Power in Transition*, p. 7.

16 Miller, 'Explaining Variations in Regional Peace', pp. 155–92.

17 See Michael W. Doyle, *Cold Peace: Avoiding the New Cold War* (New York: Liveright Publishing, 2023).

18 *Ibid.*, pp. 16–17.

19 *Ibid.*, pp. 14–17.

20 Richard Sakwa, 'The Cold Peace: Russo-Western Relations as a Mimetic Cold War', *Cambridge Review of International Affairs*, vol. 26, no. 1, March 2013, pp. 203–24.

21 See Lyle J. Goldstein, *Meeting China Halfway: How to Defuse the Emerging US–China Rivalry* (Washington DC: Georgetown University Press, 2015).

22 *Ibid.*, pp. 12–19.

23 See Robert Jervis, *Perception and Misperception in International Politics* (Princeton, NJ: Princeton University Press, 1976).

24 See Robert Axelrod and Robert Keohane, 'Achieving Cooperation Under Anarchy: Strategies and Institutions', in David A. Baldwin (ed.), *Neorealism and Neoliberalism: The Contemporary Debate* (New York: Columbia University Press, 1993), pp. 85–9, 101–3.

25 Kupchan et al., *Power in Transition*, p. 11.

26 See Axelrod and Keohane, 'Achieving Cooperation Under Anarchy', pp. 101–3; and Goldstein, *Meeting China Halfway*, p. 12.

27 See Michael Beckley, 'Delusions of Détente: Why America and China Will Be Enduring Rivals', *Foreign Affairs*, vol. 102, no. 5, September/October 2023, pp. 8–25.

28 See Claire Yorke, 'Is Empathy a Strategic Imperative? A Review Essay', *Journal of Strategic Studies*, vol. 46, no. 5, January 2023, pp. 1,082–102.

29   The Second Thomas Shoal, called
     Ayungin Shoal in Filipino and Ren'ai
     Jiao in Chinese, is an atoll that has
     been occupied by the Philippines since
     1999 and is the subject of disputed
     territorial claims by China, the
     Philippines, Taiwan and Vietnam. In
     2016, a United Nations tribunal ruled
     against China's claim of sovereignty,
     though China has refused to accept
     this decision. The Philippine Navy
     uses the grounded *Sierra Madre*
     as a base to station approximately
     one dozen Filipino marines. This
     requires frequent resupply, which
     has been a thorny issue for China.
     On 17 June 2024, the China Coast
     Guard disrupted a resupply mission,
     boarded Filipino vessels and injured
     eight Filipinos. Chinese personnel
     wielded axes and machetes, seized
     communications equipment and
     towed the boarded vessels. While the
     incident did not trigger the mutual-
     defence treaty between the United
     States and the Philippines, that
     possibility persists. See Ryan Hass,
     'Avoiding War in the South China Sea',
     Foreign Affairs, 9 July 2024, https://
     www.foreignaffairs.com/united-
     states/avoiding-war-south-china-sea;
     and Sofia Tomacruz and Rebecca
     Tan, 'Philippines Says Sailor Lost
     Finger in Sea Clash, Accuses China
     of "Piracy"', *Washington Post*, 19 June
     2024, https://www.washingtonpost.
     com/world/2024/06/19/
     philippines-south-china-sea-sailor/.
30   See Seong Hyeon Choi and Sylvie
     Zhuang, 'Why Is the US Typhon
     Missile System Being Withdrawn
     from the Philippines?', *South
     China Morning Post*, 5 July 2024,

     https://www.scmp.com/news/
     china/military/article/3269345/
     withdrawal-us-typhon-missile-system-
     philippines-viewed-gesture-china.
31   See Rosemary Foot, 'China and the
     United States: Between Cold and Warm
     Peace', *Survival*, vol. 51, no. 6, December
     2009–January 2010, pp. 123–46.
32   On procurement challenges, see
     Jennifer Kavanagh and Jordan Cohen,
     'The Real Reasons for Taiwan's Arms
     Backlog – and How to Help Fill It',
     War on the Rocks, 13 January 2023,
     https://warontherocks.com/2023/01/
     the-real-reasons-for-taiwans-arms-
     backlog-and-how-to-help-fill-it/. A
     constrained US defence-industrial
     base, complex production processes,
     the congressional contract-
     authorisation process and delivery
     inefficiencies create significant barriers
     to timely delivery.
33   See Rachel Esplin Odell et al., 'Active
     Denial: A Roadmap to a More Effective,
     Stabilizing, and Sustainable US Defense
     Strategy in Asia', Quincy Institute for
     Responsible Statecraft, QI Papers #8, 22
     June 2022, https://quincyinst.org/report/
     active-denial-a-roadmap-to-a-more-
     effective-stabilizing-and-sustainable-u-
     s-defense-strategy-in-asia/#full-report.
34   The Marine Corps' Force Design 2023
     is a good first step towards construct-
     ing a force suitable for contemplated
     Asia-Pacific scenarios. US Marine
     Corps, 'Force Design', 2023, https://
     www.marines.mil/Force-Design-2030/.
35   See Mark F. Cancian, 'Rebuilding
     US Inventories: Six Critical Systems',
     Center for Strategic and International
     Studies, 9 January 2023, https://www.
     csis.org/analysis/rebuilding-us-
     inventories-six-critical-systems.

36 See Bryant Harris, 'Congress Supersizes Munitions Production with Emergency Authorities', *Defense News*, 13 December 2022, https://www.defensenews.com/congress/budget/2022/12/13/congress-supersizes-munitions-production-with-emergency-authorities/.

37 See Charlie Campbell, 'US General's Prediction of War with China "in 2025" Risks Turning Worst Fears into Reality', *Time*, 31 January 2023, https://time.com/6251419/us-china-general-war-2025/.

38 See David Sacks, 'Why China Would Struggle to Invade Taiwan', Council on Foreign Relations, 12 June 2024, https://www.cfr.org/article/why-china-would-struggle-invade-taiwan.

39 See David C. Kang, 'Still Getting Asia Wrong: No "Contain China" Coalition Exists', *Washington Quarterly*, vol. 45, no. 4, Winter 2023, pp. 79–98; and Stockholm International Peace Research Institute (SIPRI), 'SIPRI Military Expenditure Database', 2023, https://milex.sipri.org/sipri. Japan and Taiwan are increasing their defence spending as a share of GDP, while the Philippines is holding defence spending constant.

40 See Dan Blumenthal and Derek Scissors, 'Sideline China with Free Trade', *National Review*, 22 February 2024, https://www.nationalreview.com/magazine/2024/04/sideline-china-with-free-trade/.

41 See Matt Reynolds and Matthew P. Goodman, 'Deny, Deflect, Deter: Countering China's Economic Coercion', Center for Strategic and International Studies, March 2023, https://csis-website-prod.s3.amazonaws.com/s3fs-public/2023-03/230321_Goodman_CounteringChina%27s_EconomicCoercion.pdf.

42 See US Department of Commerce, 'Readout of Secretary Raimondo's Meeting with Minister of Commerce of the People's Republic of China Wang Wentao', 28 August 2023, https://www.commerce.gov/news/press-releases/2023/08/readout-secretary-raimondos-meeting-minister-commerce-peoples-republic.

43 See White House, 'Readout of President Joe Biden's Meeting with President Xi Jinping of the People's Republic of China', 15 November 2023, https://www.whitehouse.gov/briefing-room/statements-releases/2023/11/15/readout-of-president-joe-bidens-meeting-with-president-xi-jinping-of-the-peoples-republic-of-china-2/; and US Department of State, 'Readout – Secretary Blinken's Meeting with People's Republic of China Director of the Chinese Communist Party (CCP) Central Foreign Affairs Commission and Foreign Minister Wang Yi', 26 October 2023, https://www.state.gov/secretary-blinkens-meeting-with-peoples-republic-of-china-director-of-the-chinese-communist-party-ccp-central-foreign-affairs-commission-and-foreign-minister-wang-yi/.

44 See, for example, Lanxin Xiang, 'Biden's Misguided China Policy', *Survival*, vol. 66, no. 3, June–July 2024, pp. 91–104.

45 Eric Gomez and Benjamin Giltner, 'Taiwan Arms Backlog, June 2024 Update: First Arms Sales to the Lai Ching-te Administration and New

Information About Delays', Cato Institute, 9 July 2024, https://www.cato.org/blog/taiwan-arms-backlog-june-2024-first-arms-sales-lai-ching-te-administration-new-information.

46 See Eugene Gholz, Benjamin Friedman and Enea Gjoza, 'Defensive Defense: A Better Way to Protect US Allies in Asia', *Washington Quarterly*, vol. 42, no. 4, Winter 2020, pp. 171–89; and Jared M. McKinney and Peter Harris, *Deterrence Gap: Avoiding War in the Taiwan Strait* (Carlisle, PA: US Army War College Press, 2024).

47 Although the United States has not officially renounced strategic ambiguity, Joe Biden appeared to do so impulsively early in his presidency. China strongly condemned Biden's remarks. US officials clarified that official policy towards Taiwan had not changed. See Peter Baker, 'Biden Veers Off Script on Taiwan. It's Not the First Time', *New York Times*, 23 May 2022, https://www.nytimes.com/2022/05/23/us/politics/biden-taiwan-comments.html.

48 See White House, 'Executive Order on Addressing United States Investments in Certain National Security Technologies and Products in Countries of Concern', 9 August 2023, https://www.whitehouse.gov/briefing-room/presidential-actions/2023/08/09/executive-order-on-addressing-united-states-investments-in-certain-national-security-technologies-and-products-in-countries-of-concern/.

49 White House, 'Remarks by National Security Advisor Jake Sullivan on Renewing American Economic Leadership at the Brookings Institution', 27 April 2023, https://www.whitehouse.gov/briefing-room/speeches-remarks/2023/04/27/remarks-by-national-security-advisor-jake-sullivan-on-renewing-american-economic-leadership-at-the-brookings-institution/.

50 See Deborah Seligsohn, 'The Case for Renewing the US–China S&T Cooperation Agreement', Center for Strategic and International Studies, 4 August 2023, https://www.csis.org/analysis/case-renewing-us-china-st-cooperation-agreement.

51 See The MIT China Strategy Group, 'University Engagement with China: An MIT Approach', Final Report, November 2022, https://global.mit.edu/wp-content/uploads/2022/11/FINALUniversity-Engagement-with-China_An-MIT-Approach-Nov2022.pdf.

52 See, for example, Alastair Iain Johnston, 'The Failures of the "Failure of Engagement" with China', *Washington Quarterly*, vol. 42, no. 2, Summer 2019, pp. 99–114.

53 See Loren Brandt, Debin Ma and Thomas G. Rawski, 'From Divergence to Convergence: Reevaluating the History Behind China's Economic Boom', *Journal of Economic Literature*, vol. 52, no. 1, March 2014, pp. 45–123.

Controlling Nuclear Arms in a Multipolar World

Alexey Arbatov

The goal of nuclear disarmament is a world free of nuclear weapons. The goal of arms control is to limit and reduce those nuclear weapons that still exist, so as to make their employment less likely, their costs less weighty and the consequences of their use less destructive.[1] Despite the somewhat contradictory nature of these tasks, arms control has been generally successful since the Partial Nuclear Test Ban Treaty was signed in 1963.[2]

This treaty inaugurated arms control as a multilateral endeavour, or what might be described as 'horizontal' nuclear disarmament, which quickly expanded to include the 1967 Outer Space Treaty and Treaty for the Prohibition of Nuclear Weapons in Latin America and the Caribbean, the 1968 Nuclear Non-Proliferation Treaty (NPT) and the 1971 Seabed Arms Control Treaty. A 'vertical' dimension was introduced in 1972 when bilateral negotiations between the United States and the Soviet Union resulted in the signing of the Anti-Ballistic Missile (ABM) Treaty and an Interim Agreement on the limitation of strategic offensive arms. These agreements represented a qualitatively new type of arms control since they dealt not just with the general proliferation of nuclear weapons to new geographic spaces

Alexey Arbatov is Director of the Center for International Security at the E.M. Primakov Institute of World Economy and International Relations, and is a full member of the Russian Academy of Sciences. He participated in the START I negotiations in 1990, served as deputy chair of the Defense Committee of the State Duma from 1994–2003, and headed the Non-Proliferation Program at the Carnegie Moscow Center from 2004–17. After 2004 he occupied various governmental advisory positions and participated in Russian and international non-governmental organisations for the promotion of disarmament.

Survival | vol. 66 no. 6 | December 2024–January 2025 | pp. 87–102   https://doi.org/10.1080/00396338.2024.2432195

or with specific activities in weapons development, but with the limitation, reduction and elimination of specified types of nuclear arms (in this case, deployed strategic ballistic missiles).

Thus, from the early 1970s through to 2011, the central pillar and crucial driver of arms control was a process of bilateral US–Soviet/Russian strategic-arms limitation and reduction, which in 1987 embraced intermediate-range missiles and in 1991–92 tactical nuclear munitions (by mutual politically binding initiatives). During this time, the two states concluded a second round of Strategic Arms Limitation Talks (SALT II in 1979), the Intermediate-Range Nuclear Forces (INF) Treaty (1987), the first and second Strategic Arms Reduction treaties (START I in 1991 and START II in 1993), a framework for START III (1997), the Strategic Offensive Reductions Treaty (SORT in 2002) and finally New START (2010). Four new nuclear-weapons-free zones were also created during the 1990s, and about 50 additional states joined the NPT, which was indefinitely extended in 1995. The right of the International Atomic Energy Agency (IAEA) to monitor compliance with the NPT was also consistently extended. In addition, multilateral processes dealing with nuclear testing and non-proliferation took place: specifically, these were the Threshold Test Ban Treaty (1974) and the Peaceful Nuclear Explosion Treaty (1976), and eventually the Comprehensive Nuclear-Test-Ban Treaty (CTBT) in 1996, which had been one of the key conditions for the indefinite extension of the NPT in 1995. As a result, the number of nuclear-weapons states was limited to ten (instead of dozens, as predicted in the 1960s), of which five (China, France, the Soviet Union/Russia, the United Kingdom and the United States) satisfy the definition of 'nuclear-weapon State' in the NPT as having manufactured and exploded a nuclear weapon or other nuclear explosive device prior to 1 January 1967. One nuclear-weapons state, South Africa, voluntarily dismantled its nuclear programme, including its existing nuclear weapons, in 1989 and joined the NPT as a non-nuclear-weapons state.

Article VI of the NPT obliges the five recognised nuclear-weapons states 'to pursue negotiations in good faith on effective measures relating to cessation of the nuclear arms race at an early date and to nuclear disarmament, and on a Treaty on general and complete disarmament under strict and effective international control'.[3] Yet efforts towards the physical limitation, reduction and elimination of specified nuclear weapons have largely retained a bilateral format. This has been a constant irritant in relations between the nuclear 'haves' and 'have-nots', as well as a source of discord between the two nuclear superpowers (the US and the Soviet Union/Russia) and the three other nuclear-weapons states under the treaty. In addition, it has provided justification for the nuclear programmes of the four 'outsiders' under the treaty (India, Israel, North Korea and Pakistan).

The disintegration of arms control

These problems have only been compounded by recent retreats from arms control, such as the United States' 2018 withdrawal from the nuclear deal it had reached with Iran in 2015 (the Joint Comprehensive Plan of Action or JCPOA), and the US-initiated abrogation of the INF Treaty and the Open Skies Treaty in 2019 and 2020 respectively. Other problems include a dead-locked process to establish a nuclear-free zone in the Middle East and the absence of universal acceptance of the 1997 Additional Protocol granting the IAEA expanded inspection authority. The heaviest blow was dealt by the renewal of Cold War-style hostilities between Russia and the West in the wake of the war in Ukraine, which prompted Russia to suspend New START, withdraw from the 1990 Conventional Armed Forces in Europe Treaty, recall its ratification of the CTBT (which the US had never ratified) and refuse to renew strategic-arms talks in 2024. Meanwhile, new military projects are endangering the Outer Space and Seabed Arms Control trea-ties. All this has raised the frightening prospect of the NPT's collapse and an ensuing wave of nuclear proliferation to unstable territories and terror-ist organisations.

In 2023, Russia made the engagement of the UK and France in strategic arms control (or at least the taking into account of their nuclear forces) a precondition of its return to the full implementation of New START. For its part, the United States has made involving China and its expanding nuclear arsenal a prerequisite of any follow-on strategic-arms limitation arrange-ments. Hence, apart from ending hostilities in Ukraine and alleviating the confrontation between Russia and the West, the transformation of bilateral strategic arms control to a multilateral format (minimally encompassing the five NPT nuclear-weapons states) has become a key condition of saving both 'vertical' nuclear arms control and 'horizontal' non-proliferation.

Lessons of the P5 failure

The idea of five-party arms control was first proposed by Desmond Brown, then the UK's defence secretary, in February 2008 at the Conference on Disarmament in Geneva. After that, official five-party ('P5') meetings were held in London, Paris, Washington and Beijing. The P5 adopted a number of general, wishful documents in support of strategic stability, ratification of the CTBT, progress in negotiations for a Fissile Material Cut-Off Treaty, the indefinite extension of the NPT, denuclearisation of the Korean Peninsula, upholding the JCPOA, the convening of a conference on establishing a nuclear-weapons-free zone in the Middle East and the prevention of nuclear terrorism.[4] As positive as those appeals were, the main purpose of the P5 remained unattainable: the five nuclear-weapons states did not move an inch towards the practical elaboration of limitations and reductions of their nuclear arms.

The argument of the three smaller nuclear powers was that the 'big two' – Russia and the US – should first reduce their own nuclear arsenals closer to the levels of the other three.[5] The usual response of the two nuclear superpowers implied that after 30 years of deep bilateral reductions of their nuclear arsenals,[6] they could not make any further reductions without legally binding assurances that the other three would not implement a sub-stantial build-up in their own nuclear forces.

The fundamental error of the P5 initiative was that it tried to apply the principle of multilateral, 'horizontal' disarmament – which is usually seen in relation to agreements on non-proliferation, non-deployment in specific locations such as outer space, or fissile-materials cut-off – to the 'vertical' arms-control goal of technical limitation and reduction of specific deployed and planned nuclear-weapons systems. In this sense, the NPT's Article VI was mistakenly interpreted as calling for a five-party arms-control endeav-our. It should instead be understood as committing all NPT nuclear-weapons states to engage in arms limitation and reduction in ways that are consistent with their own particular national-security positions and perceptions.

The political environment in the 1990s and 2000s was uniquely favourable for multilateral nuclear-arms limitation. Even so, the practical output of arms-control efforts during this time was minimal. It is true that the UK and France capitalised on the benign strategic environment by reducing their defence expenditure and making some unilateral reductions in their nuclear forces, but there were no formal arms-control agreements to ensure the transparency and predictability of those steps, something that Russian President Vladimir Putin pointed out later in suspending New START in 2023.[7] It is sadly ironic that in January 2022 the P5 adopted a declaration reminding the world of the Reagan–Gorbachev maxim that 'a nuclear war cannot be won and must never be fought'.[8] Only a month and a half later, the Ukraine war started and was from the very first day linked to the possibility of nuclear-weapons use.[9]

Nuclear deterrence and national security

Notwithstanding the common perception that arms races among the nuclear-weapons states set a 'bad example' to other actual or potential nuclear-weapons states, while arms reductions by the big two set a 'good example', the mechanisms of nuclear relationships are much more complicated than this formula would imply. The example set by other states is far less important than a state's own national-security interests in determining whether or not it decides to acquire nuclear weapons. Each state's national-security policies define the goals of its deterrence posture and weapons programmes. These are the criteria against which the possible effects of arms control and its desirability are usually assessed. No state would acquiesce to an agreement that it believed might be detrimental to its national security. The P5 talks, as well as the 2017 Treaty on the Prohibition of Nuclear Weapons (TPNW) and various other initiatives on nuclear disarmament, overlooked this key point.

Of the nine existing nuclear-weapons states, all except Israel see a connection between their nuclear posture and their global status and prestige. (Israel, like South Africa until 1989, treats its nuclear programme as a state secret, although its nuclear status is well known and does contribute to its regional influence and prestige, while also being a problem for non-proliferation.)

However, nuclear deterrence contributes to each state's national security in a more tangible way: the threat of employing nuclear weapons is seen to prevent undesirable actions by potential opponents. All nuclear-weapons states assign their nuclear forces the task of deterring potential opponents through the threat of nuclear retaliation in the case of an enemy's aggression using nuclear or other weapons of mass destruction (WMD). The same kind of response is envisioned by France, Russia, the UK and the US should an enemy use WMD on their allies and partners, but not by China, India, Israel, North Korea or Pakistan. All the nuclear-weapons states except China and India have signalled nuclear deterrence against aggression using conventional arms and forces (which implies a first-nuclear-strike or 'first-use' posture). Nuclear arms may also be used by France, Russia, the UK and the US in response to a conventional attack against an ally.[10]

The 'targets' of nuclear deterrence for Russia are the United States, other NATO countries, Japan, South Korea and probably Israel. For the United States, the targets are China, Russia, North Korea and possibly Iran. For France and the UK they are Russia and possibly China and Iran. For China they are India, Japan, South Korea and the US. For India they are China and Pakistan. For Pakistan the target is India. For Israel, the targets are Iran and Arab opponents. For Iran, if it acquires nuclear arms, the targets would be Israel and the US. For North Korea, they are Japan, South Korea and the US (see Figure 1).

Each state has invested massive resources in its nuclear potential. No state would agree to limit or reduce its nuclear forces if this did not buttress its national security – to say nothing of weakening it. If a state did agree, it would expect in return an adequate limitation or reduction in the military capabilities of potential opponents, foremost their nuclear forces perceived as a threat to national security. This is exactly the way the Soviet Union/ Russia and the US operated during their half-century of successful negotiations on strategic and intermediate-range weapons systems.

Otherwise, there is no reason to expect a tangible, practical outcome from any disarmament project, declaration or appeal by an authoritative public figure, international organisation or movement, however desirable or well intentioned. The eternal disputes between the nuclear big two and

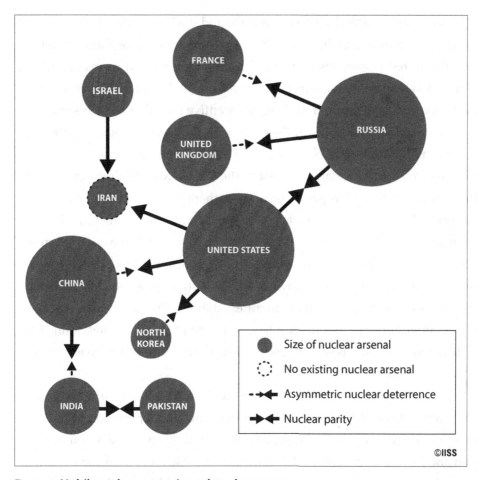

Figure 1: **Multilateral asymmetric nuclear deterrence**

smaller three, or the nuclear five and the non-nuclear others at NPT conferences, United Nations committees and other forums, about who is to take the next step in nuclear disarmament will continue to serve only as a smokescreen for the actual considerations determining states' official positions on nuclear-arms limitation.

Preconditions for practical arms limitation

To progress from never-ending discussions to business-like negotiations, it would be useful to apply the available practical experience: more than 50 years of successful strategic-arms-control negotiations between the Soviet Union/Russia and the US. These negotiations resulted in nuclear-delivery vehicles being reduced by a factor of three and nuclear warheads by a factor of seven since their peak in 1991.[11] Of still greater importance, these so-called 'stabilizing reductions' restructured the remaining nuclear forces in such a way that the capability for carrying out a disarming (counterforce) attack was mutually removed, thus eliminating an incentive for a first nuclear strike.[12]

It is notable that despite all the tension and danger surrounding the situation in Ukraine, there is no fear of a strategic nuclear attack on either side, which stands in sharp contrast to the Cuban Missile Crisis of 1962 or the missile crisis in Europe in 1983. True, there is an acute concern about the possible use of tactical nuclear weapons should the conflict in Ukraine escalate,[13] in particular via multiple deep strikes using conventional missiles on critical sites of the warring parties. Tactical nuclear attacks would undoubtedly lead to an exchange of massive strategic strikes through the dynamics of deliberate or inadvertent escalation. (Russian tactical nuclear weapons would have a strategic effect for the neighbouring states, while US tactical nuclear systems would constitute a strategic threat for the European part of Russia.)

Arms-control treaties per se cannot provide an absolute guarantee of war prevention. Instead, they are designed to reduce the temptation to initiate warfare and thus to lower the probability of war by political accommodation and technical restrictions. It is quite conceivable that the current chances of nuclear escalation in the Ukrainian conflict would be much higher were it not for the treaties (and binding political initiatives) on strategic arms, intermediate-range missiles and tactical nuclear weapons that had been implemented since the late 1980s.

The success of the SALT process, the INF and the START treaties was possible due to two principal conditions. Firstly, since the early 1960s a state of mutual nuclear deterrence had prevailed between the big two as each had the capability to destroy the other. This was not a product of will or the conscious design of either side, but was simply the outcome of an intensive nuclear-arms race between them. It was publicly recognised in the mid-1960s by the US government thanks to the efforts of then-defense secretary Robert McNamara.[14] The Soviet leadership would publicly acknowledge the situation 20 years later under Mikhail Gorbachev.[15] The second condition was the emergence of approximate equality (parity) in the superpowers' strategic forces in the early 1970s.

The first condition created the foundation for mutual interest between the parties in limiting and reducing the other side's nuclear forces, which provided for the feasibility of 'trade-offs', thus transforming the opponents into partners in the negotiated management and curtailment of the nuclear threat each posed to the other. The second condition was by no means a guarantee of security or a criterion of strategic sufficiency. However, it provided for approximately equal starting and end points in negotiations, since no party would be willing to legalise its inferiority or sacrifice its superiority for the sake of reaching an agreement.[16] Approximate equality in the weapons systems up for negotiation is very handy in facilitating such negotiations.

This analysis may explain the reasons for past failures to organise multilateral arms-limitation talks, including the P5 initiative. To be precise, the relationships between France, the UK and the US are not characterised by mutual nuclear deterrence. They are full-scale allies and thus have no interest in limiting each other's arms – they have no nuclear forces to trade off. The same is true of Russia and China. In contrast to the acute military, political and ideological conflicts that characterised their relationship in the 1970s and 1980s, they have now entered a 'strategic partnership' and thus have nothing to gain from mutual arms limitation.

Strategic relations between Russia on one side and Britain and France on the other are characterised by mutual nuclear deterrence, but there is an asymmetry in their nuclear forces, with Russia enjoying considerable superiority. The two European states value their nuclear potentials as a symbol of great-power status, and an asset in sustaining national security and relative national independence. They would not agree to legalise Russian superiority in an arms-control treaty with Moscow, nor to placing their own forces under a common ceiling with American forces. This option would be unacceptable to the US as well, since it would legalise a Russian advantage of 15% in delivery vehicles and 30% in warheads, which would be seen as even more detrimental in view of the ongoing build-up of Chinese strategic forces.

In a sense, a similar situation is emerging in US–Chinese strategic relations: mutual nuclear deterrence is present, but strategic parity is absent, with a huge American superiority expected to remain in place for at least the next ten years. Both China and Russia would reject putting Chinese nuclear forces under a common ceiling with Russia's. Under the New START cap of 1,550 warheads or something close to it in a follow-on treaty, China's projected strategic build-up would virtually nullify Russian forces in a decade or less. Otherwise, Beijing will not be able to acquire nuclear power commensurate with that of the two superpowers, which is apparently a top foreign-policy ambition.

As for the four NPT 'outsiders', they have no formal obligation to pursue nuclear disarmament as treaty signatories do under Article VI. Having obtained nuclear arms after 1967, they cannot join the treaty as nuclear-weapons states. At the same time, they would hardly agree to do away with nuclear arms in order to join the NPT in view of their own security considerations.[17]

Besides the case of Russia and the United States, the strategic balance between India and Pakistan is favourable for an arms-control dialogue. The two states have a relationship of mutual nuclear deterrence and have attained approximate parity in their nuclear-delivery vehicles (with some technical asymmetries).[18] The main obstacles to a dialogue are territorial conflicts, ideological differences, historical grievances and the fact that Indian nuclear forces are primarily directed against the third party – China.

Finally, the two nuclear states at the opposite sides of the Eurasian continent, Israel and North Korea, are exceptional cases. The nuclear forces of these states are designed to ensure their basic national existence and deter various kinds of external threats. Their forces are not a part of any particular military balance with another state and hence cannot be limited or reduced by classic arms-control agreements as a quid pro quo with an opponent.

Transition to multilateral arms limitation

Saving what is left of nuclear arms control by restoring and adapting it to the emerging polycentric world order cannot be achieved in an arbitrary way or through idealistic, universal projects. This work must meticulously take into consideration the national-security perceptions and interests of the states involved, as well as the political and strategic interactions of various nuclear arms-control regimes and initiatives.

In the political domain, the most vital task is to prevent the nuclear escalation of the Ukraine war and to facilitate a ceasefire as soon as possible, one that above all stops deep strikes into the territories of the opponents. That should be followed by negotiations on the peaceful settlement of the conflict.

In the meantime, the most important and urgent task is to sustain the CTBT and prevent the resumption of nuclear tests. Otherwise, the final collapse of the existing arms-control and non-proliferation systems would be inevitable.

In parallel, another task should be the preservation of New START, at least until February 2026 – even in a suspended format. In fact, this was done with the SALT II Treaty until 1986, after its ratification was aborted in the US because of the Soviet incursion into Afghanistan in 1979.

The end of hostilities in Ukraine and the start of a peace process there would open the way to the resumption of the US–Russia START process through the revival of consultations begun in summer and autumn 2021 in Geneva. Besides dealing with the extremely complex issues of limiting strategic conventional systems (Russia's opening position) and tactical nuclear weapons (the United States' position) – as well as addressing cyber warfare and other newly developing destructive or disruptive technologies – the parties will have to address the mind-boggling problem of engaging third nuclear-weapons states in an arms-limitation process. Preserving New START and opening strategic-stability talks between the US and Russia in a bilateral format is a necessary first step towards this goal.

In parallel, the United States should try harder to engage China in a substantive arms-control discussion. Instead of proposing agreements on 'transparency' and 'predictability', Washington should make Beijing a proposal it cannot refuse. Firstly, such a proposition should make it clear to China that the eventual treaty would not legalise Chinese inferiority in those weapons systems covered by the accord. Secondly, it should leave China's ultimate strategic stance better than it would otherwise have been. This is exactly what US president Lyndon Johnson and McNamara proposed to the Soviet prime minister Alexei Kosygin during their summit in Glassboro in June 1967. Despite the initial negative reaction (the Soviet side was taken by surprise), Moscow quickly recognised the value of the proposition, which was in line with both conditions outlined here. The summit represented the starting point of a half-century strategic dialogue that produced a dozen crucial agreements and achieved radical nuclear-arms limitation and reduction.

The same type of approach could be used by Russia in respect of the UK and France. Relying on the model of SALT I, which limited selected legs of strategic triads rather than strategic forces as a whole, Russian and European nuclear forces may be limited by equal ceilings. This would not legalise the superiority of either party, but may remove security concerns on both sides.

The prospect of limiting Chinese nuclear forces may alleviate Indian security concerns and be beneficial for its arms-control dialogue with Pakistan on the foundation of 'equality and equal security', a principle that emerged at the US–Soviet talks on SALT I and II. In dealing with technical asymmetries and the factor of a third party in a nuclear balance, the two superpowers have plenty of experience gained during decades of strategic negotiations that they could share with India and Pakistan. In the 1970s and 1980s, the Soviet Union had to plan its strategic forces to deter China, France and the UK, in addition to the US. Recently, the latter has found itself in a similar situation of aiming nuclear deterrence against both Russia and China. Still, past experience has demonstrated that such strategic problems may be successfully resolved.

After that, it might be easier to expand arms control and non-proliferation to the Far and Middle East. Untying the knots of nuclear problems implies resolution of regional territorial, political, ethnic and religious disputes, as well as conventional forces' limitation and confidence-building measures. Such accommodations, with the encouragement and guarantees of influential outside powers, should facilitate blending local nuclear arms control with the non-proliferation framework of the type implied by the idea of the Middle Eastern nuclear-free zone.

It seems inappropriate at this moment to get deeper into technical details of possible agreements among the nuclear-armed nations. Suffice it to stress that engaging third nuclear states will be an important condition for the continuation of the US–Russian bilateral strategic dialogue – just as extension of this bilateral dialogue would make it easier to achieve the participation of third nations in nuclear arms control. No doubt, it would be beneficial for fortifying the NPT and CTBT regimes, as well as the space and seabed treaties. It would also encourage fissile-materials cut-off negotiations.

The obstacles to the implementation of such measures are huge and stem not only from the tremendous objective complexity of the issues involved, but also from the emerging 'revisionist' political schools in Russia and elsewhere. Their response to the emerging polycentric world order and hi-tech innovations in armaments is the philosophy of destroying all the fruits of six decades of arms control by resuming nuclear testing, facilitating proliferation and renewing the role of nuclear weapons as an effective instrument of foreign policy and practical war fighting.[19] Although the revisionists do not propose anything sensible as a substitute to the existing arms-control framework, and their recommendations are vulnerable on moral and professional grounds, these are not to be taken lightly. Already they are tangibly affecting the moods of political elites and practical state policies.

Trump's record does not leave much ground for optimism

Donald Trump's victory in the November 2024 US presidential election has introduced still greater uncertainty for the prospects of enhancing international arms control. Trump's record during his first presidential term in 2016–20 does not leave much ground for optimism. During his presidency, the United States withdrew from the JCPOA deal with Iran, denounced the INF Treaty with Russia and abandoned the multilateral Open Skies Treaty. By the end of his first term, Trump had refused to extend New START and considered withdrawing from the CTBT (which is closely linked to the NPT).

Trump's victory could well inspire the proponents of a nuclear-arms build-up in the United States, while at the same time discouraging the advocates of lowering the nuclear threshold and dismantling the arms-control system in Russia. In any case, the future of New START and both the CTBT and NPT is now in doubt, which in turn calls into question the long-term prospects for a transition from bilateral to multilateral nuclear-arms limitation and reduction.

Even so, there could still be an improvement in the declaratory, diplomatic and economic interactions between the United States and Russia.

There is also a small chance of enforcing a ceasefire and initiating a process of peaceful settlement in Ukraine. In the long run, these developments might provide a better international environment for arms control.

*   *   *

The current confrontation between Russia and the West poses the greatest danger of nuclear war since 1945. No doubt, if such a war were to break out, all arms-control projects would be irrelevant.

However, if this Holocaust is avoided, the revival of disarmament and non-proliferation efforts will become a practical and urgent necessity given the emergence of a polycentric world order and the rapid development of new types of nuclear weaponry, conventional strike systems and various destructive/disruptive technologies. It is worth thinking through the adaptation of arms control to emerging conditions now, so that a desirable political opportunity to facilitate multilateral arms limitation is not missed, as happened during the 1990s and 2000s.

Of course, reality is always much more complex and paradoxical than any theory or 'road map'. Still, there is no doubt that saving and renovating arms control is essential for preventing a catastrophic 'end of history'. For the last 60 years, the treaties and regimes of nuclear disarmament and non-proliferation have successfully served to prevent a bipolar world order from erupting into a nuclear war. In the future, this indispensable network should be enhanced to weld a multipolar world together and preclude its slide into nuclear chaos.

Notes

1   See Thomas Schelling and Morton Halperin, *Strategy and Arms Control* (New York: Twentieth Century Fund, 1961).
2   The Antarctic Treaty that came into force in 1961 arguably included an arms-control element as it prohibited nuclear explosions and the disposal of radioactive waste in Antarctica. See 'Antarctic Treaty', available from the Nuclear Threat Initiative at https://www.nti.org/education-center/treaties-and-regimes/antarctic-treaty/.
3   The text of the NPT is available from the United Nations Office for Disarmament Affairs at https://

disarmament.unoda.org/wmd/
nuclear/npt/text/.

4   As a practical matter, a US–Chinese dic-
tionary of strategic terms was compiled.

5   The three smaller nuclear-weapons
states allegedly possess a few hundred
warheads each.

6   Each side reduced its arsenal of
approximately 20,000–30,000 nuclear
munitions to about 5,000–6,000. This
included reductions of strategic warheads from 10,000–12,000 down to
1,550 in keeping with the ceiling established by New START.

7   During the detente years of the 1990s
and 2000s the UK and France summar-
ily reduced their nuclear forces from
about 800 deployed warheads down to
510. See Stockholm International Peace
Research Institute (SIPRI), *SIPRI Yearbook
1989: Armaments, Disarmament and
International Security* (Oxford: Oxford
University Press, 1989), pp. 17–29; and
SIPRI, *SIPRI Yearbook 2021: Armaments,
Disarmament and International Security*
(Oxford: Oxford University Press, 2021),
pp. 358–68. For Putin's remarks, see
President of Russia, 'Poslanie Prezidenta
Federal'nomu Sobraniju' [Presidential
address to the Federal Assembly], 21
February 2023, http://www.kremlin.ru/
events/president/news/70565.

8   White House, 'Joint Statement of
the Leaders of the Five Nuclear-
weapon States on Preventing Nuclear
War and Avoiding Arms Races', 3
January 2022, available at https://
www.whitehouse.gov/briefing-room/
statements-releases/2022/01/03/
p5-statement-on-preventing-nuclear-
war-and-avoiding-arms-races/.

9   See President of Russia, 'Address by the
President of the Russian Federation',

24 February 2022, http://en.kremlin.ru/
events/president/news/67843.

10   Russia amended its nuclear doctrine
to this effect in September 2024.

11   The reductions achieved were in fact
much larger taking into account the
elimination of about 2,700 intermediate-
and shorter-range missiles and 3,600
warheads by the two states under the
INF Treaty in 1987.

12   The term 'stabilizing reductions' is
used in the 'Soviet–United States Joint
Statement on Future Negotiations on
Nuclear and Space Arms and Further
Enhancing Strategic Stability', 1
June 1990, available from the George
H.W. Bush Presidential Library and
Museum, https://bush41library.tamu.
edu/archives/public-papers/1938.

13   The tactical nuclear weapons of the
US and the Soviet Union/Russia were
the subject of unilateral presidential
initiatives in 1991–92, which may have
reduced their numbers substantially.
However, due to the informal nature
of the initiatives, no reliable, official
data or verification mechanism has
been available.

14   See Robert McNamara, *The Essence of
Security: Reflections in Office* (New York:
Harper and Row, 1968), pp. 51–67.

15   See the 'Joint Soviet–United States
Statement on the Summit Meeting in
Geneva', 21 November 1985, available
from the Ronald Reagan Presidential
Library and Museum at https://www.
reaganlibrary.gov/archives/speech/
joint-soviet-united-states-statement-
summit-meeting-geneva.

16   There have been exceptions to this
general principle. In the SALT I Interim
Agreement, the US accepted the Soviet
Union's advantage in ballistic missiles,

retaining superiority in heavy bombers and missiles equipped with multiple independently targetable re-entry vehicles. In the 1987 INF Treaty the Soviet Union agreed to eliminate more than twice as many missiles and three time as many warheads as the US, since American medium-range missiles could reach deeply into Soviet territory and thus posed a strategic threat, while the Soviet Union's medium-range missiles could not reach US territory and thus posed only a theatre threat to US NATO allies.

[17] In this sense, the example of South Africa is not very promising: that country abandoned its nuclear arms due to a radical change in its domestic political regime, which affected its relations with the wider world – not the other way around.

[18] Both states keep their nuclear forces secret, but independent sources estimate that each possesses about 170 delivery vehicles. SIPRI, *SIPRI Yearbook 2022: Armaments, Disarmament and International Security* (Oxford: Oxford University Press, 2022), pp. 391–403.

[19] See John R. Bolton, 'Putin Did the World a Favor by Suspending Russia's Participation in New START', *Washington Post*, 6 March 2023, https://www.washingtonpost.com/opinions/2023/03/06/russia-china-united-states-tripolar-nuclear-powers/; and Sergey A. Karaganov, 'Vek vojn? Stat'ja vtoraja. Chto delat'' [The age of wars? Article two: what should be done], *Rossija v global'noj politike* [Russia in global politics], 21 February 2024, https://globalaffairs.ru/articles/vek-vojn-chto-delat/.

Crisis and COVID in North Korea

Victor Cha and Katrin Fraser Katz

The wars in Europe and the Middle East have obscured a crisis brewing on the Korean Peninsula. While North Korean belligerence is commonplace, particularly during US election years, what is different now is a confluence of forces that increases the likelihood of militarised conflict. Crisis and negotiation has been customary between North Korea and the United States, but the normal feedback loops in the form of diplomacy are now absent. Meanwhile, North Korean leader Kim Jong-un's support for Russia's war in Ukraine with troops and weapons may embolden him closer to home – in part to distract his population from dismal domestic conditions worsened by the government's utter neglect during the COVID-19 pandemic that locked down the country for three and a half years.

Spiral of tensions

Even by its own aggressive standards, North Korea has been on a tear since the start of 2024. In October, it blew up sections of its own roads and rail lines that formerly linked to South Korea. It then threatened to shoot down any drones sent by South Korea into the North to drop anti-Kim information leaflets. North Korea also announced its intention to construct a new wall and deploy anti-personnel mines along the border to seal off any interaction

Victor Cha is president of the Geopolitics and Foreign Policy Department and the Korea Chair at the Center for Strategic and International Studies (CSIS), and Distinguished University Professor and professor of government at Georgetown University. **Katrin Fraser Katz** is an adjunct fellow in the Office of the Korea Chair at CSIS and Professor of Practice in the Department of Political Science and the Master of Arts in International Administration programme at the University of Miami.

Survival | vol. 66 no. 6 | December 2024–January 2025 | pp. 103–118 https://doi.org/10.1080/00396338.2024.2432196

with the South.[1] These actions followed the Kim regime's bombshell declaration in January that it was abandoning the goal of unification, destroying the symbolic and decades-old unification arch in Pyongyang built by Kim's grandfather, and designating South Korea as the 'principal enemy'.[2] Kim has sent 30 waves of trash-laden balloons into the South since May.[3] In June, he hosted Russian President Vladimir Putin for a summit that renewed Russia's Cold War-era security commitments, for which Kim reciprocated in October 2024 by dispatching at least one division (10,000 soldiers) to fight for Putin against Ukraine in Kursk. In September, Kim showed off a selection of new uranium-enrichment centrifuges and called for strengthening North Korea's nuclear forces. And on 4 November, North Korea launched the 89th missile test it has staged during the Biden administration, the 107th such launch since the 2018 Singapore summit, and the 186th since the collapse of the last denuclearisation agreement in 2008.[4]

Crisis cycles with North Korea usually follow the rhythm of a pendulum, swinging to one extreme until gravity pulls them back to the other extreme, with the momentum eventually settling at an uneasy status quo in the middle until the next cycle. With each iteration, North Korea's military goal is clear: it wants to develop a modern nuclear-weapons force that is invulnerable to a US pre-emptive first strike and that can threaten the continental United States and its allies at each rung of the escalation ladder, from battlefield and tactical nuclear weapons to long-range stand-off platforms. The strategic aim is to deter the United States from coming to the aid of South Korea. The diplomatic one is to win North Korea de facto recognition as a nuclear-weapons state. With each round of sanctions and denuclearisation diplomacy, Pyongyang has customarily been slowed in advancing its objectives and incentivised to consider a more peaceful path. This time, however, several forces are propelling the pendulum farther in the direction of crisis, with little gravitational pullback in the opposing direction.

The Putin–Kim–Xi axis

North Korea's blossoming relationship with Russia has afforded Kim material support and the renewal of a Cold War-era security guarantee. Putin's dire need for ammunition, ballistic missiles and military personnel from

North Korea to prosecute his war against Ukraine has gained the regime food, fuel and military technology to advance Kim's weapons programmes.[5] Perhaps even more importantly, Russia's war needs have furnished Kim with a new patron just as his regime was emerging from a long COVID lockdown and spectacularly failed summit diplomacy with the United States during Donald Trump's first presidency. Trump's walking out of the meeting in Hanoi in February 2019 was a major embarrassment for Kim, and the pandemic dashed any hope of saving face.

Historically, Pyongyang has been a supplicant who would ask Russia for subsidised oil or debt relief. Putin would occasionally throw a bone to Kim Jong-un's reclusive father by inviting him for lunch at his flat in Moscow as a gesture of goodwill. Now the tables are turned. Putin believes the outcome of his war in Ukraine may be tied to North Korean military support. This nourishes North Korean hubris, evident in its recent acts of belligerence.

The new Putin–Kim link has had a rebound effect on China. While Beijing is fond of telling Westerners who seek China's help in dealing with North Korea that it has little influence over the regime, the geopolitical reality is that Beijing jealously guards what influence it has. China grows uncomfortable whenever any other power gets too chummy with Kim. Chinese President Xi Jinping refused to meet with the rambunctious Kim for seven years, until Trump declared in March 2018 that he had agreed to meet with Kim; the first US–North Korea summit ultimately occurred in June that year. Following Trump's announcement, Xi met with Kim five times over 16 months. But after the failed Hanoi summit and a final June 2019 meeting between Trump, Kim and then-South Korean president Moon Jae-in in the Korean Demilitarized Zone, which also failed to produce results, the Xi–Kim meetings stopped. Given this pattern, the Chinese cannot be comfortable with the new Russia–North Korea security treaty, the hundreds of containers moving by rail and through the ports of the two countries, and the thousands of troops pouring into the war front to support Russia.

China appears to be trying to reassert some of its influence, which bolsters Kim's belligerent inclinations in two ways. Firstly, Kim now benefits from Chinese as well as Russian largesse. Recent studies suggest that China–North Korea trade, while not yet at pre-pandemic levels, is starting to increase.[6] High-level visits by senior Chinese Communist Party officials have also resumed.[7] Secondly, while China and Russia may be competing for North Korean attention, Kim has an opportunity to work the seams to exploit transactional cooperation among the three. Recent economic reports suggest, for example, that China's exports of petroleum coke to North Korea have increased dramatically. While this material would normally be used to facilitate North Korea's post-pandemic construction boom, increases in other types of construction materials have not been reported, suggesting that the coke is being used for other purposes – such as manufacturing munitions for Russia.[8]

The three-way axis is a win–win situation for Kim. It has facilitated, among other things, the dismantlement of the once robust United Nations Security Council sanctions regime against North Korea. Russia's veto of a resolution to renew the mandate of the UN Security Council Resolution 1718 Committee Panel of Experts terminated the 14-year initiative designed to ensure sanctions compliance.[9] China did not support reauthorising the resolution. Russia is now pushing for sunset clauses on sanctions imposed by the remaining ten resolutions applicable to North Korea.[10] Since 2020, Russia has vetoed 13 draft resolutions, abetted by China on five, effectively stymieing the UN from taking effective action against Kim's regime as it advances its weapons programme.[11]

Inter-Korean spiral

While Chinese and Russian support emboldens Kim, South Korea's policies irritate and provoke him. In North Korea's bizarre balloon offensive, started on 28 May, it has dropped more than 6,000 trash-laden balloons in all but two South Korean provinces.[12] While the payloads are not lethal, they are a form of soft terrorism, reminding citizens of how easily North Korea could jeopardise their lives were the balloons filled with more toxic contents. North Korea also accused the South of sending drones into its territory to drop anti-Kim propaganda leaflets – which Seoul denies – and has threatened a 'terrible calamity' and an 'immediate retaliatory attack' if it detects another drone over Pyongyang.[13] South Korea reciprocated the threat, warning that Kim would face the 'end of [his] regime' if he harmed South Korean citizens.

The new unification policy of conservative South Korean President Yoon Suk-yeol deeply offends the North Korean regime. Unveiled on 15 August, it replaces a traditional discourse framed in sovereign terms – which has at various times included the absorption of the North Korean state by the South and, less confrontationally, the phased integration of 'one country, two systems' – with a direct appeal to the people of North Korea. Yoon's narrative equates unification with freedom for the North Korean citizen, defined as the absence of fear, hunger, poverty and despair. It bypasses the government in Pyongyang and directly addresses the aspirations of North Korean citizens for better lives.[14] The general squalor of the country and the human-rights abominations perpetrated by the government are, of course, ample moral justification. Politically, though, the appeal directly threatens the Kim regime's control. For this reason, the regime has tried to pre-empt it by declaring the abolition of unification as a goal, designating the South as the 'enemy state' and destroying the inter-Korean family-reunion and economic-cooperation infrastructure developed over the past quarter-century.

The Yoon government, for its part, is not disposed to back away from a fight. It is very unlikely to start one, but it would certainly want to finish one. Many of its key policymakers were in office in 2010 when North Korea sank a South Korean naval vessel, the *Cheonan*, killing 46 sailors. It was the most lethal North–South military incident since the Korean War. The United States restrained South Korea from retaliating harshly. Since then, under successive conservative governments, Seoul has prepared a series of operational plans under the umbrella of a 'three-axis system', comprising the 'Kill Chain' for pre-emptively striking North Korean nuclear and missile facilities, Korean Air and Missile Defense, and the Korea Massive Punishment and Retaliation plan to decapitate the North Korean leadership.[15]

US distraction

The Biden administration has sidelined North Korea as a front-burner policy issue, encouraging Kim to be even bolder. The days when North Korean missile tests would make front-page news and cable-news headlines are long gone. On 18 December 2023, North Korea tested a solid-fuel, mobile-launched

Hwasong-18 intercontinental ballistic missile (ICBM) that registered minimally in the news cycle.[16] Its more recent launch of a new type of solid-fuel ICBM and firing of multiple short-range ballistic missiles towards the sea on 31 October and 4 November, respectively, also had little news impact, most likely because the US election consumed the media's attention.[17]

News does not drive policy, of course, and the intelligence community is hard at work analysing North Korean actions. But the American president himself has not been closely engaged on North Korea policy despite the increasing lethality of North Korea's weapons and the regime's steady drumbeat of provocations. This neglect stems from a lack of bandwidth due to the White House's preoccupation with two wars in Europe and the Middle East, US–China strategic competition, China's aggression with respect to Taiwan and the Philippines, supply-chain security, and a host of other issues that have displaced North Korea as top foreign-policy priorities. In addition, the US foreign-policy establishment has become inured to North Korean missile launches that have become so frequent as to be almost routine. Policymakers tend to express concern while offering no policy enlightenment. It would be a mistake to judge that Pyongyang does not notice this reticence. To the contrary, Kim likely sees it as evidence that he is winning a kind of attritional battle.

Reflecting Kim's confidence in his position is his abject unwillingness to engage the United States in dialogue. Biden administration officials have made almost two dozen efforts to open dialogue channels with the North, all unsuccessful. They have even seen their unopened messages kicked back out from under the door of North Korea's UN offices in New York. Whereas Pyongyang once welcomed, and even sought, dialogue and negotiations, the material and political support from Russia and China apparently have removed any urgency, allowing it to let the United States twist in the wind.[18] In fact, the US election has motivated Pyongyang to heighten provocations.[19] It is almost certain that Kim will test the incoming Trump administration just as it had welcomed in the Obama and first Trump administrations with nuclear tests. Recent commercial-satellite imagery commissioned by the Center for Strategic and International Studies (CSIS) shows the nuclear-test site primed for use.[20]

Hubris versus fragility

Amid the hostile bluster and military exhibitionism, questions remain about the North Korean regime's cohesiveness. Kim has undeniably wielded power effectively since his early and unexpected power succession almost 13 years ago. But the regime's frenetic efforts to advance its weapons programmes may belie internal stability. Although the world sees Kim being feted by Putin and holding hands with Iran and China, the COVID-19 pandemic has wreaked profound and as yet untold damage on the country.

Initial research by CSIS has uncovered new information about the suffering of North Korean citizens and their government's abuses during the lockdown from 2020 to 2023. Micro-surveys conducted at the end of 2023 indicated that the pandemic precipitated a great deal of popular anger against the government owing to its neglect of the population's health and welfare. The North Korean government denied that the virus had entered the country as it spread globally in 2020, until April 2022 maintaining it had no cases of COVID. Some 59% of those surveyed contracted the virus before April 2022 or knew someone who had, and some said the virus was 'raging like wildfire' for a full two years before the government sought outside help.[21]

Due to its poor healthcare system, the government was completely unprepared for the pandemic. Only 8% of North Koreans said they were issued a mask. Many indicated that they made their own out of cloth and washed them for reuse, which would have provided minimal protection. Only 13% of citizens surveyed said that they had access to testing. Of the 61% to whom vaccines eventually became available, only 16% said they had access before May 2022.[22] Desperation for medicine led to many reported deaths as a result of drug misuse, scams or fake prescriptions.

Without COVID testing, vaccines or anti-viral drugs, the government mainly resorted to draconian quarantines to address infections. Strict lockdowns, a worsening food crisis and extreme punishments for breaking anti-virus rules increased the North Korean population's misery. Reports of fever or sore throat were assumed to be COVID infections, prompting the government to shut down entire villages. Some 97% of respondents said they could not obtain required remedies through the market, while 81% said they suffered acute food shortages during lockdown. Those caught breaking rules were often sent to labour camps for between two days and six months.

Access to reliable information about COVID during the pandemic was limited, due to both the regime's disinclination to report the full extent of infections and local officials' hesitation to fully report cases for fear of lockdowns. The result was a double whammy of distrust between the government and the citizenry. The majority of North Koreans said they did not trust information from the government during the pandemic, and most sought it through unofficial channels. Trickles of information about other populations' access to vaccines and personal protective equipment increased North Koreans' anger and discontent and – despite the autocratic regime's predictable efforts to use the pandemic to increase social control by restricting movement and locking down market activities – created new forms of resistance. These included a willingness to circumvent quarantine rules, bribe law-enforcement officials and openly criticise the government, opening new areas of vulnerability for the regime.

Sample testimonies of some respondents give a flavour of the level of anger. One respondent from North Hamgyong province said, 'The … government developed nuclear weapons during COVID, but it didn't care about feeding its people'. Another said, 'Only my country has closed borders and doesn't allow travel between regions, and I heard that other countries offered vaccines, but we refused. They don't care whether the people live or die.' A respondent from South Hwanghae noted, 'We can make nuclear weapons and use them well, but why can't we make medicine, or is it that because we aren't thinking?' A Pyongyang resident stated: 'When I see the Supreme Leader touting his leadership, love of the people, and the superiority of the Republic while announcing that there are almost no deaths in the Republic, even though so many people have died during COVID, I think of the people who have died without being able to get the medicine they needed.'

COVID has clearly visited significant suffering on the North Korean people, and the government's cynical inaction has angered them. But the domestic fragility of the regime remains an unknown variable. It is impossible to know with certainty how it affects the leadership's behaviour. It may push the regime towards conflict. But it might instead incline the regime towards engagement on pandemic preparedness, which could be a first step to returning to dialogue on military matters with the US or its allies.

What's next?

With North Korea ensconced in a new partnership with Russia, benefiting from ongoing support from China, eschewing engagement with Washington, indulging heightened animosity with South Korea and beholding an opportunity to regain international attention with the advent of a new US administration, further rounds of escalation seem likely in the coming months. But where is the escalation cycle likely to go next, and with what impact on overall stability? Although dramatic, a seventh nuclear-weapons test by North Korea would not be a novel development and would likely be manageable by the United States and its allies. While Russia and China might block UN Security Council action, the G7 might, for instance, coordinate sanctions without further destabilising the situation.

A potentially more disruptive scenario could arise if North Korea took some unprecedented escalatory action. One possibility would be the declaration of a new maritime boundary. South Korea drew the existing Northern Limit Line during the Korean War and North Korea has never officially acknowledged it despite largely observing it. Pyongyang has threatened to redraw the line in the past, including in 1999. If it did so, North Korea might try to enforce the new line against South Korean fishing boats or coastguard vessels, prompting South Korea to enforce the old line in kind.

The complete absence of diplomatic dialogue on all fronts, thus the absence of customary exit ramps, makes the prospect of escalation from local military crises all the more dangerous. In light of its growing military and economic links to Russia and its expanding trade with China, North Korea is less reliant than before on aid from or trade with South Korea. Pyongyang has spurned the United States' and Japan's overtures for dialogue despite their having subtly removed preconditions – in Japan's case, confronting the issue of Japanese citizens abducted by North Korea in the 1970s, in America's case, addressing denuclearisation. The prospects for renewed diplomacy are likely to remain bleak.

For now, the regime seems content to rely on China and Russia for its material needs. That said, the current incarnation of North Korea–Russia ties is new and untested, and the North Korea–China relationship is nuanced and subject to fluctuation. Kim could shift towards hedging if the North Korea–China–Russia axis became shaky. North Korea's internal problems, exacerbated by the pandemic, could also spur the regime to engage the US and its allies on a narrow range of issues, such as pandemic preparedness or accepting humanitarian aid. But there are no concrete signs of such a development.

Allied options

Upholding stability and security in the Indo-Pacific is more critical than ever with wars raging in Europe and the Middle East. But these problems stretch the United States' capacities across a number of dimensions, and the onset of a fairly radical political transition will inevitably compound the challenges. Accordingly, Washington and Seoul should approach North Korea as a problem to be managed rather than solved.

Firstly, they should uphold deterrence by denial by communicating to North Korea that belligerence will not advance its strategic objectives of breaking down the US commitment to its allies and achieving recognition as a nuclear-weapons state. This means enhancing cooperation between each other and with Japan, especially in the face of North Korean provocations, and reiterating to North Korea that denuclearisation remains their long-term goal notwithstanding the expanded size and depth of North Korea's nuclear arsenal (now at an estimated 50 nuclear weapons, and with enough fissile material for 70 to 90 more). This is essential not only to disincentivise North Korea's aggression but also to help pre-empt the destabilising second-order effects of abandoning denuclearisation that would arise in the region as neighbouring powers contemplated pursuing their own nuclear-weapons capabilities.

Secondly, the US and South Korea should enable Ukraine to inflict humiliating battlefield losses on North Korean troops by providing it with the requisite equipment, sustainment and intelligence. A purported reason of Kim's for sending forces into battle is to gain his military valuable combat experience.[23] But Washington and Seoul should not permit him to harbour any illusion that his troops would be treated any differently from other combatants in a shooting war. Ukrainian forces should also be prepared to accommodate potential defections of North Korean soldiers across the Russia–Ukraine border. A fair number may be tempted to defect, as it is likely to be easier to do so from Russia to Ukraine than it is from North Korea to South Korea via China and Southeast Asia or other pathways. News of killed, captured or defecting North Korean soldiers that reaches Pyongyang or other capitals would be a source of shame for Kim and could deter him from furnishing more of his troops to Russia.

Thirdly, the allies should play on China's interests and pride to weaken the Russia–China–North Korea axis. Russia and North Korea's mutually beneficial if substantially transactional renewal of relations will be difficult to weaken as long as Putin needs Kim's help in Ukraine, and both are motivated to destabilise Europe and Asia. China's position is more complicated. For decades, Beijing has sought to maintain stability on the Korean Peninsula to avoid scenarios involving either a humanitarian crisis or US troops on their doorstep. For this reason, China has an interest in depressing Kim's appetite for disruption. For Xi himself, asserting and establishing paramount influence over North Korea vis-à-vis Russia may also be a matter of pride. The US and South Korea should appeal to China as a great power with leverage over Pyongyang and Moscow by implicitly challenging Beijing not to let Kim drive regional security in ways that conflict with China's interests. Reminding China of its own untapped ability to determine events could nudge dynamics on the peninsula towards greater stability while exposing the weak points in the Putin–Kim–Xi triangle. One concrete step Beijing might take would be withholding further exports of petroleum coke to North Korea that can be used to produce munitions for export to Russia.

Finally, Washington and Seoul should pursue initiatives for improving conditions for ordinary citizens in North Korea.[24] These could include offers of humanitarian aid even if Kim is likely to rebuff them. The offers should be conditioned on Pyongyang's willingness to accept international access and monitoring standards but de-linked from progress on denuclearisation or other security issues. CSIS micro-surveys indicated that North Koreans were aware that their government rejected outside-aid offers during the pandemic. This means that even offers that are not accepted could prompt North Koreans to question their leadership's portrayal of the US and its allies as hostile actors. Efforts to enhance North Koreans' access to outside information could also be considered. This would improve their ability to assess their own conditions relative to those outside of the country, making them less susceptible to regime propaganda.

Such actions would be unlikely to completely resolve the complex array of security and human-rights challenges that the Kim regime poses. But they could decrease the chances that Pyongyang will perceive nothing but wins from its spree of provocations and reinforce deterrence in East Asia by increasing the costs of conflict, weaken the Putin–Kim–Xi axis by diminishing the effectiveness of North Korean military support to Russia and highlight China's divergent interests in East Asia. And they would signal to the long-suffering people of North Korea that they have steadfast partners outside their borders who recognise and seek to alleviate their plight.

Notes

1 See Junnosuke Kobara, 'North Korea Announces Wall Project to Seal Border with South', Nikkei Asia, 10 October 2024, https://asia.nikkei.com/Spotlight/North-Korea-tensions/North-Korea-announces-wall-project-to-seal-border-with-South; and Chae Yun-hwan, 'N. Korea Continues to Install Mines, Barriers Inside DMZ Despite Downpours', Yonhap News Agency, 8 August 2024, https://en.yna.co.kr/view/AEN20240808006400315.

2 Hyung-Jin Kim, 'Kim Calls South Korea a Principal Enemy as His Rhetoric Sharpens in a US Election Year', Associated Press, 10 January 2024, https://apnews.com/article/north-korea-kim-rhetoric-tensions-6806461cb93ab-62d81c06d5f7922d3d0.

3 See Andy Lim and Victor Cha, 'Database: Map of North Korea's Garbage-filled Balloons', CSIS Beyond Parallel, 30 June 2024, https://beyondparallel.csis.org/map-of-north-koreas-garbage-filled-balloons/.

4 See 'Database: North Korean Provocations', CSIS Beyond Parallel, 20 December 2019, https://beyondparallel.csis.org/database-north-korean-provocations/.

5 See generally Daniel Byman and Seth G. Jones, 'Legion of Doom? China, Russia, Iran and North Korea', Survival, vol. 66, no. 4, August–September 2024, pp. 29–50.

6   See Jinwook Nam, 'North Korea's 2023–24 Trade with China: Analysis and Forecasts', paper presented at the 10th meeting of the Dialogue on the DPRK Economy, East–West Center, Honolulu, HI, 29 August 2024.

7   See 'A Chinese Official Meets North Korean Leader Kim in Pyongyang in Highest-level Talks in Years', Associated Press, 13 April 2024, https://apnews.com/article/china-north-korea-talks-6c2083d7a1d4cdeba6d72b7bc983c59e.

8   See Nam, 'North Korea's 2023–24 Trade with China'.

9   See United States Mission to the United Nations, 'Joint Statement Following Russia's Veto of the Mandate Renewal of the UN Security Council's 1718 Committee Panel of Experts', 28 March 2024, https://usun.usmission.gov/joint-statement-following-russias-veto-of-the-mandate-renewal-of-the-un-security-councils-1718-committee-panel-of-experts/.

10 See Victor Cha and Ellen Kim, 'Russia's Veto: Dismembering the UN Sanctions Regime on North Korea', Center for Strategic and International Studies, 29 March 2024, https://www.csis.org/analysis/russias-veto-dismembering-un-sanctions-regime-north-korea.

11 The recent inception of a G7 plus Australia, New Zealand and South Korea sanctions-coordination group is an effort to address this problem.

12 See Cha and Lim, 'Database: Map of North Korea's Garbage-filled Balloons'.

13 See Kim Tong-hyung, 'Sister of North Korea's Leader Threatens South Korea over Drone Flights', Associated Press, 12 October 2024, https://apnews.com/article/north-south-korea-drones-kim-7ed0c3c7e22d1d755d64a05a03f16d43; and 'North Korea Says It Recovered Crashed South Korean Military Drone, KCNA Says', Reuters, 19 October 2024, https://www.reuters.com/world/asia-pacific/north-korea-says-it-recovered-crashed-south-korean-military-drone-kcna-2024-10-18/.

14 See Kim Eun-jung, 'Full Text of Yoon's Liberation Day Speech', Yonhap News Agency, 15 August 2024, https://en.yna.co.kr/view/AEN20240815002500315.

15 See Sungmin Cho, 'South Korea's Offensive Military Strategy and Its Dilemma', CSIS, 29 February 2024, https://www.csis.org/analysis/south-koreas-offensive-military-strategy-and-its-dilemma.

16 See Victor Cha and Ellen Kim, 'North Korea Warns with Fifth ICBM Test', CSIS, 19 December 2023, https://www.csis.org/analysis/north-korea-warns-fifth-icbm-test.

17 See Kim Tong-hyung, Hyung-jin Kim and Mari Yamaguchi, 'North Korea Fires a Barrage of Ballistic Missiles Toward the Sea Ahead of US Election', Associated Press, 4 November 2024, https://apnews.com/article/north-korea-missile-launch-sea-us-elections-3c00eaae880d1cdeb79f7c9aa0aded9d.

18 See Hyung-jin Kim, 'Kim's Sister Rejects US Offer of Dialogue with North Korea and Vows More Satellite Launches', Associated Press, 29 November 2023, https://apnews.com/article/north-korea-kim-sister-us-spy-satellite-launch-1fb36f0c458b6beaf6e46c09eb78f793; and 'North Korea "Not Responding" to US Contact

Efforts', BBC News, 14 March 2021, https://www.bbc.com/news/world-asia-56391445.

19 CSIS data shows a correlation between increased North Korean aggression and US presidential and midterm election years. See Victor Cha, 'North Korean Provocations Likely Around US Presidential Election', CSIS Beyond Parallel, 23 September 2020, https://beyondparallel.csis.org/dprk-provocations-likely-around-u-s-presidential-election/.

20 See Joseph S. Bermudez, Jr, Victor Cha and Jennifer Jun, 'Update on Punggye-ri amid Increased Tension', CSIS Beyond Parallel, 14 October 2024, https://beyondparallel.csis.org/no-major-activity-observed-at-punggye-ri-amid-increased-tension/.

21 CSIS partnered with an organisation that has a successful track record of conducting discreet and careful surveys in North Korea. CSIS has commissioned this organisation to administer micro-survey questionnaires in provinces across North Korea. The questionnaires are conducted through casual, in-person conversations between interviewers and respondents. The interviewers are carefully trained to avoid leading questions or prompting specific responses to protect the integrity of the survey and the safety of all participants. The organisation administering the survey used 'snowball sampling' to conduct the survey, which involves a main group of informants bringing in additional participants. This method would be considered far from ideal under normal circumstances, as it does not constitute random sampling. The survey team's time in the field was from November to December 2023. The number of surveys completed was 100. The gender breakdown was 40 male and 60 female. Age breakdowns among survey respondents were as follows: 18 to 24 years old (12); 25 to 34 years old (20); 35 to 44 years old (26); 45 to 54 years old (16); 55 to 64 years old (18); 65 to 74 years old (6); and 75 years of age or older (2). Occupation breakdowns were as follows: student/education field (8); scientific/technical field (4); works for the party/government (6); soldier (7); company/one organisation/multiple organisations (22); business/trade (28); and other (25), a category that included dependents and homemakers. Household sizes ranged from single (9); two people (17); three people (32); four people (31); and five people or more (11). Levels of education included high school/junior high school, including dropouts and graduates (49); college/university/postgraduate researcher or doctoral students (40); other, including military academy and trade-school graduates (10); and 'prefer not to say' (1). Geographical breakdowns were as follows: Jagang province (6); North Hamgyong province (10); South Hamgyong province (13); North Hwanghae province (9); South Hwanghae province (10); Kangwon province (6); North Pyongan province (12); South Pyongan province (17); Yanggang province (3); and Pyongyang (14).

22 After the government asked for help, it appears that the general population received one dose and the military three doses. All were Chinese-made vaccines.

23 See Victor Cha, 'Crossing the Rubicon: DPRK Sends Troops to Russia', CSIS, 23 October 2024, https://www.csis.org/

analysis/crossing-rubicon-dprk-sends-troops-russia.

24 On the American side, Congress's renewal of the North Korean Human Rights Act, which was first signed into law 20 years ago and enjoys bipartisan support, would be an important step.

Israel at War, One Year On

Chuck Freilich

On 7 October 2023, for the first time in Israel's history, a war began with an attack on Israeli territory and civilians, shattering the public's sense of security. About 6,000 Gazans, of whom approximately 3,800 were Hamas fighters, broke through the border fence in 119 places, some penetrating as far as 25 kilometres into Israeli territory, about halfway to the city of Beersheba and a third of the way to the nuclear reactor in Dimona. They overran military bases and massacred, mutilated and raped civilians in some two dozen villages, kibbutzim and towns. Hamas took 251 hostages. Israeli society was already reeling at the time from five years of political turmoil and especially Prime Minister Benjamin Netanyahu's so-called judicial overhaul, which the Israel Defense Forces (IDF) and Israeli intelligence community had warned was weakening Israel militarily and encouraging its adversaries to exploit its internal disarray to launch hostilities.

The subsequent war has become by far the longest in Israel's 76-year history and the first since the 1973 Yom Kippur War that the Israeli public has regarded as an existential one. During the war's chaotic early months, an essentially absentee government failed to provide vital public services, and Israel's civil-society organisations agitated to replace it. National consensus on the existential nature of the threats Israel faces re-emerged and

Chuck Freilich, a former Israeli deputy national security adviser, is a senior fellow at the Institute for National Security Studies (INSS) in Tel Aviv and the senior editor of the *Israel Journal of Foreign Affairs*. He is author of *Israeli National Security: A New Strategy for an Era of Change* (Oxford University Press, 2018).

Survival | vol. 66 no. 6 | December 2024–January 2025 | pp. 119–130 https://doi.org/10.1080/00396338.2024.2432203

provided the government some cover, but renewed divisions then surfaced. A multifront confrontation with the so-called 'axis of resistance' – Iran, Hamas, Lebanese Hizbullah, the Houthis in Yemen and Shia militias in Iraq and Syria – has arisen, with broad implications for regional and even international security. As with other historical turning points, it is still too early to fully assess the war's ramifications, which will shape the course of events in the region for years to come. From an Israeli perspective, however, some significant conclusions can be drawn.

Short-term results

Israel has won militarily in Gaza. It has obliterated some 22 of Hamas's 24 pre-war battalions while degrading the other two, and it no longer constitutes a coherent military force.[1] Israel has also destroyed most of Hamas's rocket arsenal, as well as its military infrastructure and operationally important tunnels. The IDF has cleared a kilometre-wide buffer zone along the Gaza border and taken control of the 'Philadelphi corridor' and Rafah crossing on the Gaza–Egypt border, through which Hamas smuggled weapons prior to the war. Most of Hamas's senior and mid-level political and military leaders – including Yahya Sinwar, the mastermind behind the Hamas invasion and massacre – have been killed, as have approximately half of its fighters. In Western military doctrine, attrition of an enemy at such levels constitutes decisive defeat. In any case, Hamas is no longer capable of conducting an attack of the scale and severity of the 7 October operation, and eliminating that capability was Israel's primary military objective.[2] Palestinian Authority (PA) President Mahmoud Abbas is 88 years old and the PA is weaker and more unpopular than ever, suggesting that Sinwar's demise may have a significant impact on the battle for succession in the post-Abbas era.

For all Israel's military success, however, Hamas is the only Arab force that has ever succeeded in conquering Israeli territory, however briefly, and caused the most severe psychological trauma in Israel's history, bringing home the inherent fragility of Israel's security. Furthermore, Hamas has achieved its baseline objective of surviving Israel's counter-offensive. Israel's failure to propose and facilitate the establishment of a realistic alternative to Hamas as Gaza's governing body has left Hamas largely in political control, if significantly weakened. Hamas has channelled much of the humanitarian aid distributed in Gaza and continues to provide governmental services, especially in areas from which Israel has withdrawn, which constitutes most of Gaza. The group can still conduct isolated guerrilla attacks against the IDF and retains a small number of rockets, and a significant portion of its 800-km-long tunnel network has yet to be destroyed – and may never be. Moreover, Hamas still holds approximately 100 Israeli hostages, which have unexpectedly enabled it to restrict Israel's room for diplomatic and military manoeuvre and to exacerbate domestic Israeli tensions.

Beyond that, after more than a decade of marginalisation, Hamas has successfully placed the Palestinian issue back on the international agenda. It has also at least partially succeeded in fomenting a wider war by drawing the axis of resistance into the fighting. Hamas also, as intended, derailed and at least postponed the ongoing rapprochement between Israel and Saudi Arabia. Had the normalisation process proceeded apace, it would likely have led to further ties between Israel and other Muslim states, formalisation of the emerging US-led anti-Iranian regional coalition that includes Israel, the Gulf Arab states and European partners, and stronger international standing and overall security for Israel.

Iran provided Hamas with military and diplomatic support despite its desire to stay out of direct combat and ended up launching massive missile and drone barrages against Israel on 13 April and 1 October. If it responds further to Israeli retaliation, Iran's involvement may become even more extensive and less reversible. Hizbullah, for its part, has maintained essentially uninterrupted rocket, missile and drone fire against Israel since the war began, driving most of its northern residents from their homes. The Houthis repeatedly launched missiles at Eilat, Israel's Red Sea port, halting maritime navigation to the Asia-Pacific, and also hit Tel Aviv and its suburbs. Shia militias in Syria and Iraq have also fired missiles at Israel.

Surrounded but unbowed

Following 7 October, Israel awakened to the reality of encirclement by Iran and its allies: Hamas in the west; Iran and Shia militias in Iraq to the east; Hizbullah and Shia militias in Lebanon and Syria in the north; and the

Houthis to the south. Iran spent decades building the axis of resistance and continues to view the war as an important step towards the collective goal of Israel's destruction, setbacks notwithstanding. Hamas's ability to survive the IDF's onslaught and Hizbullah's ability to sustain nearly uninterrupted rocket and drone attacks along Israel's northern border demonstrated the effectiveness of the axis's model of irregular warfare. Moreover, by explicitly linking its willingness to establish a ceasefire with Israel in Lebanon to one in Gaza, Hizbullah increased overall pressure on Israel and the US to reach ceasefires. With the attacks by Iran and the Shia militias, Israel faced multifront warfare. A long-standing Israeli fear became a stark reality.

Perhaps even more worrisome from Israel's perspective was the axis's apparent conclusion – presumably tempered by the effectiveness of Israel's recent offensive in south Lebanon – that the asymmetric 'ring of fire' model had provided it with an effective means of countering Israel's overwhelming conventional superiority and even enabled it to gain the advantage. The war also diverted international and Israeli attention from Iran's nuclear programme, thereby facilitating its emergence as a threshold nuclear power. In addition, it confirmed Iran's growing role as a regional leader and potential hegemon, and enabled it to strengthen its ties with China and Russia.

To be sure, the war also demonstrated the axis's limitations as a coherent and effective alliance. Contrary to Hamas's expectations, in the early weeks, when Iran and Hizbullah's intervention might have made a crucial difference, Tehran repeatedly rebuffed its entreaties. Even Iran's missile attacks against Israel in April and October were in response to Israeli attacks against it and only indirectly related to the war in Gaza. Hizbullah, for its part, generally kept hostilities at a low to medium intensity in order to avoid a major escalation, while the Houthis and Shia militias fired missiles and rockets only intermittently. This collective reluctance to fully engage has continued.

In turn, Israel's military outlook has improved dramatically. It destroyed 50–66% of Hizbullah's mammoth rocket arsenal, according to most Israeli estimates, a whopping 80% according to former defense minister Yoav Gallant.[3] The IDF killed Hassan Nasrallah, the brilliant and diabolical leader of Hizbullah for over three decades. While targeted Israeli killings of top Hamas and Hizbullah leaders in the past have typically caused only temporary disruptions, and often paved the way for more effective leaders, the recent elimination of entire hierarchies may have a greater impact. Hizbullah has few senior leaders left and had to appoint a lacklustre successor to Nasrallah.

Thousands of Hizbullah fighters were either killed or wounded, a severe blow to an organisation whose total force numbers in the low tens of thousands. Consequently, Hizbullah has only been able to fire 100–200 rockets a day since Israel began its offensive in Lebanon in September, a fraction of what Israel would have expected, though still enough to hollow out Israel's northern communities.[4] Nevertheless, Hizbullah has been sufficiently confident to have rejected US efforts to bring about a diplomatic resolution of the crisis in Lebanon. Washington has proposed strengthening UN Security Council Resolution 1701 by way of Hizbullah's withdrawal north of the Litani River and deployment of the Lebanese Armed Forces and a United Nations peacekeeping force to the south. Even if agreement is reached, Hizbullah is likely to gradually dilute the new arrangements, as it has in the past, while political exigencies would likely constrain Israel from taking effective action against violations.

At a minimum, Israel's retaliation essentially destroyed Iran's air-defence system and steeply diminished its missile capabilities, clearing an aerial corridor for Israel to strike Iranian nuclear, oil and gas, or regime targets, should it decide to do so. No less importantly, the retaliation exposed Israeli intelligence's significant penetration of Iranian defences and Iran's high vulnerability to attack. Although the long-term impact of Israel's successes is as yet unclear, with Hamas also severely weakened, the axis of resistance is on the defensive and the momentum has shifted to Israel.

Israel and the US: support, dependence and friction

Throughout the war, especially during its critical early months, US support for Israel has been extraordinary. On the strategic level, extensive consultations took place continually regarding the war's objectives, conduct and endgame, with US President Joe Biden participating in one Israeli cabinet meeting and US Secretary of State Antony Blinken doing so more than once. As a show of support for Israel and to deter Iran and Hizbullah, the US deployed aircraft-carrier strike groups and other military assets to the region on four occasions. Twice, the US-led regional coalition neutralised Iranian missile and drone attacks against Israel, and US–Israeli operational cooperation, including the first-ever joint-combat operations, was unprecedented. Militarily, Washington provided Israel with over $8.7 billion in special aid, in addition to the $3.8bn in annual military assistance, much of it delivered through emergency air and sealifts.[5] Intelligence cooperation, which was already extensive, deepened. Diplomatically, the US provided Israel with strong support, including vetoes of three UN Security Council resolutions.

Israel had long believed that it was fully capable of handling the Hizbullah and especially Hamas threats on its own, possibly with limited American military resupply and air-defence support. The war's multi-front nature, however, has showed Israel's dependence on the US to be far greater. Large-scale emergency resupply was required, a shortage of interceptor missiles and operational considerations prompted deployment of American air-defence systems, a massive American military presence was needed for deterrence and a US-led regional military coalition proved necessary to defend Israel.

Israel's diplomatic dependence on the US, always substantial, was amplified in the face of growing international criticism of its conduct of the war. The high number of civilian Palestinian casualties and the physical destruction in Gaza soon produced a tsunami of support for the Palestinians, degrading Israel's already shaky international standing. Israel's bilateral ties with all of its Arab partners – including the United Arab Emirates, the most forward-looking one – took a significant hit and will likely require years to recover. But while the war postponed normalisation between Israel and Saudi Arabia and possibly other Arab Muslim states, it does not appear to have completely derailed it. When the US-led regional coalition repelled the first Iranian missile and drone attacks, and probably the second, military cooperation between Israel and the Gulf Arab states continued and even intensified behind the scenes. Israel's rapid recovery from the disarray of 7 October, its military defeat of Hamas and especially the severe blows it dealt to Hizbullah and Iran restored the Gulf Arab states' faith in Israel's military prowess and reinforced its value as a strategic partner against Iran – their primary motivation for the rapprochement in the first place. At the same time, of course, Israel's refusal to commit to a two-state solution inhibited further formalisation of the coalition and compelled the Saudis to harden their conditions for normalisation.

Leading Israeli allies such as the United Kingdom and Germany imposed partial limitations on arms sales. Efforts to promote boycott, divestment and sanctions measures intensified, and claims of genocide, apartheid and war crimes led to formal charges against Israel at the International Criminal Court and International Court of Justice. The war also spurred international support for a two-state solution, and a number of European states, including Spain and Ireland, unilaterally recognised a Palestinian state.

Although Israel took longer than the US preferred, the Israelis eventually adopted the overall American military blueprint for Gaza: high-intensity warfare during the first phase, followed by withdrawal of most IDF forces and focused operations against concrete

> *Cooperation between Israel and the Gulf Arab states continued*

threats thereafter. It similarly pursued relatively limited objectives against Hizbullah and Iran, at least partially at the behest of the US. Even so, the war also exposed the fault lines in the bilateral relationship. On balance, it probably intensified long-standing tensions over the Palestinian issue. By the spring, the US had become openly critical of the mounting civilian deaths in Gaza and humanitarian issues, as well as the absence of an Israeli plan for the 'day after'. The Biden administration shifted from full support for Israel's war aims to containing the war and bringing it to a rapid conclusion, spurred by concerns that Netanyahu was seeking to prolong the war for political reasons and had repeatedly misled the US on the hostage issue, as well as indications that Israel was seeking to depopulate northern Gaza.

The war accentuated the changing attitudes towards Israel on the Democratic left and among young people in the US, with public criticism of Israel reaching unprecedented levels and becoming a contentious issue in the presidential campaign. Even bilateral US military assistance, once sacrosanct, became controversial. The administration suspended the supply of certain munitions and warned Israel that failure to address the humanitarian issues could lead to an overall reduction in aid.

More affirmatively, the US offered a three-part 'vision' for the post-war era at the war's outset: a hostage and ceasefire deal between Israel and Hamas; Saudi–Israeli normalisation to facilitate Israel's regional integration, a stronger anti-Iran regional coalition and an impediment to China's growing regional influence; and progress towards a two-state solution to reduce regional tensions and facilitate Saudi movement towards normalisation. Israel did not fully embrace this idea and, to the US administration's mounting frustration, never presented any other long-term plan.

The war also sharpened the geopolitical divide between the US-led Western camp, of which Israel views itself an important part, and the opposing camp led by China and Russia. Whereas the US strongly supported Israel and ramped up its military presence in the region, China and Russia were extremely critical of Israel and supportive of the axis of resistance, and expanded their long-standing ties with Iran. Neither China nor Russia, however, played a significant role in regional developments, the US remaining the leading great power in the Middle East.

Israel's dysfunction

For a broad swathe of the Israeli public, including the right, the inability to save the diminishing number of living hostages through military action or negotiations, and Netanyahu's seeming lack of interest in doing so, has been the government's greatest failure. While Hamas may never have genuinely wanted a hostage deal, Netanyahu has deployed the issue for his own political purposes, casting doubt on the public's long-held confidence that the government would always do its utmost to ensure the safety and security of its citizens. Large numbers of Israelis have participated in ongoing demonstrations urging a hostage deal and demanding that the government, including Netanyahu, take responsibility for their failures. That these numbers are not as large as those reached during the attempted judicial overhaul is a measure of the public's exhaustion and disillusionment.

Israel's national-security decision-making processes at the cabinet level, unlike its outstanding operational capabilities, have been shambolic since

7 October. In the highly charged atmosphere following the attack, Israeli leaders understandably engaged in some political hyperbole, defining the war's objectives as the complete military and political destruction of Hamas and the hostages' release. Less forgivably, Netanyahu continues to speak of an obscure and unachievable 'total victory' as the only acceptable outcome. Had the war's objectives been defined more realistically as Hamas's demise as a coherent military force and a significant weakening of its political power, Israel would have already achieved them by the beginning of 2024.

Even less defensibly, after more than a year of warfare, Israel has yet to frame an overall strategy for the post-war era in Gaza and the Palestinian issue more broadly. This risks undermining and dissipating the IDF's military achievements in Gaza, has already forced it to go back into areas from which it had withdrawn, and feeds growing unrest in the West Bank. Israel has presented somewhat more coherent objectives on the northern front, but they too are elastic. As to both Gaza and the northern front, credible conjecture has thus arisen that the prime minister may wish to perpetuate low-level warfare to stay in power and stave off corruption inquiries. Israel's objectives vis-à-vis Iran are even less clear, ranging from the purely defensive to more ambitious aspirations to target Iran's nuclear programme and even its regime. The absence of a coherent strategy for the post-war order and beyond is one of Israel's most egregious wartime failures. It has already led to growing tensions with the US, as well as with international and regional partners, which are likely to worsen, and to increased international isolation. These problems are likely to intensify in the wake of Netanyahu's politically motivated firing of Gallant, the respected defence minister.

An in-depth review of Israel's national-security policies and strategy in the years and even decades prior to the war will be necessary. Some pre-war assumptions were clearly spurious – for example, that economic inducements had led Hamas to subordinate its jihadist objectives, that long-term regional normalisation could be pursued independently of the Palestinian issue, that Hamas was merely a limited threat incapable of mounting a major attack, that Israel's intelligence capabilities assured it of sufficient advanced warning, and that Israel could achieve military victory over Hamas and Hizbullah without significant American assistance.

A critical question Israeli strategists now face is whether just specific assumptions or its overall national-security strategy must be revised. For example, Israel's national-security thinking has always emphasised the importance of strategic autonomy, but the multifront nature of the future threats that Israel is likely to face may require that it marshal regional coalitions. In that case, strategic autonomy would have to give way to further development and formalisation of the US-led anti-Iranian regional coalition, and to changes in Israel's policies on the Palestinian issue.

Israel will clearly have to maintain larger regular and reserve armies, build new military and intelligence capabilities, amass larger stockpiles of weapons and munitions, and maintain a higher state of alert. This will place a premium on troop numbers and has already increased pressure on the ultra-Orthodox population, heretofore exempt from military duty, to serve. Broad support already exists for adopting a more offensive posture than Israel has had in recent years. All this will require a far larger defence budget, which would strain Israel's economy and society. Attempts to increase the size of the IDF and maintain a state of high alert following the Yom Kippur War proved economically ruinous and militarily untenable. Whether Israel can better navigate the obstacles this time around remains to be seen.

The demise of the two-state solution

Owing to the Palestinians' repeated rejection of Israeli and US peace proposals, which would have given them an independent state on essentially all disputed territory over two decades ago, and Israel's West Bank settlement policies, the two-state paradigm was moribund even before the war started. While the war has increased international support for Palestinian statehood, in the near-to-medium term, international, Arab and Palestinian attention is likely to focus on minimising hostilities in Gaza, ensuring an Israeli withdrawal and rebuilding infrastructure – not on Palestinian statehood. Moreover, for much of the Israeli population, 7 October demonstrated that Israel's bedrock condition for any peace agreement – ironclad security – is not feasible in practice. If a surprise attack and massacre of the civilian population — the very embodiment of Israel's long-standing 'security complex' and existential nightmare — could occur on the sparsely populated border with Gaza, effective security arrangements on the West Bank border, which abuts Israel's population centres, could hardly be guaranteed.

Furthermore, although some Palestinians view the war as a crushing, self-inflicted defeat comparable in magnitude to the *Nakbas* – tragedies – of 1948 and 1967, and seek a renewed peace process, others continue to support Hamas enthusiastically and view the devastation as proof of the need for ongoing and even heightened violence against Israel. What conclusions the Palestinian people will reach regarding Hamas's future place in Palestinian politics and the battle for national leadership, the peace process and ties with Israel remain to be seen.

Finally, Israel's and the Palestinians' rejection of American peace proposals has confirmed that the United States no longer has an accepted formula for a two-state solution. The US might not abandon all future attempts to achieve one – change to long-standing and fundamental policy positions does not usually occur rapidly. But the incoming Trump administration is far from wedded to those positions. Washington, in any event, may be willing to consider new approaches to separation between Israelis and Palestinians, and to the nature and shape of a final peace agreement. The traditional two-state solution may be the ultimate casualty of 7 October.

Notes

1   See Emanuel Fabian and Staff, 'Gallant: Hamas as "Military Formation" in Gaza Is Gone, IDF Focus Shifting to North', *Times of Israel*, 10 September 2024, https://www.timesofisrael.com/gallant-hamas-as-military-formation-in-gaza-is-gone-now-only-guerrilla-warfare/.

2   See, for example, Helene Cooper et al., 'In Gaza, Israel's Military Has Reached the End of the Line, U.S. Officials Say', *New York Times*, 14 August 2024, https://www.nytimes.com/2024/08/14/us/politics/israel-military-gaza-war.html.

3   Yonah Jeremy Bob and Staff, 'Gallant: Hezbollah Rocket Arsenal Down to 20%; Disagreements About How Long to Continue Invasion', *Jerusalem Post*, 29 October 2024, https://www.jpost.com/israel-news/article-826724.

4   See, for instance, Seth J. Frantzman, 'Hezbollah Rocket Fire Increasingly Targets Arab and Druze Communities – Analysis', *Jerusalem Post*, 2 November 2024, https://www.jpost.com/israel-news/article-827267.

5   Laura Kelly, 'Israel Says It Secured $8.7 Billion Military Aid Package from US', *Hill*, 26 September 2024, https://thehill.com/policy/defense/4901552-israel-us-aid-package/.

Israel in Gaza: The Quicksand of Societal War

Ariel E. Levite and Jonatan (Yoni) Shimshoni

> If you find yourself in a hole, stop digging.
>
> Will Rogers (possibly apocryphal)

> Anyone who fights with monsters should make sure that he does not …
> become a monster himself.
>
> Friedrich Nietzsche

Hamas's 7 October 2023 attack was designed to bait Israel into a response its own leadership had long believed to be against its better interests. Israeli politicians and military officials had sought to avoid a major offensive in Gaza, correctly anticipating that it would require the full occupation of the strip and would be costly, lengthy, messy and strategically counter-productive.[1] Such a war, they reckoned, would engulf Israel in a massive confrontation with Hamas and Palestinian Islamic Jihad, two relatively marginal foes, that would distract it from more formidable challengers – Iran and its powerful proxy Hizbullah, with whom Israeli Prime Minister Benjamin Netanyahu has long been obsessed.[2] Furthermore, destroying or effectively neutralising Hamas would undermine Netanyahu's strategy

Ariel E. Levite is a Senior Fellow at the Belfer Center for Science and International Affairs at the Harvard Kennedy School as well as a Senior Fellow at the Carnegie Endowment for International Peace. **Jonatan (Yoni) Shimshoni** is a Research Affiliate at the MIT Security Studies Program, an affiliate faculty member at the Schar School of Policy and Government at George Mason University, and a Global Fellow at the Woodrow Wilson International Center for Scholars.

Survival | vol. 66 no. 6 | December 2024–January 2025 | pp. 131–142   https://doi.org/10.1080/00396338.2024.2432205

of driving a wedge between Palestinian factions, deflecting demands to address the Palestinian issue.[3]

Thirteen months after the horrific attack, despite Israel's impressive operational success, the conflict has imposed multiple strategic liabilities: more than 100 Israelis in captivity facing severe harassment and mortal danger; a guerrilla war in Gaza; increasingly bloody friction on the West Bank; and an intense military confrontation with Hizbullah, which is sustaining massive attacks against Israel and paralysing life in the country's northern region. Iranian proxies in Iraq, Syria and Yemen launch daily attacks against Israel, while Iran no longer refrains from periodically targeting Israel directly. These add up to seven simultaneous fronts. At the same time, Israel faces growing international opprobrium and isolation, and Israelis and Jews abroad often experience violent anti-Semitism. Israel's domestic woes include a faltering economy, tens of thousands of displaced persons and fierce differences on fundamental issues such as universal conscription for military service.

Unlike traditional or conventional conflict, in which protagonists seek victory primarily through military confrontation, societal conflict involves directly impacting and indirectly engineering the emotions and behaviour of an entire society or critical elements of it, using a combination of tools such as economic, financial and material pressure, and informational manipulation in conjunction with military force.[4] Luring Israel into an open-ended societal confrontation was part of a deftly conceived and executed strategy capitalising on Israel's rage, humiliation and fear, and its leadership's strategic myopia. It is fighting precisely the war that Hamas wanted. History is replete with cases in which a nominally strong power ends up fighting a war of an inferior foe's choosing, sinking ever deeper into the quicksand of a long, painful and unwinnable societal confrontation. America did so in Vietnam, Afghanistan and Iraq, Russia in Afghanistan and now Ukraine.

The trap

Hamas combines a Muslim Brotherhood type of political–social movement with a formidable military organisation. Deep in its ideology is a religiously charged rejection of Israel's very existence.[5] Since it managed to consolidate control over Gaza in 2007, Hamas has focused almost single-mindedly on preparing for the ultimate violent struggle against Israel. Aware of Israel's vast military superiority and Western backing, Hamas devised a strategy – revealed by its actions and captured documents[6] – apparently based on five aims:

- to motivate Palestinians to fight Israel not just as a nation but also as a people through an Islamist ideology that justifies merciless killing and the sacrifice of their own people and resources by depicting Israel as an existential threat to Palestinians and to the Muslim holy places;
- to expose the Israeli military's weaknesses both directly and by targeting Israeli society;
- to take a large number of Israelis hostage to be used for protection and as chits in negotiations to free numerous Palestinian prisoners, underscoring Hamas's accomplishments and enhancing its appeal to Palestinians;
- to draw Israel into a major, prolonged campaign in Gaza, causing tremendous civilian casualties and damage; and
- to entice and entrap other parties in the Middle East into attacking Israel at a moment of extreme vulnerability.

Prior to 7 October, Hamas had engaged in steady low-level skirmishes and periodic bursts of intense violence against Israel, but delayed launching an all-out confrontation for some 15 years. It used the time to lay the ideological groundwork for an eventual offensive, accumulate material resources, arm itself and train for the fight while soliciting external assistance, primarily from Iran, and coordinating with other regional enemies of Israel. By autumn 2023, Hamas sensed an urgent strategic imperative to pre-empt the realisation of Israeli Finance Minister Bezalel Smotrich's 'Decisive Plan' for West Bank annexation and to prevent further Arab normalisation with Israel, which would sideline the Palestinian issue, on the heels of the Abraham Accords. Israel's internal preoccupation with Netanyahu's attempted constitutional overhaul opened a window of opportunity. Hamas expected its extraordinarily well-executed, lethal and sadistic attack to leave Israel with no choice but to conduct a major invasion of Gaza that was bound to cause extensive loss of life among Palestinian non-combatants and devastating collateral damage that would tarnish Israel's image and expose its brittleness.[7]

In Israel, the mammoth scale and heinous nature of Hamas's attack on 7 October created uncontainable shock, fear, humiliation and guilt, exacerbated by an acute sense of vulnerability. These produced a powerful drive not merely to eliminate the immediate threat and re-establish deterrence, but also to exact retribution and achieve redemption.[8] The result was a furious, massive and prolonged Israeli campaign to liquidate Hamas's military formations, fighters and infrastructure, and to break its political grip throughout Gaza. Initially, Israeli planners adhered to a narrow interpretation of the laws of armed conflict, declining to consider the fate of the Israeli hostages or the plight of Gaza's civilian population. They had no plan for the 'day after', appeared indifferent to the effect of indiscriminate collateral damage visited by urban warfare on Israel's global image, factoring in these societal considerations only later under American pressure that they had initially largely dismissed.[9] By then, however, the die was cast. Israel found itself trapped in an ever-spiralling societal conflict from which – for all its conventional military prowess and battlefield successes – it would emerge strategically battered.

Gaza's battlespace – a dense urban environment engineered and militarised above and below ground by Hamas – served as a kind of structural trap that in a sense dictated the societal nature of the war. In this setting, the campaign was an inescapable and extreme manifestation of 'war amongst the people'.[10] While the Israel Defense Forces' (IDF) active encouragement of the migration of 1.5 million people from the north and centre of Gaza served the narrow purpose of getting most civilians out of harm's way, it also dislocated and traumatised Palestinian society writ large. In addition, artificial-intelligence capabilities for identifying and simultaneously attacking very large numbers of legitimate Hamas targets, which were originally designed for relatively surgical special operations, proved insufficiently discriminating in the dense urban setting.[11] Israeli determination to destroy Hamas's remaining fighting capacity that relied on homes, schools, mosques, and United Nations Relief and Works Agency facilities as well as its extensive underground network, while minimising its own casualties translated into an intense application of firepower that led to heavy civilian casualties among remaining Palestinians and collateral damage.[12]

Key factors driving Israel's strategy

Beyond these structural factors, the slide to wholesale societal war appears to have been overdetermined, propelled by political and emotional–cognitive considerations and dynamics. Netanyahu had been committed to avoiding all-out confrontation with Hamas in order to preserve it as an impediment to political resolution, in line with his encouraging Qatar to provide Hamas with a financial lifeline. He believed that Hamas could be simultaneously appeased and deterred, and that the IDF could easily fend off Hamas aggression and overcome any challenge should these tools fail. He could maintain this policy because he had acquired the status of Israel's supreme and singularly capable champion of national security and the one leader able to prevent the establishment of a Palestinian state.[13] The shocking 7 October attack shattered this image.[14] With some initial hesitation, he elected to regain his political footing by endorsing the extensive and relentless campaign to crush Hamas politically as well as militarily, a policy that aligned at least with the wishes of other senior officials.

Despite the strategic and humanitarian calamity in Gaza, Netanyahu has resisted Western and internal pressures to seek a ceasefire or leverage Israel's operational military control of Gaza into a viable alternative political-governance structure there, secured by moderate Arab forces. One likely reason is that keeping the war going indefinitely will delay his trial for corruption, his political reckoning and an official inquiry into the war. He also appears convinced that anything other than an indefinite Israeli military presence in Gaza would lead to the revival of Hamas politically and as a threat to Israel, and to a concerted push to create the Palestinian state he dreads. On this logic, Netanyahu would retain the IDF deployment in the strip and direct control of its population for a very long time. Reinforcing this position is his dependence on right-wing extremists in his governing coalition – who insist on absolute victory over Hamas and the exclusion of the Palestinian Authority in any post-war governance structure in Gaza

– to remain in power.[15] The countervailing influence of the defence and intelligence agencies, which have historically been pragmatic, has reached a low point due to their failure to prevent the 7 October operation. Further, Netanyahu and the far right's widely accepted rhetorical characterisation of Hamas as a demonic, Islamic State-like Iranian proxy has made it difficult to moderate their stance.

Moreover, the savage 7 October assault left most Israelis consumed with a drive to avenge the mortal trauma, fear and humiliation that Hamas's atrocities had visited. The Israeli military itself harboured deep feelings of guilt and shame for its dismal failure to protect the population of the Gaza envelope and non-combat soldiers deployed near the strip, as well as a duty to free the hostages taken by Hamas by any means possible. A corresponding desire for redemption as well as revenge coincided with the military's priority of minimising its own casualties, practically guaranteeing more liberal use of force and rules of engagement, and weaker enforcement of military discipline to check excesses. Religious and nationalist segments of the population – disproportionately represented in the Israeli military as conscripts and mid-level commanders – apprehended a God-driven duty to annihilate enemies of Israel. Among the broader, less militant population, Hamas fighters' extreme and premeditated brutality and the sex crimes they committed seemed to signify an existential threat that justified an extreme and decisive response and the inference that all Palestinian Gazans were Hamas accomplices, reinforced by evidence of public jubilation at the atrocities conducted against Israeli civilians.[16]

As the high-intensity campaign drew out for weeks and months with loosely defined and overly ambitious war aims, inurement, fatigue and frustration took hold among troops as well as the senior leadership. Echoing the US military's experience in Vietnam, the IDF began resorting to body counts and leadership strikes to mark progress, even when these risked greater harm to non-combatants and endangered hostages. Israel has also indulged in deliberate pressure on the civilian population. The most vivid example was its initial refusal to allow the use of Israeli facilities and resources for the provision of humanitarian assistance, followed by grudging facilitation, indicating to many international observers that Israel was collectively punishing Palestinians.[17]

As the conflict wore on, hopes faded for a decisive military victory, but Israel dug more deeply into the societal war Hamas had initiated based on the misplaced expectation that Hamas's military losses and the growing misery of the Gazan population would induce Hamas's leadership – which had traditionally built much of its identity and mission around social welfare, for example through the Dawah – to desist. In the domestic context, Israeli leaders hoped that its purposeful and inadvertent population-targeting actions would help sustain broad popular support for extending the war effort, reduce pressure to reach a hostage deal that would require a ceasefire, and placate extremists. Israel also launched an information campaign intended to drive a wedge between Hamas and the Palestinian population by convincing it of the futility of armed struggle, Hamas's culpability for their misery, and its hypocrisy given its luxurious living standards and plundering; and by relaxing constraints on aid and agreeing to a humanitarian pause to allow for polio vaccination. Hamas, for its part, has mounted countermeasures such as inflated casualty figures and manipulated popularity polls.[18]

An eventual reckoning?

Although Israel's efforts in Gaza have had little positive and much negative and counterproductive strategic effect, it has scarcely relented in waging societal war. Its persistence will likely only add to the high strategic cost. Framing a war as an existential one against an implacably evil adversary leads to seeking absolute victory. This framing, while it may help mobilise one's own society for war, may deprive leaders of the leeway to extend leniency to the adversary's population or pursue political compromise to end hostilities.

In turn, extensively harming or immiserating civilians is unlikely to yield favourable strategic results, even in the short term, unless the per-petrator is willing to engage in conquest by annihilation, as the Sri Lankan government did against the Tamil Tigers. The militarily stronger party can, of course, rationalise societal war as an effort not only to exact revenge but also to win and deter. But international condemnation and the target popu-lation's enduring humiliation and fervent desire for retribution are likely to ultimately frustrate both goals. Unsurprisingly, the historical record does not inspire much confidence in the efficacy of wholesale societal war.[19]

*   *   *

The distinguished scholar Michael Howard viewed warfare and strategy as comprising four interacting dimensions: operations, technology, logistics and society.[20] The war in Gaza can be seen as a case in which political decisions, the structure of the battlefield and society-wide emotional–cognitive reactions combined to make society the dominant and determining dimension. Hamas made the social dimension central to its strategy and operations by using conventional dimensions of war – such as kinetic weapons, target selection, casualties, information and media – specifically for social effect. Israel, on the other hand, approached the conflict predominantly as a matter of operations and technology, often ignoring or downplaying the importance of the social dimension and thus failing to account for or manage the emotional and behavioural reactions to its actions in all of the societies relevant to the conflict, and their strategic implications.

This dynamic, of course, is hardly unprecedented; it is resonant of the Vietnam War, among others. But in Gaza it has been extraordinarily intense. That is largely because Hamas planned to leverage the plight of Palestinians to coax other parties to join the fight against Israel, and to generate Western outrage and pressure on Israel to desist. In this context, Israel's sophisticated military technology – though it dealt severe operational blows to Hamas, Hizbullah and Iran – failed to translate these into enduring strategic gains. A key reason was that its failure to articulate an appealing political vision to complement and succeed the fighting left Israel exposed to rebuke over the war's collateral consequences, the modern battlespace being largely transparent. At least in the West, most have direct access to global social media through which scenes of civilian misery in the affected societies are steadily projected, fuelling potent adverse sentiments and attitudes that, in turn, produce external pressure on combatants to adjust their tactics and strategy.

Such sentiments about Israel's conduct of the Gaza war have had an effect on the policies of its major partners – in particular, France, Germany and the

United Kingdom – inducing them to curtail the supply of some weapons and munitions, or threaten to do so. The impact of these steps on Israeli policy thus far been small. Israel has persisted and in fact, after much hesitation, has extended offensive operations to Lebanon. If these operations are sustained or expanded, their cumulative adverse effects on Israel could be significant by complicating defence procurement and significantly driving up defence costs, undermining diplomatic and legal cover, and even endangering partners' assistance to Israel in deterring and fending off aggression.

The realisation that fighting a societal war is likely to be futile or worse should lead Israeli decision-makers to focus on the dynamics and nuances of Palestinian society. Thomas C. Schelling's idea of mixing a promise with a threat could provide guidance for creating a schism between Hamas and other extremist Palestinian and Arab factions on the one hand, and more moderate Palestinians on the other.[21] The threat would be the application of military power (as selectively as possible), the promise a political path to possible statehood that many Palestinians desire and see Hamas as blocking. Until 7 October, Netanyahu rejected this approach, cynically propping up Hamas and also holding back from trying to make progress towards a political resolution of the Palestinian issue. This strategic void created the conditions for the debacle. After 7 October, Netanyahu adopted a force-only approach devoid of promise, a policy that has driven and helped sustain an open-ended, multifront conflict.

Even presented with Gaza as a vivid example of what not to do, some leaders will find the temptation of societal warfare difficult to resist owing to structural, emotional–cognitive and political forces. Nevertheless, they can be encouraged to pause and reflect on several pertinent questions. Is the looming confrontation expected to be purely military-to-military, and if so, how will it remain so confined and how will the civilian population be dealt with? What tools in addition to military force could be employed? What role does societal engagement play in the enemy's strategy? What reactions can we expect from indirectly involved but strategically important societies, and how will we balance the contradictory impacts that our actions are likely to have on the relevant societies? Most crucially: what adverse long-term effects can be expected even if short-term gains are realised? War games and simulations might be particularly helpful in teasing out answers.

Policymakers might also consider historical analogies, which can be intriguing even if leaders are predisposed – as they often are – to treat the situation at hand as *sui generis*. Such analogies could include the United States' experience in Vietnam, Afghanistan and Iraq, and Russia's in Afghanistan and Ukraine. Israeli policymakers would have been served well had they considered Egypt's sustained, at times brutal, decades-long effort to eradicate the Muslim Brotherhood movement or Turkiye's attempt to destroy the Fethullah Gülen movement.[22] These cases might have cautioned them to confine the stated goals of the operation to the significant degradation of Hamas's military capacity rather than striving to crush its political and social appeal and status without offering a viable alternative.

All of that said, if leaders still deem it a strategic imperative to engage in major societal warfare against terror armies, they need to be clear-eyed about what it would take to win. They must also prepare themselves and their own societies for a prolonged, exacting and inevitably contentious open-ended fight. A victory in such a confrontation cannot be accomplished by any one success or decisive blow. If it is possible at all, victory would result from accumulated operational successes with a minimum of setbacks in a sustained and relentless campaign, and even then only if complemented by a political initiative to leverage and consolidate these achievements.

Notes

1   See, for example, Day Lieber, 'Israel Sought to Contain Hamas for Years. Now It Faces a Potentially Costly Fight to Eliminate It', *Wall Street Journal*, 10 October 2023, https://www.wsj.com/world/middle-east/israel-sought-to-contain-hamas-for-years-now-it-faces-a-potentially-costly-fight-to-eliminate-it-aee9f211?.

2   See Jodi Rudoren, 'Netanyahu Takes a Lonely Stance Denouncing Iran', *New York Times*, 11 October 2023, https://www.nytimes.com/2013/10/12/world/middleeast/alone-and-relishing-it-israeli-leader-presses-case-against-iran.html.

3   See, for instance, Tal Schneider, 'For Years, Netanyahu Propped Up Hamas. Now It's Blown Up in Our Faces', *Times of Israel*, 8 October 2023, https://www.timesofisrael.com/for-years-netanyahu-propped-up-hamas-now-its-blown-up-in-our-faces/.

4   See Ariel E. Levite and Jonathan (Yoni) Shimshoni, 'The Strategic Challenge

of Society-centric Warfare', *Survival*, vol. 60, no. 6, December 2018–January 2019, pp. 91–118.

5   See, for example, Graeme Wood, 'Is Hamas Waging a Religious War?', *Atlantic*, 12 December 2023, https://www.theatlantic.com/ideas/archive/2023/12/hamas-israel-religious-organization/676303/.

6   See, for example, Joby Warrick, Souad Mekhennet and Loveday Morris, 'Captured Documents Reveal Hamas's Broader Ambition to Wreak Havoc on Israel', *Washington Post*, 12 October 2024, https://www.washingtonpost.com/national-security/2024/10/12/exclusive-hamas-documents-sinwar-planning-iran/.

7   See, for instance, Shira Rubin and Joby Warrick, 'Hamas Envisioned Deeper Attacks, Aiming to Provoke an Israeli War', *Washington Post*, 12 November 2023 (updated 13 November 2023), https://www.washingtonpost.com/national-security/2023/11/12/hamas-planning-terror-gaza-israel/.

8   See Rose McDermott, Anthony C. Lopez and Peter K. Hatemi, '"Blunt Not the Heart, Enrage It": The Psychology of Revenge and Deterrence', *Texas National Security Review*, vol. 1, no. 1, November 2017, pp. 68–88, https://tnsr.org/2017/11/blunt-not-heart-enrage-psychology-revenge-deterrence/.

9   See, for instance, David Alexander, 'Wednesday Evening News Briefing: Don't Repeat Our Rage-fuelled 9/11 Mistakes, Biden Warns Israel', *Daily Telegraph*, 18 October 2023, https://www.telegraph.co.uk/news/2023/10/18/wednesday-evening-news-briefing-joe-biden-israel-gaza/;

and Ron Kampeas, 'Calling Israel's Response in Gaza "Over the Top," Biden Conditions Defense Aid on Allowing Humanitarian Assistance', Jewish Telegraphic Agency, 9 February 2024, https://www.jta.org/2024/02/09/politics/calling-israels-response-in-gaza-over-the-top-biden-conditions-defense-aid-on-humanitarian-assistance.

10 See General Rupert Smith, *The Utility of Force: The Art of War in the Modern World* (New York: Vintage Books, 2008).

11 See Noah Sylvia, 'The Israel Defense Forces' Use of AI in Gaza: A Case of Misplaced Purpose', RUSI, 4 July 2024, https://www.rusi.org/explore-our-research/publications/commentary/israel-defense-forces-use-ai-gaza-case-misplaced-purpose.

12 See Yagil Levy, *Whose Life Is Worth More? Hierarchies of Risk and Death in Contemporary Wars* (Stanford, CA: Stanford University Press, 2019).

13 See Guy Ziv, *Netanyahu vs The Generals: The Battle for Israel's Future* (Cambridge: Cambridge University Press, 2024).

14 See Guy Chazan, '"Bibi's Finished": Benjamin Netanyahu Loses Core Support After Hamas Assault on Israel', *Financial Times*, 3 November 2023, https://www.ft.com/content/a92e4865-79ad-4407-a6a5-cc3266ecc214.

15 Aluf Benn, 'It's All Catching Up to Bibi Netanyahu', *Atlantic*, 25 June 2024, https://www.theatlantic.com/international/archive/2024/06/netanyahu-government-coalition-israel-war/678785/.

16 Social and political psychologists call the latter phenomenon 'outgroup

homogeneity bias'. See Eran Halperin, *Emotions in Conflict: Inhibitors and Facilitators of Peace Making* (New York: Routledge, 2015).

17 See Claire Parker, 'How Israel's Restrictions on Aid Put Gaza on the Brink of Famine', *Washington Post*, 3 March 2024, https://www.washingtonpost.com/world/2024/03/03/gaza-aid-convoy-israel-war/.

18 See 'The UN Quietly Admits It Exaggerated Civilian Casualties in Gaza', *Mosaic*, 13 May 2024, https://mosaicmagazine.com/picks/israel-zionism/2024/05/the-un-quietly-admits-it-exaggerated-civilian-casualties-in-gaza/; and Abraham Wyner, 'How the Gaza Ministry of Health Fakes Casualty Figures', *Tablet*, 7 March 2024, https://www.tabletmag.com/sections/news/articles/how-gaza-health-ministry-fakes-casualty-numbers.

19 See Alexander B. Downes and Stephen Rangazas, *Civilian Victimization During Conflict* (Oxford: Oxford University Press, 2023); and Robert A. Pape, *Bombing to Win: Air Power and Coercion in War* (Ithaca, NY: Cornell University Press, 1996).

20 See Michael Howard, 'The Forgotten Dimensions of Strategy', *Foreign Affairs*, vol. 57, no. 5, Summer 1979, pp. 975–86.

21 See Thomas C. Schelling, *The Strategy of Conflict* (Cambridge, MA: Harvard University Press, 1981).

22 See Zbi Bar'el, 'Al-Sissi and Erdogan Have Already Learned That You Can't Eradicate Ideas. Netanyahu Hasn't', *Haaretz*, 21 June 2024, https://www.haaretz.com/middle-east-news/2024-06-21/ty-article/.premium/al-sissi-and-erdogan-already-learned-that-you-cant-eradicate-ideas-netanyahu-hasnt/00000190-399a-d8cb-a19d-79dbf8ee0000.

Things Fall Apart

Benjamin Rhode

Why Empires Fall: Rome, America and the Future of the West
Peter Heather and John Rapley. London: Allen Lane, 2023.
£20.00. 208 pp.

Rome may be the 'Eternal City', but it also represents an eternal idea: that of civilisational glory and decline. Reminiscent of the wolf-suckled antagonistic twins of Rome's founding myth or the dual-faced Janus, Rome's god of beginnings and endings, these twinned processes have fascinated the political and public mind since the Roman Empire disintegrated (in Western Europe, at least) in the fifth century CE. Of course, they also obsessed the Romans themselves, who often lamented their own supposed degeneration from the more manly standards of their ancestors. Even at the time of Rome's heyday, ancient histories, religious texts and mythology in Europe and elsewhere were already replete with once-glorious cities or empires now in ruins or under water. Their doom was often ascribed to some species of internal weakness or decadence prompting a destruction that was probably divine, or at least deserved. But despite emerging much later than ruined Sumerian, Levantine or Minoan civilisations, with their fallen cities of Ur, Tyre or Heraklion, to name just a few, in the Western mind Rome has generally served as the

Benjamin Rhode is an IISS Senior Fellow and Editor of the *Adelphi* book series.

Survival | vol. 66 no. 6 | December 2024–January 2025 | pp. 143–152 https://doi.org/10.1080/00396338.2024.2432206

prototypical example of glorious rise and calamitous collapse – the 'ur-empire', so to speak.

One obvious reason for this was that, for much of the period since Rome's fall, its culture (itself in large part adopted from the Greeks), language and history underpinned the education of European and later American elites. Roman history formed the source material for any number of historical or political theories, notably in the Renaissance and the Enlightenment. America's Founding Fathers were steeped in it and self-consciously learned from it, and the fact that their new nation's capital was built in a deliberately

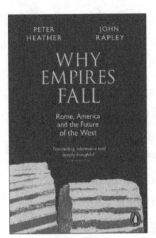

neoclassical style and its legislative seat named 'Capitol Hill', after one of Rome's own major hills, helped to ensure that the fascination with Rome's imperial narrative would survive the collapse of classical education in the later twentieth century.

Rome's compelling arc

The obsession with Rome is visible too in popular culture. In 2023, a comical online 'meme' played upon a claimed daily or near-daily male preoccupation with Rome's grandeur – and upon investigation seemed to be at least somewhat accurate.[1] The recent release of the Hollywood film *Gladiator II* suggests – regardless of its artistic merit – a continuing fixation with Roman might, violence and decline. Its wildly successful predecessor, *Gladiator* (2000), begins in 180 CE in an atmosphere charged not only with ongoing Roman military glory, represented by the thoughtful Emperor Marcus Aurelius presiding over a final victory in the Marcomannic Wars against Germanic barbarians, but also with a sense of decline from earlier, more politically virtuous days. This atmosphere is soon compounded by the accession of the venal Emperor Commodus, an event which, in his epic Enlightenment history of Rome's decline and fall, Edward Gibbon took to signal the end of Rome's (and humanity's) golden age.[2]

The fascination is understandable. Rome's story is remarkable: a hilly settlement in central Italy grew into a mighty empire stretching from Britain to the Persian Gulf. Its legacy was fundamental to so much of what was later called Western civilisation, which itself went on to colonise, shape or otherwise influence much of the rest of humanity. There can also be an unsavoury aspect to this fascination, though: perhaps almost a pornographic fixation on the power of this brutally effective conquering entity that expanded, enslaved and endured (in evolving forms) for more than a thousand years. Rome was the original fascist state, its symbols and behaviour the conscious model for twentieth-century imitators, and it remains notorious for its cruelty, slavery and violence.

Alongside the obsession with violence and force runs a parallel, twinned unsavoury element. While the urge to understand how a triumphant civilisation could crumble is understandable, one can also often observe a hand-rubbing preoccupation with Rome's emblematic degeneration and decline, sometimes paired with the historicist assumption that it is possible to derive supposed 'laws' of historical progress and decline that are applicable to the present. Rome is used as a template for contemporary civilisation's own impending collapse, which can often be invoked with a mixture of horror and vindictive glee at the perils awaiting the supposedly decadent.

Inevitably, contemporary preoccupations are projected onto Rome's fall: consider Gibbon's eighteenth-century emphasis on Christianity, his having supposedly been prompted to start his masterpiece after witnessing barefoot priests in Rome's ruins; or the Victorian denunciations of Roman sexual decadence and loss of masculine vigour (their anxieties of decline were encapsulated by the trope of a future New Zealander or another visitor from a once-peripheral state observing London's ruins, as Gibbon observed Rome's).[3] More recently, mass migration, environmental contamination, pandemics or a climate crisis, among many other factors, have been posited as the cause of Rome's downfall.[4] These various interpretations are sometimes employed to demonstrate that our civilisation is either fortuitously immune from, or similarly doomed to, catastrophe.

Over the past two decades or so, the historian Peter Heather (currently the Chair of Medieval History at King's College London) has made vital intellectual contributions to the study of Rome's collapse. He has illustrated how so many of the assumptions underlying these various civilisational jeremiads were incorrect. His argument incorporates painstaking archaeological evidence uncovered in the second half of the twentieth century that shows, for the most part, that the old narrative of Roman economic decline in the centuries before its fall was untrue: in fact, the Roman economy was at its peak in the late fourth century. Rome fell much more than it declined, at least in terms of absolute decline; and the reasons for its fall were many, complex and interweaving. There was indeed an important degree of Roman relative decline compared to the barbarians but, Heather argued, this was due more to the barbarians' rise than the Romans' decline. The shift in Rome's fortunes was less the product of some inherent corruption or weakness, and more a product of its own success: a function of an imperial system in which an original centre conquered and colonised provinces; over the course of centuries, economic and political power flowed to these provinces in a kind of imperial osmosis. A related transfer occurred from the provinces across the imperial frontiers to the 'inner periphery', a band of territory perhaps 100 kilometres deep. Archaeological evidence suggests that due to this proximity to and interaction with the Roman state over centuries, the barbarians in this zone eventually became richer and more materially sophisticated. They also became more politically sophisticated, forming larger, more cohesive and more resilient confederations, ultimately with grave consequences for the Romans.

The most obvious cause of the fall of the Roman Empire in Western Europe in the fifth century CE was a series of barbarian frontier-crossings and then settlements within the empire starting in the later fourth century. These barbarians were not originally conquerors, but refugees fleeing a fearsome nomadic people originally from Central Asia – the Huns – who were moving westward, pressing first on tribes in the 'outer periphery' and thereby on those in the 'inner periphery' until they sought sanctuary within the empire. The Romans had encountered a similar pattern in the second and third centuries, when other nomadic peoples had essentially pushed earlier barbarian groupings against the border. Thanks to ongoing asymmetries in political and military sophistication, the Romans had dealt with these threats relatively easily (including in the war dramatised at the beginning of *Gladiator*). This time around, however, the barbarians at the border had become too strong to be crushed under the imperial heel. Two years after their arrival in 376 CE, the newcomers in fact slaughtered much of the eastern Roman army in a terrible battle at Adrianople (today near the Turkish, Greek and Bulgarian borders). From the fourth century onwards, Roman military victories over various barbarian groupings had not caused them simply to disappear, as their predecessors had done in earlier centuries – often they were able to reform and remain a threat.

With barbarian confederations settling within Roman imperial territory, the Roman state faced a crisis of tax revenue and thus military capability. This combined with various other factors, notably the fact that, since the Sasanian dynasty's reform and strengthening of the Persian Empire in the third century, Rome had faced a true fellow-superpower adversary on its eastern borders. The emergence of this rival meant Rome had to grow its army by perhaps 50–100%, and boost tax revenues by about a third. Heather stressed that, even quite late into the fifth century, there remained the possibility of some kind of Roman resurgence in the West, notably if the expedition (led by the Eastern half of the empire, whose capital was Constantinople) to reconquer the rich North African provinces had succeeded. Indeed, in the sixth century under the Emperor Justinian the surviving Eastern part of the empire did actually reconquer Italy along with portions of North Africa, Dalmatia and Spain. Ultimately, though, in the fifth century, with the essential breakdown of the imperial compact in which the empire provided security in return for taxes and support from the local Roman landowner elites, wherever they could these elites made deals with the newcomer barbarians in the hope of preserving as much of their wealth as possible.[5]

Qualified modern resonance

Heather's narrative of Rome's collapse, incompletely summarised above, is elegantly recapitulated in a 2023 book co-authored with the political economist John Rapley entitled *Why Empires Fall: Rome, America and the Future of the West*. While they sensibly note that 'imperial systems unravel for all sorts of reasons' (p. 79), their collaboration was born of the belief that the various elements of imperial collapse that they had studied separately in late antiquity and in more recent times shared striking similarities. The dynamics visible in Rome's fall are, Heather and Rapley believe, equivalent to 'an imperial life cycle' in which 'large-scale economic development in the periphery', generated by an original imperial centre's effort to obtain wealth for itself, 'kick-starts a political process which will eventually challenge the domination of the imperial power that initiated the original cycle. This economic and political logic is so powerful that some degree of relative decline at the old imperial centre becomes inevitable' (pp. 4–5). The book provides a thrilling and tightly written exposition of this theory of economic development and the consequent shifts in wealth, sophistication and politico-military power visible within medieval and early modern Europe, and then from Europe to the colonial provinces of North America.

Heather and Rapley argue the West has begun to falter

Heather and Rapley argue that although the contemporary West – which they label the 'Western Empire' – rose to become the world's predominant political and economic power, it has in recent decades begun to falter. Since the global financial crisis of 2008, the West's share of global GDP has fallen from 80% to 60%. The authors contend that this is not a temporary misfortune but indicative of a structural shift in the fortunes of the West, which now faces a crisis composed of 'exactly the same moving parts' as Rome: 'exogenous shock (including large-scale migration originating in the outer periphery and beyond), an assertive inner periphery, peer superpower competition, and growing internal political stress' (p. 98).

They dismantle facile contemporary analogies sometimes drawn between the barbarian migrations of the fourth and fifth centuries and more recent immigration to the West, instead emphasising the more massive and consequential migrations within non-Western states – such as the enormous movements of people from rural to urban areas in China, South America, South Asia and Africa – which have contributed to these areas' dramatic economic growth. But this economic rise elsewhere – and the rise of the Persian-superpower analogue, China – are largely the result of Western success and stimulus: 'like ancient Rome, the modern Western Empire is facing a crisis of its own making' (p. 162). Heather and Rapley also warn that 'you can't just "make America great again" (or the UK, or the EU) because the very exercise of Western dominance over the last few centuries has rearranged the building blocks of global strategic power on which that "greatness" was based' (pp. 4–5).

The authors' arguments about the challenges to the Western economic model are persuasive and alarming, and they are careful to distinguish the character of contemporary possibilities, such as a collapse in tax revenues and the end of the essential fiscal compact binding modern states, from those of their fifth-century analogues; for instance, the latter was prompted by barbarian settlement, whereas the former derives from quite different socio-economic factors. They suggest the ultimate consequences, however, may also be existential.

Despite some impressive reasoning and the cleverness of the parallels the authors draw, as well as their important disclaimers about how the current situation differs from ancient precedents, the book's attempts to map similar explanatory factors onto today, along with its discussion of contemporary issues, can sometimes feel unsatisfying. For example, the authors recognise that much has changed in political economy over the past two millennia, notably the invention of national debt, but then argue that this 'really just means that the impending [Western] revenue crisis has been postponed' (p. 163). Perhaps, but one imagines that this form of postponement would have proved quite useful, or maybe even decisive, for many polities who had to survive before its invention.

More generally, the very concept of a 'Western Empire', although often ingeniously argued, can come across as a little tendentious. Heather and Rapley acknowledge obvious dissimilarities, including the 'reasonable' objection that the Western Empire is not 'a single entity established by a series of conquests or organised from one metropolitan centre'; but they maintain that, 'understood properly', one can discern clear parallels in how the Roman Empire and the Western Empire evolved politically. Rome 'was created by conquest, but evolved into a globally dominant (in its own context) commonwealth resting on a bedrock of shared financial, cultural and legal structures. Its modern counterpart emerged from intense internal conflict among its eventual partners', but by its late-twentieth-century zenith 'had ended up in much the same place: a self-identifying body with important common values operating through a common set of legal and financial institutions' (pp. 35–6). The analogy seems imaginative, thought-provoking, and perhaps in some ways largely correct and analytically illuminating. But it also often feels, at least to this reader, like a stretch.

The authors eschew the doom-mongering so frequently found in historical comparisons with Rome, acknowledging that it is self-evident that the West 'has not fallen, will not fall anytime soon, and in fact need never fall in the same way as its ancient predecessor' (p. 81). Still, their prescriptions can sometimes come across as unrealistic and occasionally even preachy. They discuss various policies or political shifts that Western states should adopt to adapt to the changed international environment and reform themselves. Domestically, they call (rather ambitiously) for a 'new type of functioning socio-political model, in the absence now of large flows of wealth from abroad' – a model that would essentially be based on the wealthy contributing much more money to the societies they inhabit (p. 164). Internationally, they consider the exhausting superpower rivalry between Rome and Persia, how both benefitted from periods of cooperation when facing shared nomadic threats, and how all-out war led to mutual bankruptcy and loss. Applying this history to the United States and China today, they advise the West to be wary of direct confrontation, to pick its battles and to focus only on issues that threaten the international order or 'cherished Western principles' (p. 131). This list includes China's brutalisation of its ethnic minorities and subjugation of Hong Kong, items over which, in reality, the West can exert little influence and which few observers, even those dismayed by the humanitarian plight of the Chinese Communist Party's (CCP) victims, would argue were core Western interests. Heather and Rapley's discussion of the merits of cooperation with a risen China and the need for the West's leaders to 'overturn some of the remaining detritus of arrogant Western imperialism' (p. 135) and distinguish between China's legitimate desire for a recovered superpower status and the more alarming anti-liberal behaviours of the CCP, incompatible with the more benevolent aspects of the Western model, similarly felt somewhat fuzzy, perhaps because it is increasingly clear that the CCP under Chinese President Xi Jinping does not itself distinguish between these two objectives.

The authors' recommendation that the Western Empire expand its alliances to include 'periphery' states such as Brazil, India and South Africa 'and in doing so build a larger coalition of peer states' (p. 132) with which it could better balance China (at least in international diplomacy) seems a reasonable aspiration, but it is unclear whether these states have any desire to be part of such a coalition or alliance system, or indeed whether one requires the lessons of Roman history to appreciate the merits of attracting cooperative partners.

'To ask an historian to look into and prescribe for the future is to invite a presentation consisting of as much past history as the author thinks he can get away with and as little prophecy and prescription as he thinks his audience will accept', argued Sir Michael Howard at an IISS conference in 1983. 'Historians have seen too many confident prophets fall flat on their faces to lay themselves open to more humiliation than they can help.'[6] Through his long-standing historical scholarship, Heather has already performed a crucial intellectual service in helping to debunk many pre-existing myths about Rome's fall, myths that can themselves prove pernicious in our politics through their shaping of historical consciousness and thereby contemporary policy. In this newer volume, while he and Rapley do not hesitate to look forward, they are also generally careful not to engage in too much 'prophecy', and they emphasise that all is not yet lost. But while this is a compelling and thought-provoking book, written with intelligence and verve, and which will be of interest both to historians and to analysts of the contemporary world, there is something somewhat Procrustean and ultimately wanting in their attempt to apply the earlier historical concepts onto the current age.

*　　*　　*

Heather and Rapley rightly include internal political division as a key factor in potential decline. At the time of writing, the effect of Donald Trump's second presidential term on US power, and on the international system that power has underpinned since 1945, remains ahead of us and uncertain. I have argued elsewhere, though, that it is likely to be severe, especially in

Europe, where the US-led security order over the past 80 years has allowed that continent to outshine that supposed golden age of humanity in the second century CE that Gibbon so extolled.[7] If so, it is unclear whether there is a direct historical parallel for the leader of a hegemonic state turning on its previous allies, many of whose political systems and values were modelled on that of their protector, while scarcely concealing his desire to align himself with his country's adversaries and imitate their system of government, which represents the antithesis of his country's founding values. What is clear is that the warnings of America's Founding Fathers about the inherent risk within democracies of the emergence of an authoritarian demagogue seeking dictatorial powers, which given their study of classical history seemed self-evident to them and which necessitated novel and protective constitutional measures, remain directly relevant – even if they are increasingly unheeded.

Notes

1 See Callie Holtermann and Frank Rojas, 'Are Men Obsessed with the Roman Empire? Yes, Say Men', *New York Times*, 15 September 2023, https://www.nytimes.com/2023/09/15/style/roman-empire-men-tiktok-instagram.html.

2 See Edward Gibbon, *The Decline and Fall of the Roman Empire*, vol. 1 (London: W.W. Gibbings, 1890 [1776]).

3 For a discussion of this trope, which predated the Victorians, see Vivienne Morrell, 'The "New Zealander" Contemplates the Ruins of London', 8 August 2015, https://viviennemorrell.wordpress.com.

4 For an overview of the various factors to which Rome's fall has been attributed, and an incisive evaluation of the true violence and severity of the imperial collapse, see Bryan Ward-Perkins, *The Fall of Rome: And the End of Civilization* (Oxford: Oxford University Press, 2006).

5 See Peter Heather, *The Fall of the Roman Empire: A New History of Rome and the Barbarians* (Oxford: Oxford University Press, 2006); and Peter Heather, *Empires and Barbarians: Migration, Development and the Birth of Europe* (London: Macmillan, 2009).

6 Quoted in Benjamin Rhode (ed.), *A Historical Sensibility: Sir Michael Howard and the IISS, 1958–2019* (Abingdon: Routledge for the IISS, 2020), pp. 8, 251.

7 See Benjamin Rhode, 'Europe Without America', *Survival*, vol. 66, no. 2, March/April 2024, pp. 7–18.

Playing for the Highest Stakes

Jeffrey Mazo

On the Edge: The Art of Risking Everything
Nate Silver. London: Allen Lane, 2024. £30.00/$35.00. 560 pp.

In October 1986, US president Ronald Reagan and his Soviet counterpart, Mikhail Gorbachev, met in Reykjavik, Iceland, for what George Shultz, Reagan's secretary of state, called the poker game with the highest stakes ever played.[1] Although the arms-control summit fell narrowly short of jump-starting a world without nuclear weapons, it was an important break- through towards the 1987 Intermediate-Range Nuclear Forces (INF) Treaty that lasted until 2019. It was also the first of many times Reagan quoted the Russian aphorism 'trust but verify' (*doveryai, no proveryai*), a sentiment expressed by an earlier president's favourite humourist in poker terms as 'trust everybody, but cut the cards'.[2]

High-stakes poker has often been used as a metaphor for international relations and existential threats such as nuclear weapons. Nate Silver's *On the Edge: The Art of Risking Everything* is a lengthy, often meandering but always entertaining exploration of this metaphor and its increasing salience in the twenty-first century, from the world of professional gambling through physical risk-taking, speculative investing and global existential risks such as

Jeffrey Mazo is IISS Associate Fellow for Conflict, Security and Development, and a Contributing Editor to *Survival*.

Survival | vol. 66 no. 6 | December 2024–January 2025 | pp. 153–162 https://doi.org/10.1080/00396338.2024.2432207

climate change, nuclear weapons and, especially, artificial intelligence (AI). Silver is probably America's, if not the world's, best-known and most influential statistician and data journalist, mainly due to his work on forecasting models for US presidential elections beginning in 2007. Before that, he was a successful professional sports gambler and poker player, until Congress passed the Unlawful Internet Gambling Enforcement Act (tacked on to a bill regulating port security) in 2006, which caused him both to lose his job and to gain a deeper interest in politics and the US political system. Through all the iterations of his blog FiveThirtyEight.com (launched in 2008), however,

he has retained as much focus on sports betting and sports statistics as on politics, and has written extensively about data, statistical models and the nature of prediction more widely.[3] *On the Edge* continues these themes, but takes a more personal and sociological tack. This is both its strength and its weakness.

Part One of *On the Edge* is about gambling and gamblers. It comprises two chapters on poker, one on the casino business and one on sports betting. These (especially chapter one) introduce theoretical concepts and methods, as well as some esoteric terminology, that are necessary background for Part Two on risk.

Between these two sections is a one-chapter 'halftime', a detour into 'thirteen habits of highly successful risk-takers' (pp. 217–43) based on interviews with five people who take major physical risks, including a NASA astronaut, a professional (American) football player, an explorer/adventurer, a refugee from communism and H.R. McMaster, a decorated combat veteran and former US national security advisor (and, incidentally, a former IISS senior fellow and contributing editor to this journal). The second part includes chapters on the venture-capital industry; three chapters about former multi-billionaire Sam Bankman-Fried (currently serving 25 years for fraud over the 2022 failure of his cryptocurrency exchange FTX), along with digressions into the modern rationalist, utilitarian and effective-altruism movements; and a two-chapter conclusion covering existential threats to modern civilisation and the core principles needed to survive them.

On the Edge has two entangled but not mutually reinforcing threads: a discussion on how to think about risks and risk-taking, and a central sociocultural conceit that modern elites, especially in the United States, can be meaningfully divided into two tribes or 'sprawling ecosystem[s] of like-minded people' competing for power and influence. Silver calls these tribes 'the River' and 'the Village' (p. 1). River-dwellers, with whom Silver explicitly identifies, tend to think analytically, abstractly and reductively. They tend to be competitive, critical and contrarian. The River is thus characterised by a high tolerance for calculated risk; a focus on quantitative metrics such as 'expected value'; and a penchant for game-theoretical and Bayesian statistical methods and models. The rich and the powerful – such as Bankman-Fried, Elon Musk, Peter Thiel and Sam Altman, among others – 'are disproportionately likely to be River-dwellers compared to the rest of the population' (p. 1). Broadly speaking, the River encompasses the worlds of professional gamblers (Downriver), Wall Street and Silicon Valley (Midriver), and intellectual movements such as rationalism and effective altruism (Upriver). (There is also the Archipelago, the Downriver-adjacent world of unregulated gambling and cryptocurrencies.) The Village, in contrast, is characterised by holistic thinking, left-of-centre politics, and government, media and academic institutions.

Silver's self-proclaimed motivations and inspirations for *On the Edge*, as well as his publicity and marketing material, suggest that he sees this River–Village dichotomy as the heart of the book: 'my mission is to be a friendly, informative – and occasionally provocative – tour guide to the River' (p. 2). This is unfortunate, since his valuable discussions and insights about how to think about risk do not need the dichotomy or the characterisation of the two communities to be sound. In fact, the conceit offers more distraction than insight.

Sleight of hand

One problem is that the River is not particularly well defined. The fundamental distinction between Village and River is the degree of risk tolerance, but there is a continuum across this and the other cognitive and psychological attributes Silver identifies as typical of River-dwellers. He argues, moreover, that the risk-tolerance continuum forms a bell curve, and he is focusing on the extreme right-hand tail. The argument is that risk-tolerant people also tend to show the other traits he cites, forming clusters. Thus, the River is an ecosystem of like-minded people, 'a way of thinking and a mode of life' (p. 1). Metonymic institutions such as Silicon Valley, Wall Street and Las Vegas are part of the River only to the extent that they show a high density of such people.

But this definition becomes circular. The slot-machine addicts that haunt Vegas casinos, for example, are 'not Riverians for whom modern life has become stagnant. Instead, they're seeking escape from a hazardous world' (p. 168). Although Donald Trump is competitive, risk-taking and contrarian, he is not a River-dweller because 'he's shown little of the capacity for abstract analytical reasoning that distinguishes people in the River' (p. 149). On the other hand, good poker players, River-dwellers *par excellence*, rely as much on well-honed intuition as on analytical thinking. There's a No True Scotsman vibe here.

At least the River is real in one sense. Silver identifies as a River-dweller, 'a resident of the River, and not just a visitor to it' (p. 475), albeit one who 'passes back and forth between the two worlds' (p. 27). He describes how attending a 2022 conference of 'forecasting nerds' confirmed for him that 'the River is real – not just some literary device I invented' (p. 371) – because the same people he met there had kept popping up in different contexts during his research, and he felt a sense of shared culture and camaraderie. It was 'all part of some broader like-minded community'. But the attendees were self-selected. The River is a sociological network made up of self-identifying individuals, a tribe, not an objective cultural phenomenon. This is clear from the enthusiastic way some people Silver identifies as River-dwellers have embraced the label in their own reviews and online discussions of *On the Edge*, especially on Silver's own website, even if 'residents in different parts of the River don't necessarily know one another, and many don't think of themselves as part of some broader community' (p. 18).

The Village has no such reality. Unlike River-dwellers, putative Village-dwellers will not recognise themselves or their networks in Silver's descriptions, and even the term is mildly pejorative. The Village is, rather, a fictional 'them' River-dwellers can use as a contrast to their 'us'. But there's no evidence that there is a higher proportion of people with Riverian traits in the River than in the institutions identified as parts of the Village. The IISS, for example, is in the latter group, yet its self-image (and hopefully the reality) aligns with many of the key Riverian traits in being analytical and contrarian, and in thinking outside the box. And Village institutions originally generated some of the analytical methods, especially game-theory applications in the context of conflict studies and nuclear deterrence, central to the River's own self-image. What separates the River from the Village is not so much these methods as the in-group jargon and cultural references River-dwellers use to talk about it, 'like a couple at a dinner party insulting your cooking in a foreign language they know you don't understand' (p. 3). Ironically, given a whiff of self-righteousness that can sometimes accompany the River's self-image, Silver's characterisation and critique of the so-called Village both rest on subjective observations and data-free assertions. We saw him palm that card.

Probability of doom

'Much of the River', says Silver, is concerned with 'small-world problems', like poker tournaments or developing a portfolio of start-ups, that are relatively well defined and tractable (p. 343). But the world view and skill set of River-dwellers make them tend to seek – and to assume that they can do a good job of finding – solutions to open-ended 'grand-world' problems too, especially world-altering technologies and existential threats to civilisation, or even to humanity. In particular, given the tech focus of much of the River, the risks and rewards of artificial general intelligence (AGI) loom large.[4] Associated Riverian jargon includes such terms as 'x-risk' (existential risk) and '(p)doom' (a given estimate of the probability that AGI – or, by extension, other technologies such as nuclear weapons, or natural existential threats such as asteroids or supervolcanoes – will destroy us).

Silver admits that 'when it comes to things like nuclear war and AI risk, we don't even have models so much as back-of-the-napkin estimates' (p. 442). Thus, although quantifying the probability of doom can make it easier to discuss the problem rationally, the numbers are subjective and idiosyncratic; different (p)dooms, too, assume 'doom' means different things. Expert (p)dooms for AGI in a 2023 survey of several hundred experts range from near-zero to near-certainty, with a mean of 14.4% and a median of 5%.[5] And there is huge uncertainty even in individual (p)dooms; for example, Silver gives his as 2–20% (p. 445). Another 2022 study cited by Silver tried to reach a consensus through discussion and iterative forecasting between 89 generalist and a total of 80 specialist forecasters on the x-risks of AI, climate change, nuclear war and biological pathogens. Notably, 42% of the specialists and 9% of the generalists in this Existential Risk Persuasion Tournament (XPT) were River-dwellers, in the sense that they had already participated in meet-ups of the Upriver Effective Altruism community. The group was heavily vetted for expertise, but was initially self-selected. Despite the avowed goal of the tournament to reach a consensus, there was an order-of-magnitude difference between the two groups' final mean AI (p)dooms: 0.7% and 8.8% respectively (p. 445).[6]

Silver argues that 'nuclear weapons are one of the most salient comparisons for AGI' (p. 423). The XPT study found much lower (p)dooms for nuclear risks such as a 9/11-scale event, a decimation of the human population or a near-extinction, over periods of one to eight decades (2030, 2050 and 2100), than it did for AI.[7] The difference between generalist and expert estimates for nuclear (p)doom was similar to that for AI, although the groups differed on catastrophic (rather than existential) risk by around a factor of two. The key questions affecting these differences were how to define a base rate for nuclear catastrophe using nearly 80 years of real-world experience and specific current risk scenarios such as the Russia–Ukraine war or the Taiwan Strait; to account for near misses such as the Cuban Missile Crisis or the 1983 *Able Archer* incident; and uncertainty over the additional risk of nuclear winter.

Political scientist Phil Tetlock, the study's senior author, told Silver that 'the superforecasters see the doomsters as somewhat aggrandizing, narcissistic, messianic, saving-the-world types … and the AI-concerned camp sees the superforecasters as plodders' (p. 446). Silver himself splits Riverian forecasters into 'model mavericks' and 'model mediators' whose forecasts are intended to be provocative or conciliatory respectively (pp. 446–7) – a division which closely parallels Tetlock's 2005 division of experts into 'foxes' and 'hedgehogs' (a key theme of Silver's previous book).[8] There is again a sense of the River–Village split here, however: foxes have more Village-like traits, hedgehogs more River-like ones.

Silver himself offers a bare-bones, 'half-full, half-empty', back-of-the-envelope look at the risk of nuclear war (pp. 422–9). He first posits a hypothetical panel of three experts in 1946 – Peter Pessimist, Mary Middleground and Ollie Optimist – who estimate the odds at 10%, 1% or 0.1% per year. In the absence of other evidence or any consensus, this suggests an average chance of 3.7%, or a near certainty over a 20-year period. After 78 years' experience, however, we can use Bayesian statistics to revise the estimate down to 0.35% per year, or a near-certainty within 200 years and, since it is an all-or-nothing affair with a huge downside, an averaged annual death rate in the millions. He points out, moreover, that 78 years is not enough experience to draw definitive conclusions, and that (as argued by many XPT participants) the risk is increasing, with one expert arguing that the risk had increased tenfold after the Russian invasion of Ukraine in early 2022 (p. 424).[9] Silver argues, however, that the fact that nuclear deterrence in theory and practice has been successful since 1945 is evidence that 'River types misunderstand human nature' (p. 424). The psychological and economic principles that work in poker, start-up investment or rationalism are the opposite of those that create and maintain deterrence.

'In the long run', Keynes said, 'we are all dead'; the question is whether 'we will all go together when we go'.[10] Ultimately, however, these probabilities of doom are entirely subjective, even when based on real expertise, and the XPT shows that gut feeling tends to prevail over rational argument. This shouldn't really be surprising. Reliance on even expert gut feeling, though, is one of the things River-dwellers hate about the Village, and quantifying (p)doom from small numbers of expert guesses risks creating a false appearance of precision, even on the coarsest level. 'We should be able to convey orders of magnitude' at the very least, according to Silver, who writes that 'a nuclear war is a *lot* more likely to kill humanity than a supervolcano' (p. 370; emphasis original). On the face of it, such an assertion is questionable, and a dive into Silver's cited source leads to a non-analytical article in a UK tabloid newspaper based on interviews with one expert each on nuclear weapons, volcanoes and climate change, none of whom offer any quantification of risk in their own domain, let alone a comparison between them.[11] And the three existential threats are not really comparable anyway: supervolcanoes are natural and unpredictable, climate change is caused by human activity and is at least partially foreseeable in scope and timing, and nuclear war is a secondary risk arising out of other drivers and events such as political tensions, economics and, yes, environmental catastrophes such as supervolcanoes or climate change.

Individual regimes and nations can also take existential risks. The consequences for humanity and the long term might be ephemeral, but for the immediate players that doesn't matter much. Adolf Hitler and the Japanese rulers' bets on war in 1939 and 1941 were all-or-nothing gambles, and they and their contemporary co-nationalists lost everything (although it could be argued that the long-term return for both countries was, albeit unintentionally, net positive). Neither were in a position to calculate any meaningful expected value. Vladimir Putin's gamble of winning big and quickly in Ukraine in 2022 failed, but the expected value may have been very high given that the return from success would have been significantly greater than the losses to him and his regime from failure, especially if Russia eventually prevails.

*   *   *

The same writer who told us to trust, but always cut the cards, is widely credited (but not verified) as the source of a related card-playing metaphor: 'there are no friends at cards or world politics'. The grand metaphor is more than a simple aphorism or analogy; the TL;DR for *On the Edge* could be that poker and politics are fundamentally linked at the level of game theory, even if poker is precise and politics is messy. The Riverian approach is best suited to the former. But, says Silver, 'the reason some Riverians have become obsessed with grand world problems' such as nuclear war and other existential threats 'is because the Village and the rest of the world screw them up all the time, too, in ways that often reflect political partisanship, an endless array of cognitive biases, innumeracy, hypocrisy, and profound intellectual myopia' (p. 343). Although there is a whiff of self-righteousness and straw-manning in this view, the fact is that there have been plenty of failures and are plenty of flaws in the status quo way of doing things.

This is not to say that the River-dwellers have all the answers. Silver concludes with 'a peace offering from the River to the Village – an effort to meet in the middle' (p. 469). Instead of liberty, equality and fraternity, he offers 'agency, plurality, reciprocity', foundational principles he draws from his study of successful risk-takers. So far, so good. But these are all, to Silver, quintessential Riverian principles. If the difference between the River and the Village is a Riverian social construct and not actually based on objective analysis and a clear set of principles and traits – if the Village does not really exist – there is no need for peace negotiations and no scope for gamesmanship. The healthy option is neither the River (as a Platonic ideal or a tribal construct) nor doubling down on the attributes Riverians associate with the Village, but a synthesis of the two without the tribal baggage. Since we are playing for the highest stakes, we can't afford to do otherwise.

Notes

1   See Michael Krepon, 'Reykjavik', Arms Control Wonk, 11 October 2011, https://www.armscontrolwonk.com/archive/403241/reykjavik/.

2   The original wording, using eye-dialect and stereotypes of Irish immigrants, is 'thrust ivrybody – but cut th' ca-ards'. The American humourist Finley Peter Dunne, a younger contemporary of the more famous Mark Twain, was fond of gambling metaphors. His fictional Irish bartender Mr Dooley dispensed social and political commentary and homespun wisdom in widely popular syndicated newspaper columns and books. Dunne's columns were even read regularly at president Teddy Roosevelt's cabinet meetings.

3   See Jeffrey Mazo, 'Can't Stop the Signal', *Survival*, vol. 55, no. 2, April–May 2013, pp. 163–72. FiveThirtyEight.com was originally independent; it was purchased by the *New York Times* in 2010, and by the sports network ESPN, itself owned by Disney, in 2013. In 2018 it was transferred to another Disney company, ABC News. In 2023, Silver left the site when it effectively ceased to exist other than as part of ABC's data-analytics division, and set up a new data-journalism website, Silver Bulletin (www.natesilver.net).

4   Although there are a great many very smart people who think AGI has a good chance of saving, or destroying, civilisation over a relatively short

(single- or several-generation) time frame, it should be noted that there are also plenty of smart people who think AGI is neither imminent nor earth-shattering, nor even possible. Silver would dismiss most of these as Village-dwellers, or at least No True Riverians.

5 Katja Grace et al., '2023 Expert Survey on Progress in AI', AI Impacts, https://wiki.aiimpacts.org/ai_timelines/predictions_of_human-level_ai_timelines/ai_timeline_surveys/2023_expert_survey_on_progress_in_ai#human_extinction.

6 Ezra Karger et al., 'Forecasting Existential Risk: Evidence from a Long-run Forecasting Tournament', Forecasting Research Institute, Working Paper no. 1, August 2023, https://static1.squarespace.com/static/635693acf15a3e2a14a56a4a/t/64foa7838ccbf43b6b5ee40c/1693493128111/XPT.pdf.

7 Forecasting Research Institute (FRI), 'What Do XPT Forecasts Tell Us About Nuclear Risk', 22 August 2023, https://forum.effectivealtruism.org/posts/YyBoSSaWpNacLnCji/what-do-xpt-forecasts-tell-us-about-nuclear-risk. A more detailed and recent (29 October 2024) study along similar lines from the FRI found similar results: see Bridget Williams et al., 'Can Humantiy Achieve a Century of Nuclear Peace? Expert Forecasts of Nuclear Risk', FRI, Working Paper no. 4, 29 October 2024, available at https://forecastingresearch.org/nuclear-risk.

8 Philip E. Tetlock, *Expert Political Judgement* (Princeton, NJ: Princeton University Press, 2005). Silver's previous book was *The Signal and the Noise: Why So Many Predictions Fail – But Some Don't* (London: Penguin Press, 2012).

9 Silver does note that there is no consensus on this question; others, such as H.R. McMaster, see any increase in the risk of nuclear-weapons use due to the Russia–Ukraine war as minimal.

10 John Maynard Keynes, *A Tract on Monetary Reform* (London: Macmillan, 1923), p. 80; and Tom Lehrer, 'We Will All Go Together When We Go', *An Evening Wasted With Tom Lehrer*, Lehrer Record LR202, 1959 (a live performance of this classic satire on nuclear dread is available at https://www.youtube.com/watch?v=frAEmhqdLFs). The flip side of the Riverian concern with x-risk is the transhumanist movement, an extreme manifestation of the Riverian mindset. A small subset of River-dwellers believe that, if we avoid extinction, we can in fact live forever, or for vastly lengthened lifespans, through cryonics, advances in biomedicine, uploading human consciousness and the advent of a technological singularity.

11 Joel Day, 'Experts Explain How Humanity Is Most Likely to Be Wiped Out – From Nukes to Supervolcanoes', *Daily Express*, 13 August 2023, https://www.express.co.uk/news/world/1801233/supervolcanoes-climate-change-nuclear-war-end-of-humanity-spt.

Book Reviews

Europe
Hanns W. Maull

The Lost Peace: How the West Failed to Prevent a Second Cold War
Richard Sakwa. New Haven, CT: Yale University Press, 2023.
£25.00/$38.00. 448 pp.

This impressive book offers a comprehensive account of relations between the West, led by the United States, and its principal challengers, Russia and China, from the end of the first Cold War in 1989 through to what author Richard Sakwa sees as a 'second cold war' beginning in 2014. According to Sakwa, while the end of the Cold War held the promise of a positive peace, the West failed to take Mikhail Gorbachev's 'new thinking' seriously and refused to engage with Russia (and China) at eye level. Russia, it was felt, ultimately had no alternative but to accommodate Western superiority. This encouraged the United States to seek an ambitious extension of the Western international order centred on NATO and America's bilateral security alliances in East Asia. This 'great substitution', as the author calls it, produced 'a sense of betrayal and exclusion in Russia' (p. 7) that ultimately led the world, after a quarter-century of 'cold peace' (p. 317), into a new cold war that is probably even more dangerous than the original. The author traces a shift from what he sees as US leadership of the 'Charter internationalism' that held sway after the Second World War – and that respected diversity in political systems – to US 'primacy' and the accompanying 'democratic internationalism' that sought to remake other countries in the image of America's own political institutions.

The story Sakwa tells, covering the last 35 years with considerable detail and nuance, is essentially a tragic one: the choices made by the US in encouraging former members of the Soviet bloc to join NATO while at the same time endorsing the 'indivisibility of security' were well-meaning, but their impact was corrosive. Sakwa's argument is erudite and impressive, but it is not entirely persuasive. Its first conceptual flaw concerns the distinction between 'Charter internationalism' and 'democratic internationalism'. That distinction neatly separates two international agendas that are in fact closely intertwined in the United Nations Charter and international law, which uphold states' rights such as sovereignty and non-interference but also human rights and individual human dignity. The tension between these two principles is a key feature of the UN system. Sakwa implies that a 'Charter international system' was in place during the Cold War, when in fact that conflict produced another international order with its own rules and norms that largely overrode the Charter system.

The second conceptual flaw concerns the relationship between domestic politics and international order. Sakwa tries to separate international relations from their domestic sources. His assumption seems to be that a robust international order will be able to keep revisionist states in line; his main concern therefore is with the risks of escalation resulting from foreign-policy decisions, as exemplified by the First World War. He bemoans the influence of the United States' foreign-policy establishment during the Cold War, criticising its response to Gorbachev's new thinking and its outsized ambitions to shape a new world order. Yet he fails to do the same for Russia, painting the descent into a second cold war as a consequence of Western actions to which Russia reacted. The war in Ukraine is thus ultimately attributed to NATO's eastward expansion. The alternative view, for which there also is ample historical evidence (consider the origins of the Second World War, for example), is that some regimes are inclined to challenge the status quo and overthrow the existing international order through war. Vladimir Putin's background in the KGB and the extensive influence of the *siloviki* (former colleagues from the Soviet intelligence services) in his regime suggest that Moscow brought its own Cold War biases to relations with the West, including a belief in and experience with using violence and repression to achieve its aims. Just as the failure of the Weimar Republic turned 1930s Germany into an aggressor state intent on overthrowing the European order, so the failed Russian transition during the 1990s produced a revisionist, dangerous Russia bent on overturning the post-Cold War European security order. This alternative narrative retains elements of tragedy, particularly if one assumes that the West could have prevented Russia's descent into chaos and then dictatorship, but it would apportion responsibility for the new cold war rather differently.

Austria Behind the Mask: Politics of a Nation Since 1945
Paul Lendvai. London: C. Hurst & Co., 2023. £30.00. 232 pp.

**Democratic Backsliding in Poland: Why Has Poland Gone
to the Dark Side?**
Łukasz Zamęcki, Renata Mieńkowska-Norkiene and Adam
Szymański, eds. Lanham, MD: Lexington Books, 2023.
£81.00/$105.00. 268 pp.

Poland: Thirty Years of Radical Social Change
Kazimierz M. Słomczynski et al., eds. Leiden: Brill, 2023.
€123.00. 362 pp.

Liberal democracies are fragile, and many have been damaged in what has been called a 'third wave of autocratisation' following on from a 'third wave of democratisation' starting in the 1970s. These three books explore the trajectories of liberal democracy in Austria and Poland since the end of the Second World War (for Austria) and the Cold War (for Poland). Paul Lendvai, the author of *Austria Behind the Mask*, is a towering figure in Central European journalism. Born in 1929 to Jewish parents, he survived the Holocaust in Hungary but had to flee that country in 1953. In 1959 he received Austrian citizenship, and from 1960–87, he reported from Austria for the *Financial Times* before assuming key leadership positions in the Austrian public-broadcasting system. Now 95 years old, he enjoys unparalleled insight into Austrian politics and access to its key players. The story he tells in *Austria Behind the Mask* is intended as a 'wake-up call' (p. viii). Having warned early on of Hungary's authoritarian turn under Viktor Orbán, Lendvai now believes Austria's own democratic system is under stress, and sees a need to place the country 'under observation' (p. 38).

Many Austrians enthusiastically welcomed the leadership of Adolf Hitler when Austria was made to join Nazi Germany in 1938, but after 1945 they preferred to see themselves as victims of German aggression. Their descendants – notably within the influential right-wing *Burschenschaften* (student fraternities) – appear once again to be embracing xenophobia, racism and authoritarian populism. The main political vehicle of these views is the Freedom Party of Austria (FPÖ), which in recent elections has become the country's largest parliamentary party. The Social Democrats, whose brilliant leader Bruno Kreisky dominated Austrian politics as chancellor during the 1970s despite his Jewish background, are today but a pale shadow of their former self, while the conservative Austrian People's Party (ÖVP) has also flirted with populism and Orbánesque techniques of electoral autocracy.

The government of boyish ÖVP chancellor Sebastian Kurz, in coalition with the FPÖ, crashed under the weight of its illegal and corrupt practices in May 2019. These had been exposed and resisted by a watchdog media; Alexander Van der Bellen, the country's Green president who had been elected with a razor-thin majority over an FPÖ candidate in 2017; and an independent judiciary. The checks and balances of Austria's post-war democracy thus worked – barely. How they will fare in the future against the 'real dangers' Lendvai sees to Austrian democracy (p. 210) remains to be seen. According to the author, two enabling ideological constructs underpin the 'deplorable moral picture' (p. 191) he has observed in recent Austrian politics. The first is the myth of Austria's victimhood in 1938, which has allowed Austrians to avoid the soul-searching about their behaviour during the Nazi era that West Germans have undertaken since the 1960s. The second is the notion of Austria's perennial neutrality and the way this is seen as a core part of the country's identity. This 'neutrality', Lendvai believes, has facilitated Russia's rather successful efforts to corrupt the Austrian establishment. The curtsy performed by then-foreign minister Karin Kneissl to Putin after she danced with him at her wedding in 2018 well captured this submissiveness: the bizarre episode 'damaged Austria's reputation as a pro-Western, neutral state', judges Lendvai (p. 167). At the same time, he sees forces in Austrian society that want to uphold the country's democracy, assessing that these have grown stronger too. All in all, his remarkable book is a labour of gratitude and critical love for his host country.

In *Democratic Backsliding in Poland*, the editors explore the reasons for democratic reversals in Poland under the Law and Justice (PiS) government (2015–23). Some of these, such as low levels of trust in public institutions, demands for social justice and conservative mindsets that resonate with populist ideologies, are part of a broader, global pattern of retreat from liberal democracy. Others, notably certain societal fissures going back to the 1980s, are unique to Poland. Both major political parties, the PiS (led by Jarosław Kaszyński) and Civic Platform (PO, headed by Donald Tusk), trace their origins to the Solidarność (Solidarity) movement that opposed the Polish regime in place during the 1980s. The movement brought together two different camps, originally united by their shared anti-communism, that grew into bitterly opposed 'tribes' (p. 229) with differing understandings of what democracy meant (one favouring majority rule and the other the protection of individual rights). Meanwhile, support for the procedural aspects of democracy was shallow among a significant part of the population. Polarisation was further fanned by social and mass media, notably the right-wing Catholic Radio Maryja.

It didn't help that the institutional framework of Poland's liberal democracy, which had been built after 1990, turned out to be insufficiently consolidated and in some ways outright defective. The majoritarian electoral system gave the PiS, with 38% of the vote, a majority of the seats in Poland's parliament in 2015. Once in power, the PiS started to dismantle the checks and balances that impeded its exercise of executive power, notably in the judiciary and the media, and to extend its reach into Poland's society and economy. The European Union turned out to be unwilling and unable to prevent this erosion of Polish democracy. Indeed, it may even have contributed to enhancing the PiS's power through what one of the contributors to *Democratic Backsliding in Poland* calls the 'executive aggrandizement' inherent in European integration (p. 167). Overall, this volume's eight chapters provide a comprehensive assessment of Poland's democratic backsliding, but the authors differ on its durability. Several contributors appear to view the setbacks in Poland as irreversible; only a few hold out hopes for the democratic renewal that now seems to be under way under Tusk's current PO government.

Poland: Thirty Years of Radical Social Change is for specialists only. It maps, in considerable detail, the 'radical transformation' of Poland 'from one-party Communist authoritarian rule to pluralist neoliberal capitalist democracy' (p. 1) beginning in 1990 along three dimensions: social-psychological adaptation, social inequality and exclusion, and 'votes and values' (p. 233). In doing so, it builds on the Polish Panel Survey, a comprehensive collection of empirical data collected every five years since 1988. Its analysis broadly supports the conclusions reached by Łukasz Zamęcki and his colleagues.

Germany and Nuclear Weapons in the 21st Century: Atomic Zeitenwende?
Ulrich Kühn, ed. Abingdon: Routledge, 2024.
£140.00/$190.00. 346 pp.

Germany and China: How Entanglement Undermines Freedom, Prosperity and Security
Andreas Fulda. London: Bloomsbury Academic, 2024.
£21.99/$29.95. 256 pp.

It is perhaps no coincidence that the German word *Zeitenwende* (turning point) has gained broad salience to describe the consequences of Russia's 2022 attack on Ukraine: no major country has seen its foreign and security policy thrown off course as much as Germany has by that war. Moscow, which Berlin preferred to see for many years as an indispensable partner in European security affairs – one that, to be sure, could be difficult and recalcitrant at times, but was still malleable – has now turned into an existential threat. At the same time, the credibility and reliability of the security guarantees the US has tradition-ally extended to its European allies against any threat from the east are eroding under the twin assault of China's rise and the vicissitudes of American domestic politics. Germany thus finds itself confronted with a fundamentally changed strategic environment, in which potent new threats mingle with weakening transatlantic reassurance.

How, then, has Germany coped? Two new books provide some first answers. *Germany and Nuclear Weapons in the 21st Century* looks at the country's nuclear policies and asks whether Berlin might abandon its traditional multi-lateralist defence posture and turn towards nuclear weapons as an alternative to American security guarantees. The book tackles this question by compre-hensively tracking developments in German nuclear policies, both military and civilian, between and beyond the two *Zeitenwenden* of 1990 and 2022, focusing on nuclear deterrence, arms control and non-proliferation.

In the past, these policies were marked by continuity and dependence, and Germany's nuclear policies since 2022 have followed that pattern in being incre-mental and cautious. The editor concludes that modified continuity, rather than radical change, has characterised Germany's responses to its radically altered security environment. This is most obvious with regard to its nuclear policy: Berlin so far has made no serious move towards devising a national nuclear deterrent, and the book makes a powerful case for why it is unlikely to do so in the future. While such a move might have made sense given the need to maintain deterrence in an uncertain security environment, by closing down its civilian nuclear-energy sector, Germany has lost the capacity to develop its own nuclear weapons, and any effort to revive that option would incur prohibi-tive costs and risks. Domestic political support for such a path is also highly uncertain: while Germany's traditional aversion to nuclear weapons (and to civilian nuclear energy) has recently abated somewhat, there are still wide-spread misgivings about nuclear weapons. Nor is there a credible European alternative for the deterrent function of US nuclear weapons, as Ulrich Kühn and Barbara Kunz show in their analysis of musings about a Franco-German bomb. 'Major, presently unsurmountable obstacles stand in the way of Franco-German co-operation on nuclear deterrence', they conclude (p. 122). Overall, this is a carefully edited, thoroughly researched and analytically rich assess-ment of German nuclear policies.

In *Germany and China*, Andreas Fulda looks at the *Zeitenwende* in Germany's relationship with China. He argues that Berlin has deluded itself as much about

China as about Russia, and thus ended up dangerously dependent on its economic ties with the former. As in its relations with Putin's Russia, Berlin sought commercial advantages for its corporate behemoths and put its faith in 'change through trade' in its dealings with China – or, in former foreign minister and now Federal President Frank-Walter Steinmeier's words, 'rapprochement through interweaving'. All German chancellors since Helmut Schmidt, whose influential voice as Germany's foremost elder statesman contributed to a misguided perception of China, intoned variations of this theme of business first, despite what should have been wake-up calls, such as the annihilation of the German solar industry by Chinese competitors, or the takeover of KUKA, a German producer of industrial robots, by a Chinese firm.

Resistance to this approach began to build from 2018, however, both at the European level and domestically, as China under Xi Jinping became increasingly neo-totalitarian and abusive in its repression of Xinjiang and Hong Kong. Yet by then, Germany's business-friendly approach had 'morphed from policy monopoly to dogma' (p. 201). While public discourse on China became increasingly critical and shifted in focus from opportunities to risks in the Sino-German relationship, Fulda shows that the present coalition government's approach to China has been contradictory and hesitant. Thus, ministries governed by the Greens (such as the Federal Foreign Office and the Federal Ministry for Economic Affairs and Climate Action) have pushed for a more cautious approach towards China, while the chancellor and his office prefer to adhere to the old dogma. Overall, the latter approach continues to prevail. Yet in its efforts to protect the interests of German businesses in China, Berlin finds itself increasingly isolated in Europe. While chancellor Angela Merkel managed to block sanctions by Brussels to protect the European solar industry, her successor, Olaf Scholz, was unable to prevent European tariffs on China's electric-vehicle imports.

Fulda interprets Germany's China policy as a case of 'destructive learning', criticising it for threatening Germany's freedom, prosperity and security. For this, he faults the close relationship between German government and business, Germany's federal political system and its coalition politics. Could Brussels come to the rescue, as many in Germany have suggested? Fulda is sceptical. If a coalition government in Germany lacks the unity to develop and pursue a coherent China policy, how could one expect that from an EU with 27 member states?

United States

David C. Unger

The Declassification Engine: What History Reveals About America's Top Secrets
Matthew Connelly. New York: Vintage, 2024. $22.00. 560 pp.

Matthew Connelly asks vitally important questions about whether the US government's addiction to classifying official documents, files and communications makes the United States and its legitimate secrets more or less secure. Using advanced statistical techniques along with more traditional archival research, Connelly makes a convincing case that current US practices, from reflexively overclassifying routine information to catastrophically underfunding declassification operations and archive management, do (literally) inestimable damage to national security and democratic governance.

Current practices make it harder for officials to protect real secrets and to know what other government agencies are doing, and for historians to understand the larger context of government actions. Most damagingly, they make it impossible for a sovereign people to exercise democratic oversight over a government that claims to act in its name but insists on doing so without its knowledge.

Connelly teaches international and global history at Columbia University, where he is also the principal investigator of History Lab, a project that uses machine learning, data-mining and other elements of artificial intelligence (AI) to explore how, why and which items get classified. By building up libraries of once classified, now declassified documents, and subjecting these to AI techniques, History Lab has developed algorithms that facilitate educated guesses about still redacted material. Much of *The Declassification Engine* focuses on this fascinating modern-day detective work and how Connelly's team has used it to explore secrecy practices surrounding nuclear-weapons design, code-breaking and cyber security, government surveillance of US citizens and foreigners, the role private businesses have played in government policymaking and more.

How reliable are the findings presented here? Reports of what Connelly's AI declassification engine has uncovered can only be taken on faith. His other important discoveries, gleaned from interviews, memoirs and archival research, are amply sourced in the endnotes. The extrapolations and interpretations on which he bases his findings are almost invariably worst case. That doesn't mean he's got them wrong, but his tendency to make sweeping statements such as 'the exponential growth of information, much of it secrets, all of it perishable, threatens history itself' (p. 377) invites reader scepticism.

Survival | vol. 66 no. 6 | December 2024–January 2025 | pp. 170–177 https://doi.org/10.1080/00396338.2024.2432209

I reported on some of these issues in real time during my many years as a *New York Times* editorialist, but did so without access to the since declassified material Connelly uses in this book. The discrepancies between the officially leaked and spun stories at the time and what we now know – to cite only one example, about Americans deliberately exposed by their government to dangerous levels of radiation or harmful drugs without their knowledge or consent – testifies to the value of Connelly's research. If government is now pervasively distrusted, a large share of that distrust has been all too well earned.

Connelly hopes to test and improve History Lab's algorithms and put them to constructive use in streamlining future classification and declassification decisions. So far, his hopes have been thwarted by the US government's unwillingness to partner with his project, denying him added research funding and a potential source of participants cleared to test these algorithms on still classified material.

One of Connelly's most troubling discoveries is revealed near the end of the book (p. 385), after he tries to convince government agencies to invest in further developing his declassification engine. Most of the people he meets with already know about the problems Connelly is talking about and are intrigued by the solutions he has started to uncover. But after repeated 'yes, buts' and 'yes, ifs', he concludes that the most relevant government agencies hold back because their budget processes neglect to assign a monetary value to democratic accountability.

State of Silence: The Espionage Act and the Rise of America's Secrecy Regime
Sam Lebovic. New York: Basic Books, 2023. $32.50. 464 pp.

Sam Lebovic has written a much-needed critical history of the Espionage Act, one that is carefully sourced, soberly balanced and readably written. Prosecution under this loosely worded act, backed by its intimidating threat of up to 20 years in prison, has been the principal tool used by the US government for the past century to shield much of American foreign policy from public attention and criticism, sometimes at substantial cost. The public distrust of government that has flourished under this regime of secrecy, Lebovic argues, has fuelled the politics of disinformation and the conspiracy theories that have characterised the age of Donald Trump.

In everyday usage, espionage connotes spying for a foreign power. But the specific language of the Espionage Act reaches far further, criminalising the retention or sharing with unauthorised persons of 'information related to the national defense'. Those words have proven almost infinitely applicable.

Potentially prosecutable information has included things like classified material on Hillary Clinton's private email server and in Trump's Mar-a-Lago storage rooms. Prosecutable sharing can be with anyone lacking appropriate security clearances, the press and the American public included. People familiar with the US government's classification practices readily concede that far too much gets routinely stamped 'classified', thereby opening the way to selective prosecution and barring the way to necessary democratic debate about foreign-policy choices.

Since the Espionage Act's formulation in the panicky and paranoid wartime atmosphere of 1917, its wartime-sedition clauses have been deployed against antiwar speakers such as Eugene V. Debs, and its peacetime espionage clauses against leakers such as Daniel Ellsberg (the Pentagon Papers), Julian Assange (released to Australia this summer following a plea bargain), Chelsea Manning (jailed for nearly seven years before her sentence was commuted by Barack Obama near the end of his second term) and Edward Snowden (currently self-exiled in Russia).

Government-friendly judicial decisions over the years widened the act's potential reach. The Obama administration prosecuted more leakers under its provisions than any of its predecessors. Government fear of the press's political clout has generally kept the act from being used against mainstream-media outlets that receive and publish leaked information covered by the act. But, in related cases, individual journalists such as Judith Miller of the *New York Times* have been jailed for refusing to name sources. Fellow *New York Times* journalist James Risen lived for years under the threat of similar punishment.

As Lebovic, who teaches history at George Mason University, documents, the ever-expanding classification and secret-protecting culture that has developed around the Espionage Act helped spawn a multibillion-dollar, self-perpetuating secrecy-industrial complex centred on Silicon Valley at the expense of taxpayers – and American democracy. Lebovic suggests sensible reforms to reduce over-classification abuses, but concedes that none have much chance of enactment.

American Anarchy: The Epic Struggle Between Immigrant Radicals and the US Government at the Dawn of the Twentieth Century
Michael Willrich. New York: Basic Books, 2023. $35.00. 480 pp.

American Anarchy brings welcome new attention to an often overlooked chapter in the history of the American left. Radical revolutionary ideologies such as anarchism, communism, syndicalism or socialism never gained much traction among American workers, not even among the immigrant populations where they found their greatest following. Anarchists in particular were never more than a minority within a minority, counting at most tens of thousands of sympathisers even at their peak in the three and a half decades beginning around 1885. Anarchism's association with terrorist bombings and assassinations repelled most American workers, while its defiant rejection of all laws and national loyalties held little appeal for the millions of immigrants aspiring to naturalisation and American citizenship.

Anarchist ideas did find their way to larger audiences through the antiwar, anti-conscription oratory of Emma Goldman, the labour organising of Elizabeth Gurley Flynn and Bill Heywood of the Industrial Workers of the World, and the family-planning proselytising of Margaret Sanger. The latter was a socialist, not an anarchist, but partnered with Goldman and other anarchists in her early speaking tours.

Anarchists of those days generally fell into one of two categories: terrorists like Goldman's partner, Alexander Berkman, who thought 'direct action' (violence) was necessary to inspire workers to resist capitalism, and 'philosophical anarchists', who defended violence in the abstract as a necessary tool of social revolution but confined their own political activities to oratory.

Probably the most enduring legacy of American anarchism's exhortations to live a radically free life unrestricted by laws was, ironically, a liberal, legalistic one – the greatly expanded definitions of free speech for all Americans that emerged from the legal strategies employed on behalf of anarchist defendants. The American Civil Liberties Union owes its birth in 1920 to these cases.

Willrich, who teaches history at Brandeis University, tells the story largely through the words, deeds and trials of Goldman and her closest associates, and of her creative, indefatigable defence lawyer, Harry Weinberger. Willrich's clear and lively prose makes the sometimes complex legal issues eminently readable. The book ends with Goldman's 1919 deportation to Soviet Russia, with an epilogue chronicling her disillusionment with Russian communism and its state repression, not only of anarchists.

Energizing Neoliberalism: The 1970s Energy Crisis and the Making of Modern America
Caleb Wellum. Baltimore, MD: Johns Hopkins University Press, 2023. $59.95. 264 pp.

Caleb Wellum, who teaches US history at the University of Toronto Mississauga, challenges conventional interpretations of the 1970s US energy crisis. He argues that an artificially constructed discourse of 'energy crisis' in the 1970s helped neo-liberalism become, by the 1980s, America's hegemonic frame of political thought. Wellum's arguments and supporting data enrich our understanding of those pivotal decades, illuminating how arguments for regulating or deregulating energy markets played into larger debates about the role government should play in market decisions more generally. But Wellum stretches his interpretation further than it can comfortably go. This leads him to conflate contributing factors and primary causes, and to overlook important differences between elite policy debates over neo-liberalism and the grassroots revolt against elite governance he labels 'petropopulism'.

Strictly speaking, Wellum argues, there was no energy crisis in the 1970s. Instead, there was a series of disruptive fluctuations in the available supply and wellhead price of Mideast petroleum, mainly driven by the export and pricing policies of OPEC (Organization of the Petroleum Exporting Countries) and OAPEC (Organization of Arab Petroleum Exporting Countries). He's right in the sense that available supplies of other energy sources, such as coal, remained abundant and free from manipulation by export cartels (though the petroleum-price shocks of the 1970s indirectly affected the market prices of substitutable fuels). Nor were proven petroleum reserves in any immediate danger of running out.

Wellum pushes this idea further, arguing that because the oil shocks manifested themselves in ways that mostly weren't materially visible to drivers or homeowners (consumers didn't see the gasoline flowing into their cars or heating oil flowing into their homes), the 1970s oil shocks were features of an intellectually constructed 'energy crisis' formulated by ideologues, technocrats and politicians.

The real crisis in the 1970s, according to Wellum, was geopolitical, not material. Growing Western energy consumption, shrinking US oil output and the aggressive pricing policies of export cartels resulted in an unprecedented reduction of the United States' ability to control oil prices and assure oil supplies to its Western allies – a power crisis, not an energy crisis.

While the geopolitical challenge was new, domestic American debates about energy were not. In the years following the Second World War, political leaders deliberately encouraged automobile-dependent suburbanisation and rhapsodised about a post-Depression economy of limitless abundance and consumption. But as early as the late 1940s, oil-company geologists such as M. King Hubbert warned of a coming era of peak oil, after which known reserves would start running down.

By the late 1960s, ecologists such as Aldo Leopold, Amory Lovins and Wendell Berry were preaching a New Age of limits, urging Americans to adjust their consumption downward to achieve a more sustainable balance with finite natural resources. Meanwhile, liberal politicians argued for more consumption as the glue needed to hold together what seemed to be an increasingly fraying society.

By the 1970s, elite policy debates had been joined by neo-liberal devotees of free markets, increasingly influential in both parties, who chafed at the elaborate regulatory and pricing structures that had been incrementally built around energy markets and that seemed increasingly intrusive and ineffective as the Nixon, Ford and Carter administrations struggled to respond to long lines at petrol stations and the OPEC/OAPEC challenges of the 1970s. Increasing numbers of ordinary Americans, Wellum's 'petropopulists', rebelled against what they now saw as a threat to their American birthright to unlimited energy consumption as elite liberal technocrats imposed 55-mile-per-hour speed limits and gas rationing, in league with moralistic New Age gurus preaching austere lifestyles.

In this polarised atmosphere, as Wellum tells it, an informal alliance for deregulation emerged in the late 1970s that temporarily brought together ecologists, who hoped a return to market pricing would incentivise reduced energy consumption, and neo-liberals, who expected market pricing to automatically bring supply and demand back into balance, bringing both increased production and increased consumption.

Not surprisingly, this unlikely alliance proved short-lived. Assisted by a variety of political developments, including the failure of Keynesian government economists to master stagflation, a general backlash against the reformism of the 1960s and 1970s, and the successful political salesmanship of Ronald Reagan, neo-liberalism eventually won the day. The environmentalists found themselves relegated to the political margins.

By the early 1980s, new markets for trading petroleum futures seemed briefly to reassert US power over petroleum prices. Shale oil and fracking replenished US and global oil supplies. The energy crisis that maybe never was is now over. So is the unchallenged hegemony of neo-liberalism. The crisis of US geopolitical power in the Middle East continues.

Was the energy crisis a contributing factor in neo-liberalism's ascendancy? Perhaps. But neo-liberalism's rise in both parties began earlier and is well explained by other, more powerful factors, for example the fracturing of the New Deal coalition along lines of race and class.

Founding Partisans: Hamilton, Madison, Jefferson, Adams and the Brawling Birth of American Politics
H.W. Brands. New York: Doubleday, 2023. $32.50. 464 pp.

In the late 1780s, when the new US Constitution was written and ratified, leading American political figures like James Madison, Thomas Jefferson, John Adams and Alexander Hamilton argued that the emergence of national political parties would pose a mortal threat to the new republic. Half a decade later, all four of them had hived off into two distinct and opposing national parties, with Jefferson and Madison leading the Republicans (the forerunners of today's Democrats), and Hamilton and Adams leading the Federalists. They would engage in avid partisanship for the rest of their active political lives. Once retired from the political fray, the three surviving members of this founders' quartet looked back and lamented the divisive toll partisanship had exacted among people who had shared, and continued to share, important basic beliefs. (Hamilton, fatally wounded at the age of 47 in an 1804 duel with Jefferson's vice president, Aaron Burr, never enjoyed a late-life opportunity to reflect on the costs of partisanship.) This is the story H.W. Brands cogently tells in *Founding Partisans*.

Hamilton and Madison had collaborated (along with John Jay) in writing the *Federalist Papers* of 1787–88, a series of essays promoting ratification of the Constitution. Both men then spent much of the 1790s organising and leading America's first two opposing political parties. Jefferson and Adams, members of the generation that led the Revolutionary War for American independence, became bitterly opposed presidential candidates in the new nation's first two contested presidential elections in 1796 and 1800. They reconciled before they both died on the symbolically important date of 4 July 1826, the 50th anniversary of the signing of Jefferson's Declaration of Independence.

Despite Madison's celebrated argument in *Federalist* no. 10 that a large republic would prove too vast for local factions to coalesce into opposing national political parties, Brands argues that national partisanship was all but inevitable as leading figures of the new republic fought over the nature of the newly created federal union. Would it follow Hamilton's model of a centralised national government with a strong independent chief executive assuming a wide range of powers not expressly forbidden to it? Or would it follow Jefferson's vision of originalism, based on a strict and narrow application of the constitutional text, particularly the language of the 10th Amendment (ratified in 1791) that seemed to reserve most sovereign powers besides foreign affairs to the states? That basic question continued to be fought over, in one way or another, until the American Civil War redefined the nature of the federal union. It is still being fought over today.

Behind this defining constitutional issue stood opposing interests – farmers versus merchants, creditors versus debtors, large states versus small states, states economically dependent on slavery versus those that were not. Brands, who teaches history at the University of Texas, brings these well-known battles to life by drawing on what were sometimes vituperative private letters and scurrilous public pamphlets written by the main participants. Contemporary readers may be amused to read that Hamilton nearly wrecked his political career by paying hush money in an eventually unsuccessful effort to conceal an extramarital affair, or that he tried to persuade Jay, then New York governor, to appoint false electors from an expiring state legislature to block Jefferson's route to the White House. Jay refused on principle.

Counter-terrorism and Intelligence
Jonathan Stevenson

Slow Horses (TV series)
Will Smith, creator and co-writer. Produced by Apple TV+,
2022–present.

Although spy novels seem as popular and celebrated as police procedurals and crime fiction in general, they haven't generated as much quality television. For every show that comes close to *The Bureau*, five can at least aspire to *The Wire*. The British series *Slow Horses* should therefore be prized. Based on books by Mick Herron so knowing and insouciant they hide their pained wisdom, the programme replicates that quality through veteran MI5 officer Jackson Lamb, played to louche perfection by Gary Oldman, who seems to have been born for the booze-soaked, nicotine-stained role. A fallen legend, he now oversees Slough House, a London kip far from MI5's (fictional) Regent's Park head-quarters to which the service's most incompetent and disobedient agents are banished to execute its lowliest tasks, often those requiring maximum deniabil-ity. One of them, River Cartwright (Jack Lowden, nicely measured), happens to be the grandson of revered former officer David Cartwright (Jonathan Pryce, his peremptory stodginess intact). His own cloak-and-dagger skeletons draw River – and Slough House – into high-end intrigue, to the exasperation of deputy director Diana Taverner (Kristin Scott Thomas, bloodlessly imperious), who finds the aggressively flatulent Lamb both repulsive and formidable.

Except for season three – an aberrantly preposterous story centring on an over-the-top SWAT-like assault on the MI5 records department – the storylines are credibly murky and refracted, with cul-de-sacs and red herrings as well as old grudges, rogue conduct, mordant loyalties, false-flag operations and sleeper agents that ring plausible as John le Carré without the portentousness of some of his post-Cold War work. Blackmail is the reserve currency of this crowd, and they all – especially Lamb – amass and spend it effectively. Like the best espionage fiction, *Slow Horses* leans in on glamourless bureaucracy and vicious pragmatism, and wears loftier geopolitics with discreetness verging on shame. It doesn't get to the 'special relationship' until season four, and even then pre-sents it, perhaps presciently, as a kind of votive degeneracy in the person of cashiered CIA officer turned mercenary Frank Harkness (a duly smug Hugo Weaving) who co-opts MI5 through – what else? – blackmail.

The show's very existence is an affirmation, albeit a caustic one, of the ongoing utility of British intelligence. While the special relationship has been credibly minimised as one-sided and denigrated as overhyped, it is not illusory and does embed an essential British role: that of America's strategic tutor, backed by long, hard experience. As a wise but self-loathing cynic poisoned with deflected guilt, Lamb is an acerbically poignant stand-in for the contemporary United Kingdom. Though once a force, now he's old, decadent and disempowered. But he is also a repository of unique institutional knowledge about the dark underbelly of international affairs and appears to understand the capabilities and limitations of the West and what imperils it. Over the first four seasons of the series, the precise content of that knowledge – and just what Lamb did to warrant exile to Slough House – have been withheld. The writers must now come across with a back-story nasty and believable enough to plausibly account for his benighted state and secure the legacy of this fine series.

Babylon Berlin (TV series)
Tom Tykwer, Achim von Borries and Henk Handloegten,
creators, directors and co-writers. Produced by Sky 1 and Das
Erste, 2017–present.

As recently as eight years ago, jihadist-inspired shows like *24* and *Homeland* in the United States and *The State* in the UK exemplified popular treatments of counter-terrorism. Since then, however, right-wing extremism has surpassed transnational Islamist extremism as a threat to national security in the US, and far-right movements have gained menacing traction in important Western European countries – including France, Germany and the UK – and to a degree even in the European Union, putting democracy on the defensive. It is perhaps unsurprising, then, that Sky 1's lavish melodrama *Babylon Berlin*, a brilliantly elliptical and atmospheric neo-noir television series set in the Weimar Republic starting in 1929 and based on Volker Kutscher's bestselling books, has become a cultural event in Germany and a critical hit internationally.

The series vivifies the plight of the Weimar woman in the character of Charlotte Ritter, played by the winsomely charismatic Liv Lisa Fries. By sheer force of aptitude and confidence, Ritter vaults from police typist to homicide investigator – unheard of for a woman – but still has to moonlight as a flapper and prostitute to support herself and her destitute family. Ritter's mentor and partner in crime-fighting – and at least aspirationally, her lover – is Inspector Gereon Rath, a PTSD-addled war veteran and morphine addict (Volker Bruch, stoically distressed). As subversive politicians and policemen do the clandestinely revanchist military cadre's bidding and sclerotic bureaucrats delude themselves about the integrity of the state, Rath and Ritter uncover, amid Berlin's morbidly glamourous decadence, the rot of anti-Semitism and the converging ratlines of violent extremism – communism as well as far-right fascism – that are fracturing the Weimar Republic and propelling Adolf Hitler and the Nazi Party's ascendance. Over time, of course, they confront the German people writ large. By the early 1930s, a majority of Germans supported extremist parties on the right or left, centrist parties had been marginalised and, even though very few Germans were then members of the Nazi Party, it had been normalised.

A number of analysts and scholars – in particular, Steven Levitsky and Daniel Ziblatt in *How Democracies Die* and Benjamin Carter Hett in *The Death of Democracy: Hitler's Rise to Power and the Downfall of the Weimar Republic* – have implicitly drawn analogies between the Weimar Republic and the present-day United States. These are of course very broad and subject to substantial qualification. Among other things, the United States has not just lost an eviscerating war, it does not have a worthless currency, and American militias hardly seem tantamount to the Black Reichswehr. But racist myths of cultural degeneration that stoked opposition to the Weimar Republic and the rise of Hitler in the inter-war years are comparable to those that now inspire right-wing extremists in the United States and, for that matter, in Europe. That epochal kinship – in addition to peerless style and production values, audacious plotting, assiduous research, the extraordinary chemistry between Bruch and Fries and a redemptive human-ism – explains *Babylon Berlin*'s deserved popularity and ominous resonance.

No Cloak, No Dagger: A Professor's Secret Life Inside the CIA
Lester Paldy. Lanham, MD: Rowman & Littlefield, 2024.
£25.00/$32.00. 298 pp.

In the popular understanding of the intelligence world, the ops people change the world and get the glory while the analysts and scholars who process and polish the raw intelligence are relegated to the status of support players. Nicely illustrating this phenomenon is Sydney Pollack's 1975 film *Three Days of the Condor* – a New Hollywood classic from the espionage movie's heyday – in which circumstances convert Robert Redford's Joe Turner, who just reads books for the CIA, into a danger-courting field operative to ferret out bad actors within the agency. Lester Paldy, in his engaging and enlightening – if at times cloyingly folksy, inordinately adulatory and somewhat clichéd – memoir *No Cloak, No Dagger*, provides a modest corrective. For more than 20 years, while a distinguished professor of physics at the State University of New York at Stony Brook, this ex-Marine lieutenant was a part-time CIA officer responsi-ble for, among other things, fine-tuning the wording of monitoring protocols for arms-control agreements, helping secure nuclear material against terrorist threats, and illuminating the culture and nuance of the international scientific community to intelligence officers seeking to recruit foreign scientists as agents and insulate the American scientific community against penetration by foreign intelligence services.

Despite Paldy's self-effacement about being an interloper not fully initiated, the book essentially traces his indoctrination as a professional patriot in a clandestine army. It is emphatically a memoir rather than a systematic analysis, devoid of notes and more episodic than chronological, with policy recommendations that often crop up jarringly in biographical accounts. While the author acknowledges a few CIA failures, such as the agency's process for assessing the likelihood that Iraq had weapons of mass destruction (WMD) and its torture of terrorist suspects, he rarely targets blame and sometimes endeavours to erase it. For instance, he accepts former CIA director George Tenet's claim that his 'slam dunk' characterisation of the probability of finding Iraqi WMD was 'misinterpreted' (p. 155). The overall tone of the narrative is laudatory and exculpatory, occasionally unsubtly boilerplate: 'More than a few academics criticize the CIA for its past involvement in covert actions, several of which have had unintended consequences. I shared some of those concerns, but the CIA carried out those covert actions at the direction of the president' (p. 81). But there seems to be little doubt about Paldy's earnestness.

Much of the book consists of quite familiar expository material about how the CIA works and has evolved. Some – including an entire chapter on diversity titled 'A CIA That Looks Like America' (pp. 115–24) – read like public-relations copy. But Paldy does add value on the culture and code of the US intelligence community. One lesson of his recorded experiences is that deep synergy has to exist between the analytic and operational sides of intelligence work, and between agencies with different but overlapping missions, if such work is to be effective. It is of course no secret, especially after 9/11, that 'territorial rivalries and insularity could slow progress toward mission objectives' (p. 269), but Paldy fleshes out the observation with illustrative reminiscences from an unusual vantage.

The CIA: An Imperial History
Hugh Wilford. New York: Basic Books, 2024. $35.00. 378 pp.

Nothing Is Beyond Our Reach: America's Techno-spy Empire
Kristie Macrakis. Washington DC: Georgetown University Press, 2023. $29.95. 282 pp.

Whether the post-war United States has been an imperial power and what role its intelligence services might have played in any quest for empire has preoccupied a fair few historians and political scientists. In *The CIA: An Imperial History*, Hugh Wilford of California State University, acknowledging but downplaying

American denials of designs on empire, casts the CIA of the Cold War and, parenthetically, the 'global war on terror', as following the lead of mainly the British in anointing an elite, distinctly WASP and at times apparently Anglophilic class to shape and lead US intelligence operations. Decolonisation 'became enmeshed' (p. 47) with the Cold War, reinforcing the perceived value of the European experience while also imbuing Americans with some of the counterproductive prejudices of their predecessors, including Orientalism. It's a breezy and confidently written book, focusing on colourful personalities while covering well-trodden ground from a refreshingly simple, though perhaps somewhat tendentious, perspective. Wilford does offer some sharp insights. While legendary CIA counter-insurgency maven Edward Lansdale purportedly 'abhorred European colonialism' (p. 123) and strained to differentiate American efforts in Vietnam from it, these efforts still degenerated into 'a dirty war of the sort that the European colonial powers were waging in their former colonies – only much more conspicuous because of its scale and the extent of US domestic opposition it was arousing' (p. 135). The fact that the US overreached in Vietnam and elsewhere, and that America consequently found extrication difficult, doesn't, of course, quite prove the proposition that the CIA was purposefully imperialist. Nevertheless, Wilford concludes that 'the imperial history of the CIA is likely not over yet' (p. 313).

Kristie Macrakis, a Georgia Institute of Technology historian who sadly passed away two years ago, takes a more nuanced view in *Nothing Is Beyond Our Reach*. With a flair for atmospheric frou-frou that rivals Wilford's and a gift for finely sifting topical material from the abundant post-war history of intelligence, she argues that, owing to the inherent limitations of human intelligence, a growing fear of a Soviet surprise attack early in the Cold War and plain 'technophilic hubris', a tech-oriented American network for enforcing international security evolved 'piecemeal … with no central blueprint', but still amounted to 'global dominion' whereby 'technology replaced territory' (p. 237). The US has not dominated populations or land but has, less intrusively, controlled military bases and listening posts. Even so, says Macrakis, because allies that were once colonial powers facilitated the development of this network, and the United States has used its far-flung assets to lethally project power – for instance, via drone strikes – its international image and standing have suffered as others perceive it as imperial.

To split the difference between the two books, it seems reasonable to conclude that the United States' approach to intelligence is not intrinsically imperial, but has often taken on that appearance due to strategically over-ambitious policies. In turn, it is arguable that, although at the start of the post-war period the

US intelligence apparatus did take shape as an aggressive expeditionary enterprise, geared to confronting the Soviet Union and later adapted to tackle jihadist threats, it could now become a more defensive and selective tool for protecting US interests against multiple great-power rivals and non-state adversaries.

We Are Proud Boys: How a Right-wing Street Gang
Ushered in a New Era of American Extremism
Andy Campbell. New York: Hachette Books, 2022. $29.00. 311 pp.

In early 2020, many counter-terrorism analysts regarded the Proud Boys as little more than a nuisance – white, male Western chauvinists and misogynists bandwagoning on a presidential philosophy and style they considered sympathetic to their own. This made sense: at that point, though Proud Boys founder Gavin McInnes had helped organise the deadly Unite the Right rally in Charlottesville, Virginia, in 2017, the group hadn't done much more than menacingly brace people its members judged to be liberals 'like a roving crew of bullies shaking down passersby for lunch money at recess' (p. 6), as investigative reporter Andy Campbell puts it in his pointedly casual and conversational *We Are Proud Boys*. It was hard to take a gang of flabby boors carrying cans of beer in their tactical vests seriously as potential insurrectionists. A year later, along with the Oath Keepers and the Three Percenters, they helped orchestrate the 6 January 2021 assault on Capitol Hill. As Campbell declares, 'the first person to breach the US Capitol was a Proud Boy' (p. 239). His book seeks to chronicle and explain the group's 'meteoric rise' (p. 10) as the most overt and unabashed among contemporary right-wing militias.

Though essentially episodic rather than systematically analytic, and heavy on hackneyed journalese and breathless modifiers, it furnishes a valuable early blow-by-blow treatment of an important player with commitment and brio. While the book keys on illustrative anecdotes showcasing the group's bigotry, ignorance and juvenility, and on biographical sketches of representative members, it also marshals revealing information about the Proud Boys' societal advance. A key development was the replacement of McInnes – an undisciplined, obscene clown – with Henry 'Enrique' Tarrio, who 'was more than just a loudmouth … with an axe to grind' and 'viewed the Proud Boys as marketable to the mainstream right' (p. 129). Donald Trump's nod to the group with his 'stand back and stand by' remark during his first debate with Joe Biden in September 2020 afforded the group 'a veil of political legitimacy' (p. 145). Frenetically raising money, in part through Tarrio's online-merchandising outfit 1776.shop and a GiveSendGo campaign based on fictitious accounts of Antifa violence, the Proud Boys dispatched hundreds of members to Washington during the run-up to 6 January.

Washington DC's Metropolitan Police arrested Tarrio on 4 January and he subsequently pleaded guilty to misdemeanour weapons and flag-burning charges. He was later convicted of seditious conspiracy for his part in the Capitol insurrection and received a prison sentence of 22 years – the longest of any 6 January conspirator. But these facts belie the cozy relationship between right-wing militias and some members of the wider US law-enforcement community. Campbell recounts several examples, and a particularly telling one arose in May 2023 – after the book appeared – when Shane Lamond, a Metropolitan Police lieutenant and head of the department's intelligence unit, was arrested for obstruction of justice for warning Tarrio he was about to be arrested and then lying about it. Anti-federalist police and elected law-enforcement officials at the county and local levels are broadly susceptible to militia co-optation, and the Proud Boys, among other groups, have successfully recruited quite a few. Although several local chapters of the group split from the national organisa-tion after 6 January and it appeared weakened, Campbell argues that as 'the most successful political extremist group in the digital age' (p. 267), the Proud Boys have provided a playbook for normalising political violence.

War, Conflict and the Military
Franz-Stefan Gady

Braddock's Defeat: The Battle of the Monongahela and the Road to Revolution
David L. Preston. Oxford: Oxford University Press, 2015.
£14.99/$20.99. 480 pp.

As I walked along the brick-marked outlines of Fort Duquesne in downtown Pittsburgh on a humid afternoon in July 2024, the discrepancy between the tactical disadvantage and strategic significance of this site for French and British forces during the French and Indian War (1754–63) became apparent. Constructed by the French as a military strongpoint in 1754 at the point where the Allegheny and Monongahela rivers converge to form the Ohio River, the fort was meant to control the Ohio Country west of the Appalachian Mountains. While the site may have looked formidable on a map, in practice it was nearly indefensible. Fort Duquesne was dominated by heights across the Monongahela River, from where even eighteenth-century artillery could quickly reduce it to rubble. The site of the fort was also swampy and prone to flooding, making it difficult to keep the gunpowder dry and to maintain the palisades and entrenchments that marked French domination of that part of colonial North America.

In summer 1755, the understrength garrison there, composed of French marines and Canadian militia, and supported by a large contingent of Native Americans, learned of a British-American military expedition comprising more than 2,220 men under the command of General Edward Braddock. The expedition's goal was to destroy the fort and expel the French as part of a larger campaign to break French military power in the region. The garrison realised it would be tactically impractical to defy the British behind the ramparts. At the same time, the French knew that if they stood any chance of maintaining their position in the Ohio Country, they could not give up their stronghold at the forks of the Ohio River, a major gateway to the West and a crucial pivot connecting French colonial possessions in Canada with Louisiana.

Consequently, under the initiative of the French-Canadian officer Daniel Hyacinthe Liénard de Beaujeu, the French and their Native American allies, which constituted two-thirds of the total force, set out to ambush the larger British-American flying column of around 1,460 men in a pre-emptive strike. The Anglo-American force consisted of elements of two British regular regiments and colonial troops, accompanied by, among others, a young Virginian colonel named George Washington. These troops had forced their way from present-day Maryland 180 kilometres over the daunting Allegheny Mountains into what is today western Pennsylvania. The ensuing Battle of the Monongahela on 9 July 1755 was won by the Native American and French forces, which displayed 'superior discipline, tactical decisions, and leadership', according to David L. Preston in *Braddock's Defeat* (p. 5). The battle was significant not only because it marked the French Canadians' greatest victory of the war, but also because, more importantly, it helped to lay the foundations of an independent American identity.

As Preston writes, the battle 'fostered an already nascent American consciousness, defined by colonists' prolonged relationships to the continent and its Indian peoples, and sharpened by the friction they experienced while fighting alongside British regulars' (p. 328). Such 'friction' included the fact that, during the battle, the Americans largely stood their ground, sniping at the enemy from behind trees, while the British regulars, unfamiliar with French and Native American irregular warfare, broke and ran. Above all, the military defeat – in which, according to one calculation, 66% of, or 976, British and colonists became casualties – shattered the colonists' 'exalted ideas of the prowess of British regulars and assuaged their fears of becoming independent', to quote Benjamin Franklin, who had a hand in providing Braddock's forces with desperately needed supplies during the doomed campaign in 1755. The Battle of the Monongahela is thus arguably one of the most important battles fought on the American continent, though it seems little remembered today. Even a city tour guide who led me on a historical tour of downtown Pittsburgh was not aware of it.

Preston's history stands out for two reasons. Firstly, his reliance on French and, where available, Native American sources enables readers to gain a good understanding of the intricacies of French colonial society and culture, including the pivotal role played by the French-Canadian aristocracy and their tenuous yet symbiotic relationship with their Native American allies, who provided the real martial sinew of New France. Secondly, the book succeeds in reconstructing mid-eighteenth-century Anglo-American relations and the already broiling tensions between native-born colonial and British-born administrators. The outcome of this relationship apparently supports the dictum that revolutions or periods of political instability can be the product of elite overproduction, whereby elite aspirants – such as Washington, who desperately wished to become a regular British officer – find themselves vying for power positions that are denied to them due to their birth.

Braddock's Defeat also holds lessons for present-day military leaders and thinkers by demonstrating the consequences of failing to achieve lasting institutional adaptation in the face of defeat. The British did indeed transform their forces after the disaster at Monongahela by introducing light infantry and ranger tactics, adaptations which gave British forces 'a formidable degree of fighting prowess' and 'the capacity to engage Native American forces in woods they had once so greatly feared', according to Preston (p. 316). This would allow them to emerge victorious from the French and Indian War. However, the author notes that once 'the greatest theorists and practitioners of light infantry tactics were all dead … their veteran experience died with them' (p. 316). This threw the British Army back to square one in terms of its ability to success-fully engage American insurgents unwilling to meet in open battle, a regression that was most evident in clashes such as Lexington and Concord during the opening stages of the American Revolutionary War (1775–83). This experience demonstrates the consequences of an overreliance on informal methods to pass on valuable lessons and adaptations to force structure and tactics, and holds a warning for those who believe that being battle-tested alone increases the chances of winning future battles.

The New Nuclear Age: At the Precipice of Armageddon
Ankit Panda. Cambridge: Polity Press, 2024. £25.00. 256 pp.

Ankit Panda's *The New Nuclear Age* impresses with its meticulous research, inci-sive analysis and chilling relevance. This sobering yet accessible work delivers a stark message: to paraphrase Winston Churchill, relying on nuclear deterrence in today's 'third nuclear age' is the worst option, except for all the others.

Unsurprisingly, Panda presents a compelling case for the need to guaran-tee the continued effectiveness of deterrence, despite its inherent risks. As the book's subtitle ominously suggests, when stripped of sanitised defence jargon, the fundamental premise of nuclear deterrence remains the spectre of global annihilation. As Panda puts it: 'Nuclear deterrence cannot be neat and anti-septic because it is precisely the possibility of Armageddon – of plunging into the unknown, but assuredly and intolerably painful – that keeps the world humming along' (p. 219).

The current nuclear age had two predecessors. The first concluded with the end of the Cold War and the collapse of the Soviet Union, events that sig-nificantly reduced the risk that high-intensity conventional warfare between military blocs would escalate into a thermonuclear war. The second nuclear age, emerging in the 1990s, saw reduced US–Russia nuclear competition, smaller arsenals and some de-alerting measures (such as the United States' removal and storage of nuclear weapons from bombers). While optimism grew for advances in arms control and confidence-building measures, new challenges arose from nuclear proliferation in South and East Asia and the Middle East, alongside concerns about terrorist access to weapons of mass destruction.

The defining feature of the third nuclear age is the rise of China. Beijing has been rapidly expanding its nuclear arsenal: in 2021, the world learned that China was building 100 new missile silos in its western desert. The country has maintained a no-first-use policy since 1964, but US nuclear strategists have long harboured doubts about its true intentions. Moreover, the prospect of a two-front war pitting the US against both China and Russia has complicated American deterrence efforts against these nuclear peer adversaries, adding a perilous escalatory factor to the rivalry between them.

Further challenges include multipolar deterrence relationships involving the US and its allies, China, India, North Korea, Pakistan and Russia; emerging technologies such as hypersonic weapons and cyber capabilities; and general-purpose technologies, such as artificial intelligence, that could potentially affect nuclear command and control. Meanwhile, the painstakingly constructed arms-control architecture and confidence-building measures of the previous age are unravelling, with little prospect of revival.

Deterrence appears to be humanity's last best hope, though maintaining it will be challenging. Panda highlights what may be the most dangerous aspect of this new era: the merging of conventional and nuclear capabilities, and the ensuing risk of rapid vertical escalation. He writes:

> The implications could be particularly destabilizing in a conventional war where such systems may be used for warfighting ends well below the nuclear threshold. For instance, U.S. long-range strikes on certain missile bases in China hosting both conventional and nuclear missiles could be interpreted by Beijing as the start of a potential disarming strike, leading to potential escalation to nuclear use. (p. 89)

This subject deserves deeper exploration, given increasing US–China tensions over Taiwan and both sides' reliance on long-range strike capabilities in East Asia.

Panda does well to emphasise that deterrence is not solely about payloads, missile ranges, effective command and control, or survivable second-strike capabilities from a functioning nuclear triad. While these factors contribute to instilling escalatory fears in opponents, Panda argues that dialogue is equally crucial to prevent a catastrophic outcome. 'Nuclear deterrence', he writes, 'absent any supporting mechanisms built on negotiated restraint, is simply too dangerous' (pp. 194–5). Yet engaging in constructive dialogue with adversaries is increasingly seen as politically impossible. As Panda notes:

In Washington, it would not be too far-fetched to suggest that any arms control arrangement – legally or politically binding – that may be acceptable to Vladimir Putin, Xi Jinping, or Kim Jong Un would be politically a nonstarter. The mere idea of shared interests with adversaries, even with the risk of nuclear conflict looming, is controversial. In Beijing, Moscow, and Pyongyang, meanwhile, skepticism will abound about any proposals emerging from the United States. (p. 198)

Panda argues that nuclear deterrence is not a permanent solution for preventing large-scale wars between powerful nations. Instead, it should be viewed as a 'temporary salve – giving the states that possess these weapons, and humanity as a whole, sufficient time to seek a better world' (p. 221).

Panda acknowledges that this vision may not align with current trends. Therefore, a tailored deterrence strategy is the most realistic approach to increasing the likelihood of finding off-ramps during a nuclear crisis. Since deterrence occurs in the mind of an adversary, understanding that mindset is crucial. However, this can only happen through dialogue. For that insight alone, Panda's book is a must-read for any policymaker of a nuclear-armed nation.

World on the Brink: How America Can Beat China in the Race for the Twenty-first Century
Dmitri Alperovitch with Garrett M. Graff. New York: PublicAffairs, 2024. $32.50. 400 pp.

Sinae deterrendae sunt: China should be deterred. According to Dmitri Alperovitch and Garrett M. Graff, this principle should inform the United States' foreign, defence, trade and industrial policies in the twenty-first century. Much like Cato the Elder's rallying cry 'Carthage must be destroyed' (*Delenda est Carthago*) was intended to energise resistance against what he saw as the principal security threat to Rome in the 150s BCE, Alperovitch and Graff seek to deter Xi Jinping's China. In particular, they wish to dissuade China from invading Taiwan, a move that could have potentially devastating consequences, possibly including a global war. Unlike Cato, however, the authors are not alone in raising the alarm: a growing chorus within the US foreign-policy and defence establishments is calling for more concerted actions by the US and its partners to prevent China from ever attempting to seize the island, even bloodlessly.

The authors make the case that Taiwan matters because it is the twenty-first-century equivalent of West Berlin during the first two decades of the Cold War. They cite familiar strategic and economic interests, including Taipei's critical role in global semiconductor production. What sets their book apart, however, is its focus on how Xi's personal ambitions could influence China's approach to Taiwan. 'Over his last decade in power', say the authors,

> Xi has positioned himself as one of the great historic leaders of modern China – on par, according to the Communist Party's telling of his story, with the founder of the PRC [People's Republic of China], Chairman Mao. And what better way to put himself on par – perhaps even exceed – the greatness of Mao than to achieve the goal that Mao himself could not and complete the conquest of Taiwan? (p. 121)

This personal ambition, especially in autocratic systems with few checks and balances, can override broader strategic and economic interests. It's an insight worth considering when evaluating Chinese intentions. Personal ambition, often culminating in hubris among elderly autocrats, combined with revisionist goals can result in tactical and strategic surprises for Western leaders. Vladimir Putin's decision to expand his war in Ukraine to a full-scale invasion in February 2022 is a case in point. Simply asserting that any Chinese attempt to take Taiwan by force might devastate the Chinese economy, or raising doubts about the combat readiness of the Chinese People's Liberation Army (PLA) for a complex military operation like an amphibious invasion of Taiwan, might not be enough to deter Xi. His ego might still drive him down an escalatory path, without regard for the potential consequences for China and the world. Certainly, the growing size and frequency of Chinese military manoeuvres near Taiwan make it increasingly difficult to distinguish between build-ups for exercises and preparations for an actual attack. One of the highlights of Alperovitch and Graff's book is their invasion scenario set in 2028, which envisions a full-scale military exercise turning into a full-scale invasion of the island.

What is to be done? The authors, perhaps unknowingly, draw from the strategies of Ancient Rome. Specifically, they advocate for a Fabian strategy, named after Quintus Fabius Maximus Verrucosus, a Roman statesman and general. This strategy was designed to outlast the Carthaginian general Hannibal by avoiding pitched battles and slowly wearing down the enemy while Rome rebuilt its military power. 'Ultimately, America's goal is to buy time – delay, delay, and delay – for the Taiwanese', say the authors (p. 360). 'Taiwan must build up its forces, mobilizing, training, and arming itself, and demonstrating to China that a war will be too costly and likely result in a disastrous defeat of the invasion fleet' (p. 360).

Whether a strategy centred on outlasting an autocrat, while building up American and Taiwanese military power to deter the PLA from attempting to seize the island, is realistic given the current political climate in the US remains to be seen. Nonetheless, the book makes a compelling case that the status quo cannot be maintained indefinitely.

War in Ukraine: Conflict, Strategy, and the Return of a Fractured World
Hal Brands, ed. Baltimore, MD: Johns Hopkins University Press, 2024. $32.95. 328 pp.

Beyond Ukraine: Debating the Future of War
Tim Sweijs and Jeffrey H. Michaels, eds. London: C. Hurst & Co., 2024. £45.00. 432 pp.

If journalism represents the first rough draft of history, then edited volumes on ongoing wars – such as Russia's full-scale invasion of Ukraine – represent a preliminary sketch of military analysis. Writing on France's Grande Armée in 1805 or Germany's Wehrmacht in 1940 would likely have contained different analytical conclusions than writing on those same organisations in 1815 and 1945 respectively. For one thing, it matters significantly for military analysis which side is perceived to have won at the end of a conflict. Perceptions of victory increase the likelihood of post hoc analysis, whereby analysts may interpret facts in retrospect to align with the conflict's eventual outcome. Post hoc analysis is less prevalent at the beginning of a conflict, though it can never be completely eliminated, and indeed was present in the early stages of the Russia–Ukraine war following the initial failure of Russia's attempt to impose regime change on Ukraine. Before solid facts emerged, the fighting in Ukraine served as a proverbial blank canvas upon which analysts and commentators projected their own interpretations, informed by their innate biases and bearing little resemblance to the actual operations on the ground. This is not unusual. In fact, the myths that emerge from hyperbolic yet fact-poor analysis during a war's initial phases are often the hardest to dispel and frequently impede a more nuanced understanding of the emerging character of warfare.

The volumes *War in Ukraine* (edited by Hal Brands) and *Beyond Ukraine* (edited by Tim Sweijs and Jeffrey H. Michaels) both serve as excellent antidotes to these analytical pitfalls. Most importantly, the editors stress the preliminary nature of each book's findings. Brands describes *War in Ukraine* as 'history in real-time', comparing it to 'shooting at a moving target' (p. 2), while Sweijs and Michaels admit their own book 'will probably get some aspects right and some aspects wrong' (p. 9) when it comes to drawing lessons from the fighting in Ukraine about the future of war.

The focus of the two volumes differs. Brands's focus is more explicitly on the origins and wider geopolitical implications of the conflict. It offers a first assessment of US policy in the run-up to the war, including discussions on the degree to which the latter contributed to a failure to deter the full-scale Russian invasion in 2022. The book contains military analysis of events that unfolded in 2022 and 2023, including the role played by nuclear weapons in shaping the character of the conflict and Western military support in the first year of the war. Sweijs and Michaels's volume is more directly concerned with the future of war and how the first few months of the high-intensity conflict in Ukraine have led to the revision of some views on the subject. It contains excellent discussions on the assumed growing dominance of the defence in land warfare; the role played (or not) by offensive cyber capabilities in state-on-state warfare; and how thinking on systems warfare, largely absent in Ukraine, may still shape the future battlespace beyond the traditional domains of warfare to include society at large.

At the same time, beyond the tentative nature of the analyses, both volumes note that there are some things we can know with relative certainty about the fighting in Ukraine. We can also draw some general lessons for future warfare, while acknowledging the limitations of insights gained from two Soviet-influenced militaries fighting a land war in Europe for combat operations between great powers in other parts of the world. For example, it can be said with some confidence that the war in Ukraine will remain a grinding war of attrition, blending legacy technological capabilities with emerging tech. Attrition will also likely be an important characteristic of any future great-power war. The conflict also demonstrates the importance of magazine depth and reserves in general, as well as the significance of advantages in the electromagnetic spectrum for command-and-control purposes. It further illustrates the importance of volumes of fire to enable manoeuvre on the battlefield, with implications for the doctrines and future force structure of NATO forces. The most tentative lessons concern vertical-escalation dynamics and the degree to which any useful insights on this subject can be drawn from the conflict. The mere involvement of a nuclear-armed combatant calls for constant re-evaluation of risks that, depending on the perspective, either leads to a prudential, crisis-management approach or self-deterrence. Humility in analysis may thus be the most important takeaway from these two works.

The Return of Donald Trump

Dana H. Allin

I

Philip Roth's *The Plot Against America* is a nightmarish alternative history in which aviation hero Charles A. Lindbergh defeats the incumbent, Franklin D. Roosevelt, in the 1940 United States presidential election.[1] The novel's ingenious ambiguity is that the nightmare is experienced through the eyes and fears of a child – young Philip Roth, who is the same age and living in the same small apartment in the same small house in the same lower-middle-class Jewish neighborhood of Newark, New Jersey, and with the identically named brother, mother and father, as the novelist Philip Roth in the real 1940. In part because he is a child, it is never entirely clear how much of the nightmare is real and how much is imagined.

The young Roth knows the world as adults presented it to him. He cannot understand everything that adults understand and, anyway, the adults themselves cannot be sure about what is happening and what might be coming. The Jews of Newark know that dark walls have closed in on the Jews of Europe, but they cannot imagine the full horrors of a Holocaust that has not yet happened. They know that Lindbergh's 'America First' slogan means ending Roosevelt's policy of supplying Britain for its fight against Adolf Hitler's armies. They know that Lindbergh accepted a medal from Hitler's number two, Hermann Goering, and that he has blamed

Dana H. Allin is an IISS Senior Fellow and Editor of *Survival*, and an adjunct professor at the Johns Hopkins School of Advanced International Studies (SAIS–Europe) in Bologna, Italy. This essay is adapted in part from Dana Allin, 'The Return of Donald Trump', IISS Online Analysis, 7 November 2024, https://www.iiss.org/online-analysis/online-analysis/2024/11/the-return-of-donald-trump/.

Survival | vol. 66 no. 6 | December 2024–January 2025 | pp. 193–202 https://doi.org/10.1080/00396338.2024.2432214

American Jews for lobbying to drag America into Europe's war – as did, in both cases, the real Charles Lindbergh.

The Roths and other Jews feel threatened when President Lindbergh establishes the Office of American Absorption (OAA) to speed up assimilation by giving urban Jews the experience of life in the rural heartland. Yet, when Philip's older brother Sandy is selected by the OAA to spend the summer on a tobacco farm in Kentucky, he has the time of his life.

Sandy was chosen for the programme because Lionel Bengelsdorf – the erudite, eloquent and nationally famous rabbi who endorsed Lindbergh for president, became his adviser, conceived of the OAA and now heads it – is courting his voluptuous Aunt Evelyn. These connections bring bitter tumult to the Roth family, because Philip's father – Evelyn's brother-in-law – is passionately pro-Roosevelt, fiercely anti-Lindbergh and furious that Evelyn, Rabbi Bengelsdorf and, by extension, Lindbergh himself have reached into his household for a project that he considers anti-Semitic. Here is another dimension of ambiguity, for although the entire novel unfolds under the shadow of Lindbergh's transformation of America, the plot's dramatic conflicts are almost entirely between and among American Jews. Towards the end of the novel there are, to be sure, pogroms across the South and Midwest killing 122 of them. These aren't ordered by Lindbergh – they coincide with his mysterious disappearance – and they are no greater or more vicious than the anti-black lynchings and massacres that actually took place in this era.[2]

At about this point in the novel, a baroque plot contrivance switches the train of history back onto its familiar track. Roosevelt is re-elected and, with the Japanese attack on Pearl Harbor, America goes to war. The country that will emerge from it will be Roosevelt's America, not Lindbergh's.

II

The Plot Against America was published in 2004. Its author lived for another 14 years, long enough to be asked, more than once, if he thought Donald Trump embodied the threat that he had depicted in the book. 'It is easier to comprehend the election of an imaginary president like Charles Lindbergh than an actual president like Donald Trump', Roth responded to one of these queries. 'Lindbergh, despite his Nazi sympathies and racist proclivities, was a great aviation hero who had displayed tremendous physical courage and aeronautical genius in crossing the Atlantic in 1927. He had character and he had substance … Trump is just a con artist.'[3]

Calling him a con artist did not mean failing to take him seriously. But a problem of comprehension – that is, comprehension of the historical phenomenon of MAGA and Trump – is that he has effectively flooded our consciousness with outrages too constant and too numerous to organise in any hierarchy of menace. Meanwhile, many American voters may have reassured themselves that in the first Trump term nothing cataclysmic happened to America, if you omit 2020, the year of COVID-19, as many apparently do. Even the 6 January 2021 insurrection and attempted coup against constitutional government appeared to be rendered harmless by its comic-opera incompetence, though the families of Capitol police officers who died as a consequence would not see it quite that way.

Trump certainly has been far more explicit in his threats to American constitutionalism than the real or fictional Lindbergh or other America Firsters of the 1930s. During his first administration and in the recent campaign, he espoused ideas that his former chief of staff, retired Marine Corps General John Kelly, and his handpicked top general, former Joint Chiefs of Staff chairman Mark Milley, called 'fascist'.[4] Trump vowed to go after the 'enemy within', among whom he explicitly named Democratic politicians Nancy Pelosi, the former House speaker, and congressman Adam Schiff, now a senator, who chaired the committee that twice voted to impeach him, as well as Kelly and Milley.[5] He said he would use the military forces under his command to do so, if necessary. Many former Trump officials warned that, in a second term, the personnel and institutional guardrails that restrained him in his first term would be gone. *Atlantic* magazine editor Jeffrey Goldberg, who had reported on the alarm of these officials, pointed to the 'problem of the colonels': while most American military generals might continue, in Trump's second term, to balk at carrying out unlawful orders, there is a vast substratum of officers just below general and flag rank – inevitably including some who are not so rigorously trained in and inculcated with constitutional norms –

whom Trump can promote at will.[6] Milley, for his part, told journalist Bob Woodward that he feared being called back to active duty for the purpose of being court-martialled.[7]

The question raised by the 1930s analogy is whether xenophobia and anti-constitutionalism at home, plus a species of isolationism and affinity for an aggressive dictator abroad, can converge to make the fight against one tantamount to the fight against the other. That's the case that President Joe Biden made in his State of the Union address to Congress in January of this year. He invoked Roosevelt's speech of January 1941 and in substance argued, as Jonathan Stevenson and I put it in an earlier issue of this journal, that the 'Russian forces that invaded Ukraine in February 2022 belonged to the same historical threat and malignancy as the violent acolytes of Donald Trump who stormed the US Capitol in January 2021'.[8] When Biden stepped down from his party's nomination and Vice President Kamala Harris took over, she carried the same civic argument into her campaign, albeit leavened with more traditional pocket-book appeals. In any event, she did not carry the day.

Ukraine, obviously, is immediately vulnerable to her failure. While its president, Volodymyr Zelenskyy, was prophylactically quick to offer Trump congratulations for his victory, Trump has repeatedly disparaged Zelenskyy as a too-successful 'salesman' who took unreasonable advantage of American largesse and promised to end this arrangement by settling the Russian war against Ukraine in 'one day'.[9] This presents America's European allies with their first crisis: do they go along with what would be, in effect, an imposed settlement that Russian President Vladimir Putin would find gratifying, or can they offer somehow to continue supporting Ukraine's defiance without American help?

More plausible, perhaps, is a scenario in which European allies of the United States would not be able to defy Trump's desire for an immediate deal, but might summon the material and political wherewithal to help guarantee whatever settlement is reached. In this new Trump era, such commitments are even more unlikely than they had been to involve Ukraine's admission to NATO. But a set of bilateral or multilateral commitments from European countries could drive the development of coordinated and autonomous defence capabilities – that is, those that would be independent of the United States.

This admittedly optimistic scenario is based on the reasonable assessment that in the 2020s, unlike the 1930s, the balance of economic and military capabilities now favours the status quo powers of Europe over the revisionist power, which today is Russia.[10] But it does not account for the dynamic disruptions of which Trump is capable. Probably not enough attention has been paid to his campaign pledge of 10–20% across-the-board tariffs on imported goods.[11] Trump has even mused that revenues from these tariffs could replace income tax, apparently genuinely unaware that the tariffs will be paid by American consumers in the form of higher prices. In any event, he will either impose them or use the threat of doing so to cut trade deals with various partners; the European Union has already readied an offer. Even successful deal-making would mean the further fragmentation of world trade. The more dire possibility is that Trump's use of the trade weapon would actively, and intentionally, harm Europe.

Such intentional harm would mark a fundamental change in transatlantic relations. During the Cold War, America's forward military presence and its nuclear deterrent spared Western Europe the high costs of wholesale rearmament and thus enabled the construction of social-democratic, and Christian Democratic, welfare states. In America too, despite heavy investments in Europe's defence as well as Asian wars, the New Deal version of social democracy expanded, due in large part to a stroke of historical and geographical luck. Territorially safe from the war's devastation, marshalling heretofore untapped potential through the wartime mobilisation of resources gifted America with its extraordinary share of global wealth. This geopolitical serendipity allowed both a military protectorate over Western Europe and continued economic growth and social spending at home to flourish.

In the United States' Cold War grand strategy, European economic and social success was central. As George Kennan put it in 1948:

> if economic recovery could be brought about and public confidence
> restored in western Europe – if western Europe, in other words, could

be made the home of a vigorous, prosperous and forward-looking
civilization – the Communist regime in eastern Europe ... would never
be able to stand the comparison, and the spectacle of a happier and more
successful life just across the fence ... would be bound in the end to have
a disintegrating and eroding effect on the Communist world.[12]

In the world view informing Trump's tariff plans, the economic
strength of Europe is no longer a vital American interest. On the contrary,
an economically strong Europe is bad for the United States; by logical
extension, a weak Europe is good. There have of course been economic
tensions between the United States and Europe throughout the post-war
era. Actual enmity, however, is something new. Moreover, the Trump
administration could very well tacitly join forces with Putin's Russia
in promoting the fortunes of Europe's right-wing populist parties. The
success of these parties would greatly diminish the prospects for Europe
to pull itself together for long-term support of Ukraine. That, at least for
Russia, is very much the point.

III

In its final week, members of Harris's presidential campaign described
themselves as 'nauseously optimistic' about the election.[13] There had been
at least two reasons for their upbeat mood. Firstly, they and their candidate had run a very good campaign, while in the final weeks Trump's
campaign seemed to be imploding. Secondly, to borrow from Charles de
Gaulle, these Democrats held a 'certain idea' of the United States.[14] It was
a patriotic idea embodying former president Barack Obama's rhetoric of
struggle towards 'a more perfect union'; Biden's channelling of Roosevelt's
coalition, which was social-democratic in ethos if not in name; and Harris's
own theme of confronting civic danger by grasping 'joyful' American possibilities, while reaching out to conservative, constitutionalist supporters
such as former congresswoman Liz Cheney and her father Dick Cheney,
the former vice president.

In this idea of America, Trump's presidency was a one-term set of
parentheses, his return to office therefore unimaginable. Yet, by the

numbers, his victory should have surprised no one. Polling averages showed a basically tied race, with movement back towards Trump in October. Insofar as someone had to win such a tight race, the polls turned out to be accurate.

Trump will either do the things he has promised to do, or he won't. It is hard to imagine why the former is less likely than the latter. In this light, the US will likely be convulsed by civil and constitutional disorder.[15] On the assumption that the election results reflect not a full embrace of Trumpian ideas but rather rising prices, a COVID-19 hangover, Biden's unpopularity and a degree of racial depolarisation, journalist Josh Marshall predicts 'a series of major public and political confrontations over the next four years, much as we had the first time Trump was president, only more intense'. But Marshall also acknowledges a different scenario, stemming from the fact that 'anti-Trump America has been at this for a decade', and that

> people are truly exhausted. People can choose simply to withdraw back into their private worlds – their families, their hobbies, the private, insular world of non-involvement, civic passivity. I don't think that will happen. But I think many people will be having that conversation with themselves. That is very much how autocracies take hold. People get tired of fighting. Mass withdrawal from the public sphere is the foundation of autocracy.[16]

The international consequences of Trump's victory will be downstream of its effects on America's domestic stability. While the effects of some Trump administration policies on the international order may be predictable, those of America's general demeanour may be more difficult to foresee. Whatever the effects, they will be substantial given the United States' central global role.

Overall, we are about to resume a historical experiment. Can there be stable global order without the US playing its traditional leadership role? The truly frightening prospect is that this human, and partly notional, construction will be destabilised at the same time as our planetary ecology is ruined by global warming, and that the two processes will converge. Among his many promised disruptions, Trump is especially enthusiastic about destroying Biden's legacy of massive investment in renewable energy.

Trump's supporters will argue that the global order was already unravelling, which is true, and that the reason was the policies of Biden and all the presidents before Trump this century, which is a more debatable proposition. Some self-styled restrainers, mostly critics of Trump, may nonetheless hope that the international system will find its own balancing mechanisms even in this third iteration of 'America First'. There are reasons to be sceptical.

Notes

1   Philip Roth, *The Plot Against America* (New York: Random House, 2004).

2   In the most devastating episode, white-supremacist vigilantes killed up to 300 blacks and destroyed 35 city blocks over the course of two days in Tulsa, Oklahoma, in 1921. See White House, 'A Proclamation on Day of Remembrance: 100 Years After The 1921 Tulsa Race Massacre', 31 May 2021, https://www.whitehouse. gov/briefing-room/presidential-actions/2021/05/31/a-proclamation-on-day-of-remembrance-100-years-after-the-1921-tulsa-race-massacre/; and Yuliya Parshina-Kottas et al., 'What the Tulsa Race Massacre Destroyed', *New York Times*, 24 May 2021, https://www. nytimes.com/interactive/2021/05/24/us/tulsa-race-massacre.html.

3   Quoted in Judith Thurman, 'Philip Roth Emails on Trump', *New Yorker*, 30 January 2017, https://www. newyorker.com/magazine/2017/01/30/philip-roth-e-mails-on-trump.

4   See Michael S. Schmidt, 'As Election Nears, Kelly Warns Trump Would Rule Like a Dictator', *New York Times*, 22 October 2024 (updated 6 November 2024), https://www.nytimes. com/2024/10/22/us/politics/john-kelly-trump-fitness-character.html; and Ruby Cramer, 'Trump Is "Fascist to the Core," Milley Says in Woodward Book', *Washington Post*, 12 October 2024, https://www.washingtonpost. com/nation/2024/10/12/mark-milley-donald-trump-fascist/.

5   Jack Forrest and Veronica Stracqualursi, 'Trump Calls Schiff and Pelosi "Enemy from Within" Even After Allies Defend Past Comments', CNN, 20 October 2024, https://www.cnn.com/2024/10/20/politics/trump-enemy-from-within-schiff-pelosi/index.html.

6   See 'Jeffrey Goldberg and Catherine Rampell: The Un-American', *Bulwark Podcast*, 23 October 2024, available on Spotify, https://open.spotify.com/episode/1Nh7NeewlHB6Bjfd4iTv9T.

7   See, for example, Martin Pengelly, 'Mark Milley Fears Being Court-martialed if Trump Wins, Woodward Book Says', *Guardian*, 11 October

2024, https://www.theguardian.com/us-news/2024/oct/11/bob-woodward-book-mark-milley-trump.

8 Dana H. Allin and Jonathan Stevenson, 'Will America Fail Ukraine?', *Survival*, vol. 66, no. 2, April–May 2024, pp. 189–90.

9 See, for example, Veronika Melkozerova, 'Ukraine Braces as Triumphant Trump Vows to "Stop Wars"', *Politico*, 6 November 2024, https://www.politico.eu/article/ukraine-reaction-donald-trump-victory-us-election-2024-russia-war-volodymyr-zelenskyy/.

10 See, for example, Barry R. Posen, 'Europe Can Defend Itself', *Survival*, vol. 62, no. 6, December 2020–January 2021, pp. 7–34.

11 See 'Trump's Tariff Plan Could Cost Americans $78 Billion in Annual Spending, NRF Study Shows', Reuters, 4 November 2024, https://www.reuters.com/markets/us/trumps-new-tariff-proposal-could-cost-americans-78-bln-annual-spending-nrf-study-2024-11-04/.

12 Quoted in John Lewis Gaddis, *Strategies of Containment: A Critical Appraisal of Postwar American National Security Policy* (New York: Oxford University Press, 1982), p. 45.

13 Matt Viser and Yasmeen Abutaleb, 'Harris Wraps Up Her Historic Bid Amid a "Nauseously Optimistic" Mood', *Washington Post*, 5 November 2024, https://www.washingtonpost.com/politics/2024/11/05/kamala-harris-historic-campaign-finish-anxiety-optimism/.

14 See Philip H. Gordon, *A Certain Idea of France* (Princeton, NJ: Princeton University Press, 1993).

15 See, for example, Jonathan Stevenson, 'With Election Day Near, Here's a Reminder that a Second Trump Term Could Mean Mayhem', *New York Times*, 31 October 2024, https://www.nytimes.com/2024/10/31/opinion/donald-trump-second-term-election.html.

16 Josh Marshall, 'Status Check Just After Midnight', TPM, 6 November 2024, https://talkingpointsmemo.com/edblog/status-check-before-midnight.

Correction

Article title: : Britain in the Pacific: Staying the Course?

Author: Nick Childs

Journal: Survival

Bibliometrics: Volume 66, Number 5, pages 147–158

DOI: https://doi.org/10.1080/00396338.2024.2403226

This article was originally published under a single author byline as UK Ministry of Defence clearance for named published work by serving personnel was still in process. The amended online version now lists two authors, Nick Childs and Callum Fraser.

Printed in the United States
by Baker & Taylor Publisher Services